Business cost-benefit analysis

Business cost-benefit analysis

R F J Dewhurst
Senior Lecturer
School of Industrial and Business Studies
University of Warwick

McGraw-Hill

London · New York · St Louis · San Francisco · Düsseldorf
Johannesburg · Kuala Lumpur · Mexico · Montreal · New Delhi
Panama · Rio de Janeiro · Singapore · Sydney · Toronto

Published by

McGRAW-HILL Book Company (UK) Limited
MAIDENHEAD · BERKSHIRE · ENGLAND

07 094171 8

PRINTED AND BOUND IN GREAT BRITAIN.

Contents

Preface

'I don't care what the figures say, I know what the decision should be', is a remark that has been heard not infrequently in boardrooms. It has an interesting parallel in case work at business schools. There, the teacher may initially concentrate discussion on the figures, and get the class to assess the situation on this basis. At some point he will say 'That is the "*Q*" (quantitative) answer, now what about the non-"*Q*" factors involved?'

In one sense this book is dedicated to the idea of eliminating this dichotomy between 'figures' and 'non-figures'. Put more precisely, its aim is to reduce the non-figure area and convert as much as possible of it to fertile figure ground!

It is NOT, however, the thesis of this book that figures matter and people do not. The reverse indeed is the truth. Only people matter and figures not at all, other than to serve their masters. But figures can be powerful tools. All that this book is trying to do is to extend the range of tools available to human beings and trust and believe that they will be used wisely.

Inevitably much of the writing has a mathematical flavour. Almost all the detailed mathematical work has been condensed into one chapter (chapter 4), and the book can be read without following through every example in this chapter. However, for those who wish to do so, and who are unaccustomed to matrix algebra, an explanatory appendix has been included at the end of that chapter.

The main thesis running throughout the book is my approach to decision making. (Indeed in one sense the whole book is just the argument in favour of a cost benefit or input output approach to all decision making, and the working out of its applications to various functional areas). But no man is an island. I am very conscious of my debt to certain people. In particular, I have been much influenced by the work and writings of Professor R. N. Anthony, Professor M. Bromwich, Messrs Draper and Smith (on regression analysis), Paul E. Green, Doug Lang, Professor M. H. Peston, Lawrence L. Schkade and the authors of I.C.I. pamphlet No. 3. No doubt there are others. I am grateful to them all.

After chapter 1, the introductory chapter, chapter 2 discusses the current social/economic applications of cost benefit. Chapter 3 sets out briefly the problems of applying the decision making process to an organization. These problems are discussed in detail in chapters 4, 5, 6, and in chapter 7 (the summary chapter on decision making). The latter part of the book deals with the applications of these problems to the real life situation. Chapter 8, the lead chapter in this part, attempts a solution of the vexed problem of measuring management. Chapter 9 deals with the general problems of research and development, and chapters 10 and 11 with the detailed applications in the marketing and training areas.

I would record with thanks the help I have had from my colleagues, particularly Professor Ian Tricker, Douglas Garbutt, Bob Hurrion, my brother, Dr Vivian Dewhurst, and also his wife, Mrs Margery Dewhurst, for a very comprehensive index.

I have had the good fortune to get the services of another colleague, Mel Hirst, who has written the chapter on marketing. An expert on this field, he is well qualified to do this.

A number of people and organizations have kindly allowed me to include references and quotations. I am especially grateful to Mr Arthur Webb, Editor of *The Accountant.*

Finally, I would like to express my thanks to Miss M. Joy Brown, Mrs Audrey Bond, Mrs Phyllis Comley, Miss Carol Cunion, Mrs Sheila Griffiths, Mrs Barbara Stanton, and Mrs Tod Wye for secretarial help.

1971 R. F. J. DEWHURST

1. Introductory

1.1 The decision maker and the need for cost-benefit analysis

It has long been noted, if little remembered, that whenever figures have entered into any area of decision making they have never subsequently been displaced. Once a foothold has been obtained, it seems they are there to stay. Ten years ago Discounted Cash Flow, Critical Path Analysis, and Linear Programming were esoteric techniques known only to the mathematically minded few. Today, Linear Programming is taught to teenagers in schools! Some areas of decision making, however, have until now utterly defied quantitative analysis; maybe their days, too, are—if the phrase be allowed—finally numbered!

The earliest provider of quantitative information for a business organization was the accountant. (In general, we concentrate rather on the private than the public sector though our conclusions apply *mutatis mutandis* to organizations of any sort.)

Until recently, the main job of an accountant in any business was to record accurately, in money terms, transactions that had already taken place. The basis was the yearly profit and loss account and the balance sheet at the end of the year. These statements of accounts were prepared by the accountant for the board and checked by independent auditors. They were then presented to the shareholders, the *de jure* (though not, in reality, the *de facto*) controllers of the company. Since the shareholders supplied the money in the first place, it was argued that it was right that they should be told what use was being made of it.

These yearly profit and loss accounts were used by the board and by management too. It is easy to see, however, that, because of the long time lag, their use was limited. The figures for any year might well not be available until several months after the year end. If something had gone wrong in the first month of the accounts year, it could well be over a year before this situation came to light.

Obviously the time element had to be reduced. Quarterly or monthly profit and loss accounts, with their emphasis more on speed of preparation than a too precise accuracy, became standard practice in all large organizations. Another breakdown of elements, in which the cost of a particular job or process were recorded, was provided by cost accounts. Both monthly profit and loss accounts and cost accounts are obviously of great use in management. They come under the generic classification of management accounts.

But all these accounts are historical. They record profits or costs for periods *after* they have happened. No one can doubt their importance, but equally no one can change the past. For practical purposes what matters is to be properly informed in advance. Correct decisions can then be made before it is too late. Top management must surely wish to be provided with information and advice relating to the future. This is the really useful work that an accountant can do.

What sort of decisions will top management have to make? Presumably those involving the allocation of fairly large sums of money. Such a decision might be, for instance, whether to spend more money on increasing production. Would the additional revenue justify this investment? Or perhaps a decision is required on whether a replacement machine be purchased? Would the saving in labour costs justify the expenditure? Or is it sensible to set up a new factory? Would the increased profits make up for the heavy initial outflow of cash? Table 1.1 sets out the problem.

Table 1.1

Cash flow out from investment in:	*Cash flow in from:*
Additional production machine	Additional net revenue
Replacement automatic handling machine	Savings in labour costs
New factory	Increased profits

The essence of all these decisions is a comparison of the money cost of the investment with the expected incremental cash flow over the years. If, for instance, the cost of a new factory is £100 000, and the increase in cash flow from profits is expected to be £20 000 for the first year, and for all the years to come, then the return on investment is 20 per cent. (Even before tax this is a pretty reasonable return.) Unfortunately, however, profits do not usually behave in this straightforward way. They tend to start low, build up as the factory gets into full swing, and then terminate after a number of years. To determine the true return on the money invested, taking account properly of the time factors in the cash flows, requires a Discounted Cash Flow (DCF) calculation. The computation requires some care, in practice, and the steps are gone into in detail in chapters 5 and 6. The theory, however, is simple. In every case the rate of return on the investment is calculated. Table 1.2 is Table 1.1 expanded to include the rates of return on each investment.

Table 1.2

Cash flow out from	*Cash flow in from*	*Rate of return on investment*
Additional production machine	Additional revenue	8%
Replacement automatic handling machine	Savings in labour costs	14%
New factory	Increased profits	10%

Which of these possible investments is the best proposition? Clearly the replacement automatic handling machine. This gives the highest return for our money. Provided 14 per cent is regarded as a reasonable return (this point is also dealt with in chapters 5 and 6), and provided enough cash is available for one of these investments, the controller/accountant would advise expenditure on the automatic machine.

How, then, should he advise when he has to consider investment in such items as:

1. Research and development
2. Training
3. Any additional staff expenditure, such as setting up a new O.R. department
4. Advertising
5. A canteen or any other welfare expenditure
6. A public relations department
7. A new computer
8. A new assistant chief executive

The investment expenditure on such activities, since it is pre-determined, is known; the benefits, however, are indirect and not readily assessable in terms of the hard cash received, for instance, from sales. Yet management has to decide whether to spend money on these items or to spend it on something with an immediate and calculable cash benefit, such as the handling machine. Cash is never available in unlimited quantities. A choice has to be made. *The only way any fair comparison can be made is by putting a cash value on these benefits.*

1.2. The origins of cost-benefit analysis

Cost-Benefit Analysis (CBA)—a social/economic technique which seeks to enable such comparisons to be made—really started in America in the 'thirties in connection with large Federal schemes like the Tennessee Valley Authority. Why, it was argued, should the Tennessee Valley scheme be adopted rather than some different hydro-electric scheme? The investment cost of the various schemes could be arrived at fairly accurately, but before any comparison could be made, it was necessary for the benefits in terms of reduced unemployment, the provision of electricity and water to the local population and to industry, the irrigation of farm land and so on, to be reduced to quantitative terms.

Yet another early use of CBA was in traffic studies in the State of Oregon just before the Second World War. Although it was not until quite recently that much interest was shown here in this application, there are some grounds for thinking that this field promises to be one of the most fruitful of all. The Victoria Line underground extension and the M 1 motorway were both analysed in terms of costs and benefits. The Ministry of Transport has recently developed new criteria for allocating their funds both in road planning and in accident preventative measures. If, as is of course the fact, only a limited sum of money is available, the problem (taking the latter case) is to find the best way to use it to reduce road accidents. How? By better roads, better lighting, improved car safety measures, better police control, more exhortation on the T.V. or radio? All these cost money. Which gives a better saving for every pound spent?

In the last few years CBA has been applied in many areas never before the subject of any analysis which attempted to quantify the benefits as well as the costs in money terms. The public sector is currently responsible for some 40 per cent of total capital investment. Almost the whole of this sector can be regarded as fertile CBA ground. To date, applications of CBA include:

Water development and supply
Transport (roads, accidents, etc.)
Town planning and land usage. Regional planning
Airport planning
Military defence
Health expenditure
Education

Some of these will be discussed more fully in chapter 2. Here we are only concerned with those general characteristics which apply to all problems in CBA.

1.3. Techniques of analysis

Broadly speaking the initial approach is to split benefits into two groups:

1. those whose value cannot apparently be measured directly in any quantitative terms whatsoever (e.g., spoilation of a view by a new power line). In chapter 2 an attempt is made to put some figures on the value of these benefits.
2. those which, though they cannot be measured directly in money terms, can be measured in some other units (e.g., decrease in number of deaths due to an improved medical treatment, increase in height or weight of children, or number of students who pass at 'O' or 'A' levels).

Let us—very briefly, at this stage—consider a simple example of this second group. Suppose London Transport is considering the installation of a new escalator at a tube station which will convey people up and down a good deal faster than of old. This benefit may be measured directly in quantitative terms, i.e., in passenger-hours saved. If the alternative investment is in a new lift, then both benefits can be expressed in the same quantitative terms and comparison is possible.

When, however, the benefits are not expressed in the same units—for example, when the alternatives are faster tube trains, safer trains, more routes, better lighting on platforms, better ventilation, and so on—they must be converted into the same units for comparison. Cash is the obvious choice, for it has the especial advantage that the benefit in each case can be compared directly with its own investment cost.

1.3.1. Direct approach

We have already noted that traffic studies were an early application of CBA. Let us consider how to calculate the benefits that arise from providing better travelling facilities by the construction of a new road between two towns. Since charges are not usually levied on all and sundry for travelling by road, the benefits cannot easily be measured directly.* It is possible, however, to analyse the expected benefits. The potential users can be split initially into two groups:

* Even this is not quite true. In some countries, such as Italy, new motorways with toll charges, run almost alongside the old inter-city roads.

(*a*) commercial lorries and vehicles, and

(*b*) private cars

(though, of course, there will be others, e.g., buses).

Traffic surveys will give an estimate of the numbers of each of these main types. If the proposed road shortens the distance between the two towns by (say) twenty miles, then each user will benefit to that extent from the saving in distance and time. The problem therefore resolves itself into transforming these figures into money terms. The commercial group will be comparatively easy. Some sort of average figure for a cost per mile, supplied perhaps by British Road Services, would provide a good basis for this assessment.

Private cars, however, present a difficult problem. It is fairly easy to arrive at the saving in terms of petrol and depreciation, but the real gain is the social benefit in terms of leisure hours saved. Since private car mileage is the dominating factor, no real estimate of the overall benefits can be arrived at without putting some money figure on the benefit from a leisure hour. Can we equate leisure hours with office earning hours—on the basis that a man is prepared to contribute his time to his employer at an average rate of (say) 50p an hour? Probably this is a fair guide when the time is spent travelling to and from work, since the overall hours given to the employer, in exchange for wages, include these unavoidable journeys. In fact in any cost benefit analysis these work journey hours are separately assessed and costed, usually at a rate of around 30p or 40p an hour.

The problem of costing genuine leisure hours still remains. In practice, the figure used by cost benefit traffic economists is about 15p or 20p an hour, that is, about half the work journey rate. How can this figure be arrived at? Another method, of great importance, considered below, shows one way.

1.3.2. Yardstick approach

Earlier it was said that charges are not usually levied on road-users. But the railways do charge, and road and rail are alternative possible means of travel. Now it is not suggested, of course, that the rail figures can be used directly and exclusively for the pricing of road benefits; many other considerations need to be taken into account. Nevertheless, a comparative quantitative basis can be established.

This example is only included in order to illustrate the means by which apparently intractable cost-benefit problems may be tackled. In brief, find some yardstick (which can itself be costed) with which to compare the benefit in question. As a physical illustration of the method, suppose we wish to measure the height of an object, but that for some reason it just is not possible to do this directly, e.g., by putting a measuring tape against it. It can, however, be compared with an object whose height is known to be a little under 10 feet, and perhaps with another object, which is a little over. Obviously if it is higher than the first object and shorter than the second, its height must be around 10 feet. It has been measured, not directly, but by comparison.

1.3.3. Historical and pragmatic approach

Decisions have, of course, been made many times in the past where benefits in both the main groups outlined in §1.3 above have been set against their costs. Since the costs were usually known, they indicate what the corresponding benefits were regarded as being worth at that time. They provide, therefore, an historical basis for setting some figures against them. Obviously if such figures are to be used as the basis for cost-benefit analysis today, the effect of inflation requires to be taken into account.

Such decisions have invariably been personal or emotional in the sense that they have been made without figures to support them. It does not follow from this that there is anything wrong in using them as the basis for costing benefits. After all, the worth or value of an emotion—arguably, its utility—is the cash value we put on it ourselves. A good view, for example, has no meaning at all unless there is someone to look at it. The value of a good view to us is the value that we ourselves place on it.

Not infrequently throughout this book the problem of solving intractable cost benefits problems *involving human feelings* will be dealt with by this method.

1.4. Recapitulation

The conclusions reached in this chapter may be summarized like this:

(*a*) apart from his purely recording work, the job of an accountant in a business is to advise and to assist in making financial decisions;
(*b*) such decisions involve weighing a payment made now against its anticipated cash inflow later (sometimes the payments are 'negative', as in a cost-cutting exercise);
(*c*) some decisions of business accountants—e.g., for expenditure on research, advertising, publicity, personnel, welfare and public relations—and nearly all decisions of administrative officers in nationalized industries and Government departments, are difficult to evaluate on this basis. One side of the 'equation'—the estimated expenditure on investment—is comparatively easy to determine in money terms; the other side—the expected benefits—can usually only be expressed (if at all) in non-cash quantitative units, such as leisure hours.

(*d*) when the benefit from alternative investments can be expressed in the same quantitative units (as in the lift and escalator problem) a direct comparison is possible. But whether investment in either is justified is still not proven;

(*e*) when the benefits from the alternative investments are not in the same quantitative units, they must be converted to a common unit. Cash has the overwhelming advantage that it enables the benefit from the investment to be compared directly with the cost, and hence makes possible an assessment as to whether the expenditure is justified or not.

(*f*) converting benefits into cash terms is difficult. Techniques do, however, exist, and progress becomes easier as we proceed into this almost uncharted area. When one or two agreed figures (such as a leisure-hour* rate) have been established as landmarks, other figures can be related to these;

(*g*) conversion of benefits into money terms is not the final step; the time element must be taken into account. That discount rate which, when applied to the benefits, will make them equal to the investment amount, must be determined. This return on investment rate is an easy measure for comparison purposes. Its incidence is quite general. It applies both to decisions at macroeconomic level, and to business decisions.

* Social cost-benefit analyses commonly use a leisure hour rate. Less easy to define, but also of great importance, is a unit to measure the annoyance or exasperation which people feel when they want something at a given point in time and expect to receive it immediately (or within a short prescribed period). Telephone connection delay time is one example, traffic hold up time due to unexpected construction work, or indeed almost any unexpected or excessive queuing, are others. The common denominator of all these is that no waiting—or very little—is expected. Zero base waiting time (ZBWT) is difficult to assess in any terms. Its worth is probably exponential with time. In the past the G.P.O., for example, has made many decisions which involved cost (e.g., for telecommunications equipment) against ZBWT. All these decisions *implied* (cf. §1.3.3, last paragraph) a figure for ZBWT, though, of course, no such figure was actually used in the analysis. No doubt in future an agreed figure, based originally on these decisions, will be used in such calculations.

Appendix on mathematical formulation

The various approaches are:

1. *When the benefits can all be measured in money terms.*

   (*a*) If a suitable interest rate has already been determined, then the investment is worthwhile if the discounted stream of benefits exceeds the discounted investment costs. (This is present value analysis.)*

   or,

   (*b*) Determine that interest rate which equates the discounted value of the investment costs with the discounted value of the stream of benefits. (This is 'discounted cash flow'; or 'internal rate of return analysis'.)* This technique makes comparison between several alternatives easy, since the best investment is that which gives the highest interest rate.

2. *When the benefits can all be measured in terms of one performance characteristic,*† *even though this cannot be converted into money terms.*

   The investment that has the highest ratio of benefit to cost is the best on this criterion.

   Take for example, the escalator/lift problem (§1.3). Suppose the investment cost of the escalator is £100000, but it saves 100 leisure hours per day. Assume that it will last for the same length of time as the lift, and that this leisure hour saving is the only benefit. Suppose the lift costs £50000 and its leisure hour saving rate is 40 per day. The escalator has a benefit–cost ratio of 100/100000, and this is higher than the benefit ratio of the lift, i.e., 40/50000.
   N.B. If *some* of the benefits can first be determined in money terms, then these can (after discounting) be deducted from the gross cost of the investment. The resulting net investment cost can then be used as the 'investment cost' above.

3. *When the investment amounts are equal, and it is possible to express the benefits from each investment in terms of a number of similar performance characteristics.*

   If one investment gives better performance characteristics for *each* benefit, then that investment will be the best.

* See chapters 5 and 6 for a full description of capital investment appraisal techniques.
† 'Performance characteristic' is here defined as any measure of performance or activity, i.e., it is any suitable unit of measurement (e.g., a leisure hour).

Take again the escalator/lift problem, but assume this time that the investment amounts are the same. The benefits, too, have been altered, and now read:

Performance characteristic	*Escalator*	*Lift*
Leisure hours saved per day	150	100
Work journey hours saved per day	120	110
Labour hours saved per day (on operation, maintenance, etc.)	10	4

Judged by each performance characteristic the escalator is better than the lift. Since the costs are the same, the escalator is the better investment.

Restated Mathematically

(1) (*a*) Investment is worth while if

$$I = \sum i \frac{1}{(i+r)^n} \leqslant \sum b \frac{1}{(i+r)^m}$$

(*b*) Investment in I_1 is better than in I_2 if

$$I_1 = \sum i \frac{1}{(i+r_1)^n} = \sum b \frac{1}{(i+r_1)^m}$$

$$I_2 = \sum i \frac{1}{(i+r_2)^n} = \sum b \frac{1}{(i+r_2)^m}$$

and

$$r_1 > r_2$$

(2) Investment in I_1 is better than in I_2 if

$$\frac{a_{11}}{I_1} > \frac{a_{12}}{I_2}$$

(3) Investment in I_1 is better than in I_2 if

$$I_1 = I_2$$

$$a_{p1} \geqslant a_{p2}$$

for each value of p from 1 to ω.

I_1 I_2 are the alternative investments, i and b are the yearly investment costs and benefits respectively.

n and m are the number of years of these costs and benefits respectively,

a_{p1} a_{p2} are the amounts of the performance characteristics for I_1 and I_2 for each value of p from 1 to ω.

r is the interest rate.

2. Cost-benefit analysis and social/economic problems

2.1. Business and social costs and benefits

The difference between private (business) and social costs was first clearly stated by Professor Pigou in his *Economics of Welfare.* To quote his, by now classic, definition:

> The essence of the matter is that one person A in the course of rendering some service for which payment is made to a second person B incidentally also renders services or disservices to other persons of such sort that payment cannot be exacted from the benefited parties or compensation enforced on behalf of the injured parties.

In our crowded, highly integrated island examples abound; one illustration will suffice. Consider the position of a detergent manufacturer. For his business, the costs are the costs of producing the detergent, and the benefits are the revenue received from customers. However, producing a detergent in bulk provides a serious effluent problem, since the by-products tend to pollute any river into which they are dispersed. This may well present quite a costly problem to the local river authority. From the overall (social) point of view this cost will be a disbenefit. Yet the detergent manufacturer, when deciding whether to produce or not, does not have to consider this, and may think it no concern of his. Public authorities, he will say, are there to deal with it. But should we be concerned with these (public) social costs. Whose side are we really on?

To some extent there is an analogy in the benefits accruing from the services of an *individual.* In our free-enterprise economy, payment to a worker is related to that amount by which he benefits his company. In theory, if the value of his services falls below his salary, his firm will try to get rid of him. If his services exceed his salary he should be able to get another job elsewhere. But from a social point of view is this, indeed, all? Should we not take into account the benefit that he gives to his wife, to his children, and his friends and indirectly through them to the community at large? His children—to pursue the most emotionally significant of these three—will presumably benefit society later, and perhaps very substantially—and this benefit will be affected by what he gives them now. From a social point of view this matters. Should we therefore be judged solely by what we earn (that is by what we benefit our firm), or as well by what we give to society through our children and other emotionally significant relationships? What is our real net benefit? What maximizes total overall benefit? Should we, even in this free enterprise society, solely consider the restricted benefits that we give to our business?

Such considerations, though fascinating, are outside the scope of this book. Let us return to the basic differences between the private (business) cost and the social (overall) cost. We can represent these by a simple diagram:

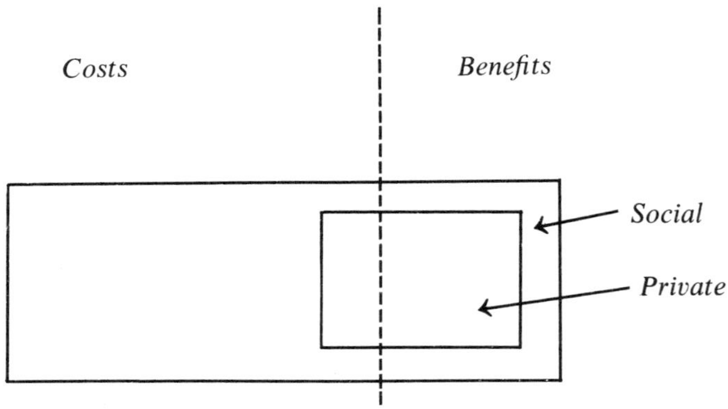

From this (almost Venn type) diagram it is easy to see that, although the private benefits exceed the private costs, in this case, the overall social position is the other way round. If we wish to maximize social benefits in a society which operates under free market conditions, how can we go about it? The use of the term 'free market' implies that one obvious solution, namely that the (private) business should be *made* to act in the best social interests by government decree, is not available. Even in the free capitalist society of the western world, this is of course not strictly true. Plenty of government interference and regulation does occur. But the aim is to keep such action to a minimum. What other way round the problem, therefore, exists?

The Pigovian answer is quite simple. If these additional* social costs (called externalities since they are external to the private business) exceed

* Sometimes in economic writing the term 'social cost' is used so as to include private costs; sometimes it relates only to those *additional* social (non-private) costs. We are using it here in this latter sense. In set theory notation if U represents the universal (social) costs and benefits, and A represents the private costs and benefits, then A' the complement of A in U represents these additional social costs.

the social benefits, then the remedy is to tax the private operator. If, on balance, the externalities are favourable, then, so the theory runs, the private operator should be encouraged to go ahead by being given subsidies. All this, of course, is an attempt to maximize social benefit, though not by interfering with the economy, other than by the use of monetary measures.

The practical difficulties inherent in the application of solutions of this type are enormous. In many cases it is almost impossible to measure the social disbenefits at all, let alone to convert these measurements into money terms. How do we measure the effect of pollution, congestion, or noise—three of the unpleasant consequences of being part of a rapidly increasing population living on an island of a fixed size? Consider noise. Until recently the accepted unit of measurement of noise was the decibel, but this unit only measures the pressure intensity of the sound. It does not attempt to differentiate between those sounds which are comparatively pleasant or unpleasant to the human ear. Some sounds are so high that the human ear cannot hear them at all, yet presumably they must have a decibel value. Some sounds are intermittent; some go on for a long while. Is a sound, repeated ten times at intervals of several seconds, less unpleasant than one which lasts longer but which, since it is continuous, is over much sooner. How do we quantify the effect of duration? These points are taken up in the appendix to this chapter.

Even when it is theoretically possible to measure the externalities, the practical problems of taxing the private firm or person, in a manner proportionate to the unfavourable effects that it or he is causing, are tremendous. Consider traffic congestion in relation to individual persons. The Pigovian theory is that a person creates unfavourable external effects by reason of the delay he causes other persons. But how much delay does he cause? If he travels to his work every day he may cause a lot. If he uses his car mainly for journeys into the countryside, he will probably cause little, if any. Yet in both cases he pays the same Road Fund Licence. Perhaps when he arrives at his work in the city, he will have to pay car park fees or else put money in a parking-meter. In this case, we do have some parallel between the social disbenefit (congestion), and the tax on the individual. Here, however, the correspondence ends, since the level of application of fees, licences, and parking-meter payments is almost certainly determined by other considerations than a desire to offset the social value of these unfavourable externalities.

2.2. Applications of CBA

The major applications to date of cost-benefit analysis (in the broad social economic sense in which we have been using the term in this chapter) were listed in chapter 1. Water development and supply have already been mentioned as providing the first practical applications of cost-benefit analysis techniques. Transport is perhaps the single, most important, present-day application. Both the M 1 and the Victoria Line in the U.K. were appraised very carefully by means of cost-benefit analyses. It is doubtful, however, whether the results of these analyses, in any way at all, affected the decisions to go ahead with either of the projects. Worse still—from the point of view of trying to justify the importance of cost-benefit analysis—this gap was caused by two distinct factors, each of which would have been sufficient in itself to preclude any connection between the cost-benefit analysis and the final decision. The first factor was the overriding political and social importance of the two projects. Too many people, too many bodies, were emotionally concerned and politically committed to the projects for them to have been turned down, whatever the results of the cost-benefit analysis had shown. It had to happen, whatever the figures said. (This pattern is analogous to that in a company when a detailed DCF calculation is carried out to determine what the real rate from a new machine will be, although everyone knows that the machine must be got in any case. The explanation of this difference lies in the fact that the conventional DCF calculation in such a case only takes into account the simple, easily quantifiable factors involved. A full DCF calculation, in which all the factors were taken into account, would give results in line with the commonsense appraisal of the situation.) The second factor is that many of the assumptions made in the analysis were blatantly arbitrary. For instance, most of the traffic, using a new motorway, will be traffic which has been diverted from other roads. The motorway provides a clear benefit to such users in the form of a shorter, quicker road. But some of the users of a new motorway (and even the volume* of these, let alone their money value, is hard to estimate) will use it because it is available. 'Why try and climb Mount Everest?' asked the interviewer of the Himalayan mountaineer. 'Because it's there' was the reply. Some of the traffic using a motorway does so for this same reason. Presumably such generated traffic—as it is called—can hardly be valued so highly from a social point of view, as the traffic which is using it because it provides a positive benefit compared with other available routes. But how do we quantify 'hardly as highly'. The authors of the M 1 analysis decided that the ratio of the social benefit of generated traffic to non-generated traffic should be half.

2.2.1. The Victoria Line

In any cost-benefit analysis the main problem usually arises on the benefit

* Such figures as are available indicate that it may well be as high as 30 per cent.

side of the 'equation'. Yet the benefits from operating a new underground line might seem at first sight to be fairly easily arrived at, since the underground charges fares to its customers. In a free market these fares would accurately reflect the value of the service operated, that is the benefit. Unfortunately, however, these fares are not arrived at by determining what people will pay for the transport service offered. London Transport is not a free enterprise commercial concern operating in competition with other similar bodies, but a monopolistic public corporation whose fares are fixed by completely different, quasi-political, criteria which bear no relation to the market situation. One approach would be to impute shadow prices on these fares, that is to determine, presumably by market research, what people would pay for this service. But since, as we have seen, there are no direct commercial alternatives, the problem of determining the free market rate is almost insoluble. In fact, given the present mandatorially fixed fare levels, the estimated loss for the Victoria Line is around two or three million pounds per annum.

The only practical alternative, from the users point of view, to a London Transport tube or bus, is private transport—that is a car. And no correlation at all exists between the price that car owners pay by way of licences and tax on petrol, etc., and their heavy social costs, that is, the costs of the roads.

We have therefore no option but to ignore the actual fare prices. To determine the social gain we must use the more general cost-benefit techniques of analysis. How then can we evaluate these benefits? C. D. Foster and M. E. Beesley in their exhaustive study* argued that the benefits would be available to three separate groups:

1. *Diverted traffic*—that is, users of the new Victoria Line who were users of other methods of traffic (either private transport or other tube lines or buses).
2. *Non-diverted traffic*—that is, users of the other routes who would continue to use them but who would be able to do so faster, more safely, and more cheaply because of the reduced congestion on these routes.
3. *Generated traffic*—that is, as we have seen, traffic which would not exist at all had the new facility not been available.

The first problem was to determine the physical amounts of each of these types of users, i.e., working time and leisure time users. Most of the early work for the Victoria Line was done at the Road Research Laboratory. Nowadays, results arrived at by test marketing techniques

* C. D. Foster and M. E. Beesley, 'Estimating the Social Benefit of Constructing an Underground Railway in London', *Journal of the Royal Statistical Society*, Series A. Vol. **126** Part I, 1963.

—discussed in broad outline in chapter 7—and used in conjunction with computer control simulation models, can give fairly accurate answers to these problems of determining the quantity.

The working time proportion presented no problem, since it was assumed that this time could be valued at the same rate as the average hourly rate of pay of those travelling on the Victoria Line. Leisure (non-working) time was valued at 25p per hour. The authors remarked that this was 'arbitrary but perhaps not unreasonable'. No doubt. But much the same comments could reasonably be made about figures of 10p, 20p, 30p, or 40p. Obviously all these would give results which would be widely different.

Not all the social benefit would arise, so the authors argued, from the time saved. London Underground has a duty to provide a certain standard of comfort to its customers. To see that this, too, must be expressed in money terms, it is only necessary to take an extreme case. If all trains were to travel very fast, but no lights, seats, heating or fresh air were to be provided, all the benefits from the speed would be lost since no one could even find their way in the dark to the trains, let alone use them. London Transport—indeed any public authority—must consider how to allocate its expenditure between comfort and technical efficiency. The valuation

Table 2.1

Costs		*Annual amount (£m)*
A. Annual working costs		1·413
Benefits		
B. Traffic diverted to V.L.:		
1. Underground: Time		0·378
Comfort		0·347
2. British Railways: Time		0·205
3. Buses: Time		0·575
4. Motorists: Time		0·153
Cost		0·377
5. Pedestrians: Time		0·020
	Sub-total	2·055
C. Traffic not diverted:		
	Sub-total	3·916
D. Generated traffic:		
	Sub-total	0·822
Total benefits		6·793
		1·413
Total benefits less running costs		5·380
Value of capital expenditure		38·810

of comfort on the underground is a good example of the indirect yardstick approach (see chapter 1). Since comfort cannot be estimated directly in money terms it must be compared with something that can be. The authors compared the observed behaviour of those faced with a choice between fast services (with low comfort, e.g., poor seating) and slow services (with good comfort, e.g., a high probability of obtaining a seat). On this basis a substitution rate of comfort for time can be obtained. But time had already been expressed in money terms. Hence, comfort, too, can be given a cash value. Table 2.1 gives in summary form the results of the Victoria Line cost-benefit assessment.*

The estimated net annual benefits—that is the total benefits less the running costs—amounted to £5·380m. The authors considered that the scheme would last for some fifty years. This amounts to a return of just under 15 per cent on the total estimated capital cost of the line of £38·81m.

A full discussion of how such rates can be calculated is given in chapters 5 and 6. We must, however, add here that this return does not take into account the rate of inflation. It is inconceivable that fares ten years in the future—let alone fifty—will bear any resemblance to current fares. The equivalent rate of return, taking into account inflation at only 4 per cent per annum, would be 19·6 per cent. On all these counts it seems hard to escape the conclusion that some of the calculations and certainly the resulting rate of return in the Victoria Line analysis had a rather limited meaning. This is in no way to deny its very great importance as a pioneering effort. All social cost-benefit analyses these days follow along much the same lines—if that is the right phrase—as this work!

Sub-optimal and optimal solutions. The estimated capital cost (£38·81m) for the Victoria Line was very high. In practice this money would be partly supplied indirectly by the Government, but in theory it comes from London Passenger Transport Board sources and must compete with other possible schemes of theirs for the limited funds available. This is strictly true for problems similar to the example given in chapter 1 when London Transport was considering the alternatives of the installation of a new escalator, or a lift, with other forms of expenditure giving benefits to the public, e.g., faster, safer trains, better lighting or ventilation on platforms and so on. In a simple cost-benefit analysis such as this, the area within which the decision will be made is fairly narrow. The cash will come from London Transport resources and comparison will only be made with other underground schemes which give benefits to the public. Such a restricted solution is sub-optimal.

But all the benefits provided by London Transport are in the last analysis paid for out of public money. Other transport utilities such as the buses,

* Taken from C. D. Foster and M. E. Beesley, op. cit., p. 49.

British Railway trains, etc., afford similar benefits, and their money, too, is provided from public funds. An optimal solution would require that the costs and benefits be compared—not only within the underground system—but across the whole range of public transport facilities.

Ideally, it seems, all public money benefits should be compared and schemes should only be adopted if they give value for money when related to all civil service, local government, etc., expenditure.

One general example of the extreme uselessness of sub-optimal solutions is worth mentioning. At a crossroads near to Hyde Park Corner the traffic density some years ago was as high as anywhere in London. To relieve the congestion an under-tunnel was suggested. Analysis showed that this would result in an immense speeding up of traffic. In terms of time saved, the benefits appeared to outweigh the costs very substantially. Accordingly the tunnel was constructed. The net effect was to move the traffic congestion a couple of blocks farther down to the next traffic intersection point. The overall gain in transit time for all through traffic was negligible. The planners had concentrated on a sub-optimal solution and had not been able to see, almost literally, beyond their noses.

2.2.2. Land conservation and town planning

To some extent transport, and the use of land for town planning purposes, are similar problems. Part of the benefits from both must be expressed in leisure hours saved. Efficient town planning will seek to minimize wastage in leisure hours by providing good communications, e.g., road, rail and buses both within the town and for travel to places outside the town. However, in town planning, there are many other additional factors to take into account. Land in the U.K. is already in very short supply, and it is certain that it will become an increasingly scarce resource as the years go by. Land used for town planning generally means land taken away from agriculture (there are some exceptions to this, for instance it is probable* that London's third airport will be built on reclaimed land near Foulness). As a result of the increasing application of scientific methods to farming, the output per acre rises each year between 1 and 2 per cent in real terms. Such an increase is doubly welcome. First, because the population is growing and more people need more food. Second, because food imports are about 6 per cent of our total imports in money terms and the main U.K. financial problem lies in its net negative trade balance; additionally, when the U.K. does get into the Common Market, a critical factor will be the ability of the U.K. farmer to stand up to free competition from his E.E.C. competitors. So town planning requires land, and agri-

* Perhaps this view is an exception to that coldly analytical approach which hopefully pervades this book. The author happened to live on the edge of one of the inland sites!

culture requires land, and land is in short supply. Who then, shall have it, and what shall be paid for it? In theory, any price for a commodity reflects the difference between the annual revenue and the annual costs discounted to today's value. So far as farm land is concerned this is utterly meaningless. Neither farm costs nor farm revenue are at all realistic. Artificial fertilizers are heavily subsidized (something like 40 per cent is paid by the Government) and grants are available on drainage, fencing, afforestation, clearing, etc. Farm revenue, too, is heavily distorted by the subsidized prices that marketing boards pay for the produce. The current value of agricultural land has been so affected by legislative provisions that it no longer bears any resemblance to the true market value. Once again it seems that cost-benefit analysis has got to rely on imputed shadow prices. Yet the problem of getting such a price is almost insuperable. The gap between the open market, free enterprise position and the real life situation is so wide that no proper reconciliation between the two can be made.

Within the closed circle of 'official' farm produce prices, artificial rents, subsidized services to farmers, and the limitations put on availability of land by planning regulations, sub-optimal solutions regulating the use of land have perhaps some meaning. Alternative town planning schemes can be evaluated on this basis. It is more difficult to believe that any basis exists for a meaningful comparison between the uses of land for either farms and dwellings, or motorways, or Government offices, for instance.

2.2.3. Education

All social/economic applications of cost-benefit analysis seem to bring their own special problems. Education is no exception. The particular problem here is with time. In the case of expenditure on schools—and this constitutes the main bulk of the money involved—the return may not start for some ten or more years and may go on for another forty or so. Prima facie it might seem that this is just a rather extreme example of those problems that time differences in cash flows always bring. On this argument it is just a question of determining what extra rate we are prepared to pay for the fact that the jam will be available tomorrow and not today. In other words, we need to arrive at a social time preference rate (see chapter 6). But are we really comparing like with like here? We (the present adult tax payers) are providing the money now, not for our own later benefit, but for the benefit of our children. Yet the children have no say in the matter; we decide for them!

The most simple and straightforward applications of cost-benefit analysis of education therefore naturally lie at the other end of the spectrum, that is in adult education. Here the situation is 'comparatively' simple. Let us take an example. The total social cost of an engineering degree at a university is probably around £10000. This may not be quite the right figure. At any rate it will not be too difficult to arrive at this total cost, since all the cost components, e.g., lecturers fees, cost of college buildings, etc., can be fairly precisely determined. Now figures could be obtained to give the average* salary level amongst those engineers with degrees and those without. Assuming that salary level is a good indication of the individual's value to the community—and this assumption we have so far made all along—then the difference between this salary level, taken year by year throughout the whole working life, will give the value of university education to the community. This is most easily expressed as a rate of return on the initial cost. Most of the work so far done along these lines points to a social rate of return on education in the U.K. of between 8 and 12 per cent.

However, even this apparently simple example bristles with problems. Just to compare the salaries of those who have taken degrees with those who have not is blatantly wrong. The degree-takers, in any case, were almost certainly much more intelligent or pushing than the non-degree-takers. Because of this high intelligence and determination they were given, or they got, the opportunity to take the degree. This relatively high intelligence might even have resulted in their having just as high a salary differential over the non-degree-takers. Perhaps their intelligence got them their extra money, and not the degree. Almost certainly this is putting the position too strongly, but it does point to the fact that the control groups in the analysis must be selected with great care to eliminate the differential intelligence factors and only leave the value of the increase in working ability specifically due to the university education.

One further distinction must also be made. By degree costs we mean the total social cost to the community, that is, what the taxpayer in the long run will have to stand. From the individual's point of view, the benefits, i.e., the salary differential over the years of his life, will be the same, but his costs (his father's perhaps!) will be only those extra fees and accommodation expenses that he has to pay out. These are likely to be much less than the true social costs. Some recent studies indeed indicate that the private rate of return may well be as high as 20 per cent. In both cases, of course, the loss of earnings during the period of study at the university, must be taken into account. For these years the non-degree-taker will have a differential advantage exactly equal to his salary. Alternatively, and equally correctly, this can be regarded as an opportunity loss from the point of view of the university degree student. In chapter 11 the rate of

* About the only bright star in the fog that surrounds cost-benefit analysis is the fact that average figures *can*, in general, be fairly used, since we are dealing with large numbers of people. Contrast with the story of the man who had one foot in a bucket of frozen ice, and the other foot in a bucket of boiling oil, but said that 'on average' his feet were cosy!

return on industrial training—a particular type of education obviously of special importance to business—will be considered further.

2.2.4. Health

As a nation, how much money should we spend on health, and how should this money be allocated among hospitals, general practitioners, research establishments, and so on?

The first of these two problems seems almost impossible to solve, even using a theoretical cost-benefit analysis approach, since both global costs and benefits of health expenditure are almost impossible to identify, let alone measure. It might seem at first sight that the total costs of health for a country are just the costs of medical services together with the costs of drugs, medicine, etc. But is this indeed all? Clean towns are germ free towns with, consequently, much less spreading of infectious diseases. So, presumably, we should include part of the cost of sewage disposal, rubbish removal, clean water (almost all the costs of adding fluoride to the water should be included since reduced dental charges will form the sole benefit), and clean air—as opposed to smog—the most potent factor in respiratory diseases such as bronchitis. What 'part' should be taken is not clear. And, just to take the last of these problems, how does one even attempt to evaluate the social cost of smog abatement schemes, the rules and regulations regarding factory smoke, and transport regulations relating to exhaust fumes from cars?

It is evident that the costs of health expenditure are inextricably tied up with other social costs. Unfortunately, this applies equally, or perhaps with even greater force, to health benefits. The apparent social benefit from health expenditure is the extra work that the individual is able to perform as a result of being well. All we have to do, it might seem, is to estimate the reduction in the amount of working time lost as a result of our health programme. But how can we do that? We certainly cannot assess it in terms of number of days off work. Many people's work is left on their desks if they are absent for just a few days, and the understanding is that on their return they put this right themselves; overall nothing—or very little—is lost. Some people, too, happily take time off whenever they wish to, and present a certificate, signed by a harassed doctor, to support their statement that they were run down, just had a bad cold or 'flu, or had gastro-enteritis (that is, they told the doctor that they had a pain in the stomach!). The real problem is that time spent off work is, in any case, only the tip of the iceberg. The main benefit from good health expenditure must be in a generally higher level of health, a feeling of well-being, a healthy mind in a healthy body, all leading, without doubt, to far better performance at work. And how can one even hope to quantify this?

To arrive at the costs and benefits of health, looked at from the overall point of view, is therefore a very difficult problem. This is unfortunate, since, as we have seen earlier, the benefits from all public monies should, ideally, be compared, and expenditure should only be justified if the value of the benefits compares favourably with other civil service government expenditure.

The problems of allocating the available funds *within* the health service are equally difficult. It is not easy to decide what amount to spend on preventative medicine, which illnesses to concentrate on, and in general where to spend the money to the best advantage. Almost no work at all has been done on comparing the relative values of money spent on preventative medicine and curative medicine. In parenthesis it seems odd that imaginative schemes which aim to give people thorough overall medical checks at fairly frequent intervals, with a view to detecting illnesses in their early (and, therefore, probably curable) stages, and advising on general fitness so that good resistance can be maintained, have not met with a ready acceptance in this country as yet. Most of the schemes that do exist are either privately run (e.g., by the large industrial companies such as Shell, or by bodies such as the Institute of Directors), or they are a specific against some particular illness, e.g., cervical cancer. We all recognize that the most simple way to preserve our car is to have it serviced regularly, rather than to wait till a breakdown occurs, and then have to put it in a garage for major repairs. Apparently we are not prepared to adopt such a realistic attitude to our own internal machinery. Perhaps part of the reason lies in a strong subconscious desire not really to want to know if anything is wrong. Medical check-ups are worrying things. We can cope with the thought of a bad report on our car but not on ourselves.

Allocating money to medical research presents very difficult technical problems. (In practice, the problem often does not arise, since a good deal of research money is given by foundations and trusts for specific purposes.) Once again the problem of jam today or jam tomorrow arises. Shall we spend money today to save lives in ten years time, or shall we spend it now on costly treatment for patients? Even setting aside this problem of time (until chapters 5 and 6), how do we compare medical treatment for everyday illnesses which just keep people off work, with medical treatment which really saves lives? As we have already seen, there are great problems in determining the value of medical treatment for everyday complaints, since time spent off work is generally not at all a good guide to value. Moreover, since housewives, too, catch diseases we need to attach a value to housewives services. What is the value of their 'time off work'? Even if we can find a value for these imponderables, how can we compare them with the value of a life saved? It is no good, at this stage, saying that life is so precious that it cannot be valued. The plain facts of the matter are that it must be, and that it is. Every time a sum of money is allocated to a research project on some incurable illness, an estimate is made as to its cost and the probability of its successful outcome. Since the number of lives that will be saved must also be assessed, it follows that these lives are being costed.

The truth of the matter is that these sorts of decision are being made all the time. Sometimes they are made at a very high level; sometimes, as in the case of the purchase of a single kidney or lung machine for some £7000, they are very personal. Both the Ministry of Transport and the Ministry of Health have the same problem of saving lives; the former by reducing death on the roads, the latter by medical treatment. Who shall have the limited money available? Both cost money; the only rational way of choosing is to decide who saves more lives for the same money, i.e., whose cost per life is the lower. Now it is not suggested, of course, that this is the sole, or even the major criterion in allocating funds between Ministries and other organizations. Nevertheless, some figure for lives saved must be used for cost-benefit analysis of this type. Figures between £4000 and £10 000 have perhaps been the most commonly used.

Let us now turn our attention from the general health framework to the problem of individual illnesses. Most of the work to date in the application of cost-benefit to specific illnesses, has been on the effectiveness of preventative methods and measures. For instance, the cost of covering areas of water in which the malaria mosquito bred, was compared with the benefits from the expected decrease in malaria victims. More recently, considerable research has been done on comparing the costs and benefits from different ways of treating a particular illness or complaint. Ulcers, for example, can be cured either by surgical treatment or by diet, or their effects can be suppressed by drugs: sometimes a combination of these is used. Figure 2.1 shows a diagram of health costs against time.

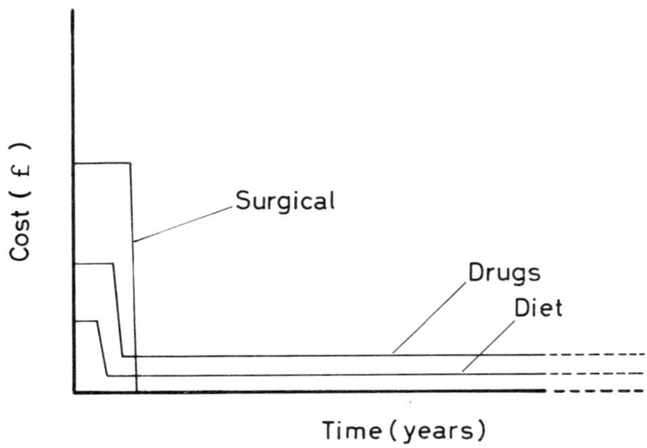

Figure 2.1.

In trying to decide on the appropriate treatment a National Health doctor will not feel himself constrained by the cost of any drugs he prescribes. The restrictions which do constrain his action will mainly be those of long hospital waiting lists. On this basis he might well decide on drugs or a diet. However, if we take the broad cost-benefit view, the picture is not so simple. Treatment by surgery will mean hospitalization for a number of days. The precise cost to the National Health Service can be easily determined. The patient's loss of output in terms of days off work will probably only be a few days more. Treatment by diet or drugs, on the other hand, will not mean that any appreciable number of days off work will be lost, but the general level of performance of the individual at his work may suffer appreciably for a long while—perhaps even for the rest of his working life. If the hospital decides on a diet as the best treatment—probably because of the shortage of available beds—it does not, and cannot take into account all the social costs of this decision. Within its own limitations its decision may be correct; in the wider context it can be seen as a suboptimal solution.

Appendix on the measurement of personal and social disbenefits

Note on the measurement of personal and social disbenefits
The questions to which we would like to provide an answer in this section can roughly be put as follows:

First, to what extent are we affected by direct personal disbenefits such as unwelcome noise, smell (air pollution), vision. Even much more indirect disbenefits, such as the possibility of suffering damage from flood, lightning, fire, water pollution, etc., need some sort of consideration.

Second, how can we measure these disbenefits in any terms at all, and particularly how can we measure them in money terms?

Excessive and unpleasant noise and air pollution are both increasing rapidly in parallel with the growth in population and the number of technological inventions available such as, for instance, the motor car. Not too long ago both the air and the sea were regarded as practically limitless in size and therefore capable of absorbing any number of waste products. We now have to face up to the fact that this is not true and that both these elements are showing signs of approaching saturation level. No doubt in the years to come the same problems will arise with outer space! Since noise and air pollution are of such substantial and growing importance, these two will be considered in some detail, and particular attention will be paid to noise.

Noise. Noise is a human being's awareness of unpleasant sound. Sound is caused by radiation of energy in the form of pressure waves from a vibrating source. The waves need a medium, such as air for their transmission. Sound, therefore, cannot travel through a vacuum.

There are three basic units of measurement:

1. *Decibels*. Strictly, a decibel is a ratio of one sound pressure level to the sound pressure level of a reference base. Consequently, a decibel, being a ratio, is a dimensionless unit. It is defined as follows:

Given a reference sound of power n_{ref}, then the value in decibels of a sound of power n is:

$$10 \log_{10} \frac{n}{n_{\text{ref}}}$$

It will be appreciated that the effect of expressing the relationship in this form is to reduce the ratio to a logarithmic scale. Thus if n is $10 \times n_{\text{ref}}$, the value in decibels is

$$10 \log_{10} \frac{10n_{ref}}{n_{ref}} = 10 \times 1 = 10$$

But if n is $100 \times n_{ref}$, the value in decibels is

$$10 \log_{10} \frac{100n_{ref}}{n_{ref}} = 10 \times 2 = 20$$

Increasing power by ten times, therefore, doubles the decibels, increasing by 1000 trebles the decibels, and so on.

The basic reference (n_{ref}) is usually defined in terms of the *power* of the actual source of sound. The internationally accepted standard is 10^{-12} watts. With this standard set as it is, it so happens that the smallest change in sound level usually discernible by the human ear is about one decibel, and further, what would usually be regarded as about a doubling of loudness is equivalent to a change of around ten decibels. This logarithmic scale is indeed convenient for many reasons and especially since the range in the figures of power used in practice would otherwise be too wide for convenience.

So far now we have been discussing sound in the physical sense, that is by its propagation in sound pressure waves. What we are really concerned with, of course, is how these variations in pressure affect ourselves. The receiving device by which the human being hears sound is the ear. However, only sounds with frequencies between about 25 and 15 000 cycles per second can be heard by the ear. Even within this range the reaction of the ear to sound varies considerably. With the exception of sounds of extremely high frequencies, the ear is a good deal less sensitive to low

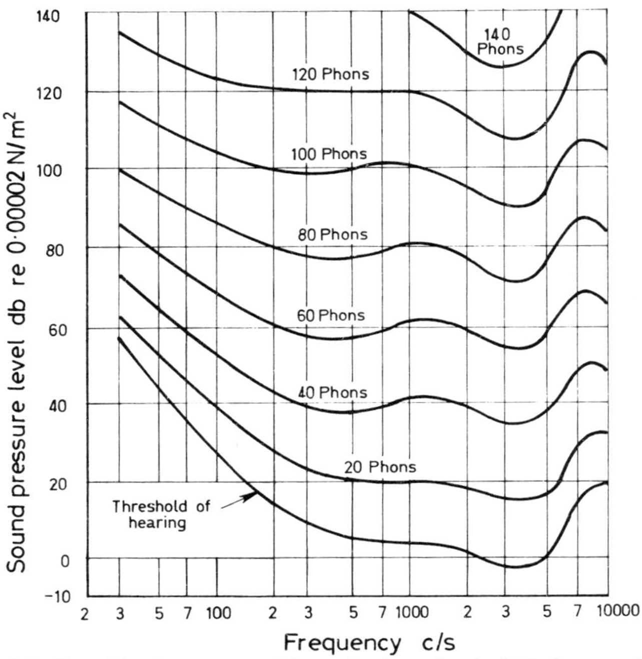

Figure 2.2. *Equal loudness curves.* Note: *Loudness level of 40 phons = 1 sone.* Institute of Heating and Ventilating Engineers Guide

than to high frequency sounds. It follows that more sound in terms of decibels is required at a low level than at a high level of frequency to give the same impression of loudness.

2. The *unit of loudness* is a *phon*. This is a subjective, *ad hoc* unit. In experiments with relatively large numbers of people the relationship between loudness and decibels for various frequencies was established. The results are shown in Fig. 2.2, where 'equal loudness' curves are given.

Unfortunately the situation is further complicated by the fact that some sounds, though regarded by the human being as of equal loudness, are not regarded as being equally unpleasant. Another, even more subjective, method of assessment is therefore required.

3. *Noise criteria* (NC) have been established which are defined as showing equal human tolerance (though perhaps intolerance would be a better word!) to noise. Figure 2.3 shows the relationship between decibels and noise at various frequency levels.

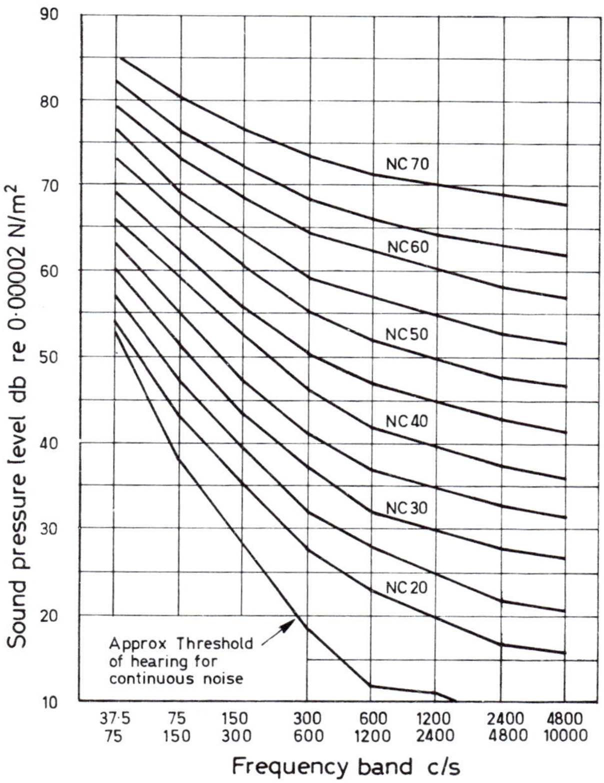

Figure 2.3. Noise criteria curves. Institute of Heating and Ventilating Engineers Guide

As can be seen from this figure, the noise criteria have been established by starting in each case from a standard noise within a fixed frequency band of 1200–2400 cycles. For instance, noise criterion 30 was established by listening to a sound of 30 decibels at a frequency of 1200–2400 cycles and then finding those decibels which gave an impression of equally unpleasant noise at other frequencies.

To sum up we have so far discussed the use of three units:

1. *Decibels*—an objective unit for measuring sound pressure
2. *Phons*—a subjective unit for measuring loudness
3. *Noise criterion*—a subjective unit for measuring the unpleasantness of noise. (The phrase 'perceived noise level' is frequently used as a synonym for 'noise criterion'.)

Clearly we should only be concerned with the last unit. In fact the use of decibels to measure noise is a vast oversimplification of the problem to say the least. To attempt to assess the disbenefit of noise by saying that it can be roughly measured by the excess of actual decibel units of the noise over (say) 90 decibels is unscientific, if not to say unsound.

Fortunately, instruments are now available which can measure noise criteria. These instruments are basically decibel meters whose readings have been weighted to correspond to the human being's varying tolerance to noise over the frequency bands.

Now that we have arrived at a method of assessing and measuring the unpleasantness of noise, are we in a position to proceed further? Can we lay down reasonable noise criteria limits, and can we evaluate the disbenefit from exceeding these limits? Unfortunately, there are still some further considerations that must be taken into account before we can do this.

Firstly, some allowance must be made for the background noise and the type of environment. What is perfectly acceptable in a foundry or heavy engineering works (recommended design noise criterion of 70) would certainly not be tolerable in a concert hall, recording studio or ballroom (recommended design noise criterion of 25). Between these two extremes lie these:

NC 30*	Private dwellings, conference rooms.
NC 35	Small executive offices.
NC 40	Halls, corridors, restaurants, large staff offices, design offices, small stores.
NC 45	Department stores, supermarkets, canteens, general offices, workshop offices.
NC 50	Typing pools, offices with business machines.
NC 60	Light engineering workshops.

It follows that in considering any excessive noise our reference level must first be determined. Thus the measure of the excess of unduly loud noise (for example NC 70) in relation to the staff office (recommended design criterion of 40) when it occurs is the ratio:

$$\frac{\text{excess}}{\text{reference base}} = \frac{30}{40} = 0{\cdot}75$$

This is the *noise index*.

Second, it is not only the relative excess which is important but the time and more particularly the conditions under which it occurs. For example, the noise criterion for houses is 30. If the house lies under the glide path of one of London's airports it is likely that every so often the noise level will rise to 90 or even higher. This gives a noise index of 2 which is, in any case, very high. However, at night time the criterion

* Taken from the *Institute of Heating and Ventilating Engineers' Guide*.

is probably lower than 30 since background noise at night is less than in the daytime. The noise index may then rise to 3 or perhaps 4. Even this high figure, however, does not give a true indication of the adverse effect of this noise since it is not just the noise itself, but the loss of sleep which follows when the noise is so great that it wakes one up, that is the real nuisance.

Unfortunately (from the point of view of quantifying noise) there are, it seems, other consequential effects of noise, not all of which are so obviously apparent to the person concerned. There is, for instance, almost overwhelming evidence that noise has an unfavourable effect on the entire physique causing tension and rapid fatigue. The World Health Organization (W.H.O.), has estimated that four million dollars are lost in the U.S. every day from noise induced fatigue in offices alone. The biological effects of noise are probably far greater than is usually thought, particularly in heart and nervous ailments. The French Academy of Medicine estimates that noise is a contributory factor in 52 per cent of such diseases. Sometimes sharp sudden noises can have dangerous consequences out of all proportion to the noise level. The proportion of road accidents which have startle noise as a main or contributory factor is probably as high as 25 per cent.

Other than quoting the figures above as a guide, no attempt is made here to quantify the material disadvantages of consequential noise damage. It can be seen that they are already substantial and are apparently growing year by year. What we are primarily concerned with (at any rate in the business context) is the adverse effect of undue noise on people at work or at home. At work this effect will be felt in two ways. First, it may well result in inefficiency due to fatigue. The W.H.O. figure quoted above is apposite here. Second, it will be felt by the staff as one of the factors they should take into account when deciding whether the conditions of work are satisfactory or not. In the U.K. there is considerable evidence from welfare surveys that staff now place a good deal of emphasis on living conditions, fringe benefits and the like, when deciding where they wish to work. However, figures are immensely difficult to arrive at here. The only reasonably reliable figures are those for the adverse effect of noise on people in dwelling-houses. We can use these figures for our purposes if we *assume* that excessive noise (over and above that which is expected and to which people are accustomed) is equally annoying and intolerable to the person concerned, whether experienced at home or at work. Only then can the figures for one be properly used for the other. We have already seen that daytime noise in a glide path near an airport gives a noise index of around 2. The material effect of this can be measured by the fall in value of house property in the areas subject to this extreme noise. On average this fall is of the order of 10 per cent or a little over. Medium-priced houses in the range £6000 to £9000* are regarded as selling at about £1000 below their true market rate, that is the rate that they would have fetched in an area which is similar but free from aircraft noise. Rents generally are between £50 and £100 per annum cheaper, and this gives a more direct assessment of the current value of noise. Taking the mean figure, we can put a money value of £75 per annum on a noise index of 2.

We have, or course, ignored any number of important factors in arriving at this figure, which must be regarded as being a first attempt on which, later, more serious efforts to arrive at a proper assessment could be based. We have ignored the problem of noise at night. Probably this is justifiable, since the fall in value of property on the glide paths where frequent jet flights take place at night (e.g., at Heathrow) is substantially higher than the figures given above. We have also ignored the problem of the duration of the noise. Continuous and intermittent noise can be unpleasant

* *Report to the Roskill Commission by the British Association for the Control of Aircraft Noise on property around Gatwick.* Reported in *The Daily Telegraph* of 5 February, 1970.

though in a rather different way. A continuous noise of around NC 90 would prevent normal conversation, destroy concentration and generally would make life pretty unbearable. On the other hand it is possible to adjust to continuous noise. The best known example of this is the roar from the Niagara Falls. The noise close to these falls is incessant and, to a visitor, intolerable. But the inhabitants of houses in the vicinity regard it as just background noise, and barely noticeable. Their ears have become quite accustomed to it.

The problem of adjustment is closely allied to the problem of individual tolerance to noise. It can be held that any noise tolerance figures based on the drop in value of property (or increased wages demanded at work) because of excessive noise, do not give a true value for the disbenefit of excessive noise to the average person. The argument is that as people are relatively free to choose (within limits) both their dwelling-place and place of work, only those people who are comparatively unaffected by noise will choose to live immediately under a flight path, or to work in a foundry, a milk bottling plant, or a heavy engineering works. Consequently, the real money value of excess noise necessarily endured to an average person is considerably in excess of the figure quoted above.

It would be interesting to try to go further with this attempt to evaluate the disbenefit from noise. Many problems still remain, many arbitrary assumptions have been made to arrive even as far as we have. For instance, is it really true that excessive noises at work and home are both felt to be equally unpleasant? Maybe we feel that we must be prepared to tolerate more at work than we would do in the privacy of our own home? Or is the reverse perhaps the case? Home conditions must be accepted since we can do little about it once we are there, but at work—well, what are shop stewards for! We may accept gladly what we have to, or we may complain about it bitterly. It is all a matter of temperament, a very subjective matter—a comment that applies, unfortunately to most of the problems in this section!

Air pollution. Although air pollution is a great social problem, it is not a particular problem for most businesses. The incidence of smog or clean air will remain substantially the same for locations within a distance of several miles of each other. All industries, dwelling-houses and cars within this broad area will provide their quota of harmful and noxious gasses and fumes to the atmosphere, and all will suffer equally from this general contamination. On the other hand, noise, as we have seen, is much more local in its effect. Even noise from a jet engine is a serious nuisance for only a short distance each side of the flight path. Most noises, even those from a foundry, a traffic intersection, or a pneumatic drill, have a very limited range. They affect a business or a dwelling-house in a much more individual way and consequently they require individual treatment. Contaminated air has a social or group cause; it affects all members equally and it requires a social remedy.

It is interesting to note the way that inborn beliefs and prejudices affect the rational treatment of problems such as these. Air has always been thought of as pure, free, available to all, indeed as being nature's gift to mankind. No need to question its supply; like mother's milk or the sun's heat it is there in limitless quantity. Unlike water it does not even need to be turned on and off at the tap. The cleanliness of water, indeed, has always been a consideration in people's minds, and water purification schemes have long been the subject of much scientific and commercial work. Although the disadvantages of dirty water and the diseases that it can spread have long been known and feared, the effects of dirty air—which have been with us ever since the industrial revolution—have not been at all widely understood until quite recently. Undoubtedly it is this apparent easy and universal availability which has caused the rather sluggish reaction to air pollution. The great smog of 1952 first roused public opinion to the terrible effect of polluted fog on respiratory diseases.

In just a few days in that black December, the increase in the number of deaths in the Greater London area was around the figure of 4000. Nowadays almost everyone is intellectually aware of the danger to health from polluted air, yet the measures taken still do not really face up to the problem. Air pollution legislative measures always seem designed to deal with the problem as it was some ten years or so before that particular statute became law. The Clean Air Act 1956 is both the outstanding piece of clean air legislation, and the best example of this time lag. Under the Act any local authority could declare the whole or any part of the district of the authority to be a smoke control area. The Act was widely framed so that the emission of smoke from almost any building in a smoke control area constituted an offence. Further, in a declared area, only the use of authorized fuels or equipment was allowed. All these measures taken together would probably have been quite adequate if they had been introduced shortly after the war. However, converting fireplaces to burn smokeless fuel and replacing the direct use of coal in industry by oil all take time, as even those enlightened authorities who did make use of their powers under the 1956 Act soon found out. It was not until about 1958 at the earliest that the Act really began to be effective. The Act suffered therefore not only because it was permissive, but more importantly because its approach was piecemeal. It ignored the fact that the problem was a national one and that dirty air can carry over into a clean zone. The situation is analagous to the allotment holder who allows his ground to be covered with weeds, blind to the effect that this has on the holders of the other allotments adjacent to his. Most allotment authorities insist that the owner responsible for each area keeps his section free from weeds. The same cannot be said of the Clean Air Act.

Because of the wide range of both the sources and the effects of polluted air it is exceedingly difficult even to attempt any quantification. There is evidence that people are prepared to pay substantially more for house property in clean areas and to put themselves to the considerable discomfort and expense of travelling long distances to get there. Areas such as Tunbridge Wells or even the South Coast are now 'commuter' distance from London, and prices of houses some fifty or sixty miles out from the City are correspondingly high. But it is impossible to determine what proportion of this increase is for the benefit from clean air, and what proportion is due to all those other additional facilities that these areas provide. The only approach that offers any hope of giving meaningful figures for the disbenefit from smoke and smog is from a survey of the insurance records for premiums paid against respiratory diseases.

There is one specific problem in air pollution which is met with in those industrial or chemical plants where dust, noxious gases or fumes are given off during the processing work and to which the workers employed there are exposed. Figures are available* giving the maximum concentration to which staff in these plants should be subjected. It is not clear, however, whether the high wages paid at a brick works, for instance, are due to the adverse effect of the dust and excessive heat, or are paid because the work is excessively hard, or are given because the labour employed there has been traditionally of a certain character and therefore continues to attract labour of a similar type for its new recruits.

Conclusion. From what has been said it is evident that the quantification of social or personal disbenefits is an exceptionally difficult job. Noise has been treated in some detail, partly because it is in any case such an important item, and hopefully because showing how to go about measuring the effects of one typical disbenefit and transferring these units into money values does provide some guide to how such problems in general can be treated.

* For example, see the *Institute of Heating and Ventilating Engineers' Guide.*

Many other personal disbenefits exist and are experienced in varying degrees by all of us at home or work. For instance:

Excessive heat.

Excessive cold.

Excessive humidity.

Water pollution, or excess in hardness or softness of water.

Food pollution, e.g., from cumulative effects of pesticides, herbicides, or one chemical such as DDT.

Lack of comfort, e.g., a badly designed seat for a typist or executive, or an ergonomically unsatisfactory control panel for an operator.

Excessive concentrations of people, i.e., people pollution. This is a growing problem in the U.K. and elsewhere.

We could continue this list almost for ever. It could be argued that excessive solitude, such as that from which a lighthouse keeper suffers, or even perhaps a research assistant working on his own at an isolation unit, constitutes a personal disbenefit. After all, human beings find sense deprivation far more emotionally disturbing than overstimulation. But we must draw the line here. Otherwise this appendix would have to cover all conditions and relationships at work, at home, indeed almost everywhere.

3. Alternative courses of action

3.1. Introduction

In this chapter we are proposing to discuss the various factors that must be taken into account when evaluating alternative possible courses of action. Some of these factors, of course, will be difficult to measure. Even in a book, such as this, dedicated to the idea of increasing the proportion of '*Q*' (Quantitative) as opposed to 'non *Q*' factors in any decision-making situation, we have to accept that some considerations cannot be measured in money terms. Some businesses for example seem really to exist just to 'institutionalize the values' of the directors and ruling executives. By this, we mean, that the firm's size, importance, prestige, high quality, security, and local or national patronage are more important to these men than the maximization of profit, and the operation of their business reflects these views.

In this chapter too, we are restricting our analysis to the deterministic situation; for example, we are assuming that the answer to a question such as what would be the likely labour saving in switching to some new numerically controlled machinery is a single figure—say £10 000 a year. Later the idea of a range of figures for future estimates, with probabilities associated with each estimate, is considered. For the moment, only the one figure representing the best available estimate is used in the analysis of costs and benefits. Initially, we concentrate our attention mainly on the cost side of the cost-benefit 'equation'.

3.2. Past and future costs. Opportunity cost

As Omar Khayyám said, 'The moving finger writes, and having writ, moves on: nor all your piety nor wit shall lure it back to cancel half a line'. In decision-making terms a translation of this would read: 'No decision made by man can alter what has already happened', or—more briefly—'sunk costs (or benefits) are irrelevant'. It follows that the only costs that are relevant are differential costs and benefits, that is those incremental or additional items which will occur if one alternative rather than another is decided on.

It is extraordinary how little this obvious precept is observed in practice. It is common to hear given as a good reason for retaining a share investment the fact that the price is currently lower than the purchase price. 'I mean to keep it till it shows a profit' or some such phrase is usually given in justification. But, of course, what has happened in the past, whether this share has made a loss, and others perhaps a profit, is irrelevant from the point of view of deciding if it should be kept or not. For that decision the *only* consideration is how the respective share prices are expected to behave in future. The past is irrelevant.

Nothing is more nauseating for readers than to be regaled with some boring personal experience. Nevertheless, it is interesting to note how preaching and practice do differ. The author has taken his family on a continental camping holiday for a number of years. This has entailed putting a hook on each car for dragging the luggage trailer. The cost, including the electrical lead, is fairly substantial. This conversion was duly made on changing to a new car and used for one year. The following year the alternative of a package tour holiday for the family was heatedly opposed on the irrational grounds that the trailer must be used for another year to justify the high conversion cost!

Sometimes the term marginal cost is used as a substitute for differential cost, and is generally understood to have the same meaning in context, though in the strict sense marginal cost should be confined to additional or incremental units of output only. Opportunity cost is a synonym for differential cost, with the proviso that the two alternatives are restricted to the one under consideration and the next best available choice. The logic of this terminology is that if the decision is taken to go ahead with the alternative under consideration, then the advantages (and disadvantages) of taking the next best choice must necessarily be given up. The measure of this loss is the opportunity cost.

3.2.1. Book value of assets

One figure that often causes problems in a practical consideration of the costs of alternative courses of action is the book value of fixed assets, such as a piece of machinery. Let us suppose that the two alternatives we are considering imply the continuing use of the machinery or its disposal. Other costs and factors will no doubt enter into the calculation but we shall confine our attention here solely to the machinery cost. To take an example, supposing that a machine cost £20 000 some seven years ago and has been depreciated at the rate of £2000 a year, so that the book value now is £6000. Let us assume in the first place that the scrap value is nil (or more precisely equals the cost of disposal). We can make the comparison between the two alternatives in two possible ways. We can compare costs with costs, that is the effect that each has on the profit and loss account, or we can compare cash and cash. The latter comparison is remarkably easy. No cash enters in either case, so that from the point of view of the machinery disposal, the two alternatives must be equal. If we compare cost with cost, then, in the event that we carry on using the machinery we shall continue to debit the profit and loss account with £2000 per annum for three years. It follows that the total charge over three years will be £6000. In the event that we get rid of the machinery, as we will no longer have the asset, we shall have to write off the book value of £6000. The total charge to the profit and loss account will still be £6000. Now it is true that there is a slight difference between the two, due to the time factor. In the first case, the charge is spread over three years, and not over one. Nevertheless, in total, the charge is the same. Hence, even on a cost for cost comparison basis the effect of book value is the same for each choice. Consequently, it is not an incremental cost. It is, therefore, *irrelevant* for decision-making purposes.

If instead of having a scrap value of nil, the machinery had a salvage value of (say) £1500 after the cost of removal, then this figure will be a genuine incremental benefit in the event that we decide to get rid of the machinery. In cash terms we receive an extra £1500; in cost terms the charge to the profit and loss account is reduced from £6000 to £4500, that is a benefit of £1500. In both cases the incremental benefit is £1500. A similar analysis applies in the event that there is an expected net salvage value if the machinery is retained for a while and then sold. In both cases the incremental benefit will be the scrap value. The book value, therefore, is still irrelevant.

Although the book value can be left out of the calculation, the same cannot necessarily be said of tax written down value. If the machinery has a scrap value now of £1500 and a tax written down value of £4000, then the tax allowance will be 45 per cent (assuming a 45 per cent corporation tax rate) of £2500 (£4000 minus £1500). If the machinery is retained for the remaining years of its life and then disposed of at nil scrap value, the total allowance for tax will be 45 per cent of £4000. The difference (45 per cent of £1500 = £675), is substantial. However, there are two caveats. First, the assumption is implicitly made that there are taxable profits available against which the allowances can be set. If there are no taxable profits no tax in any case is payable, so there is no differential gain. Second, if the final scrap value is not nil, then the tax gain will be correspondingly decreased. Strictly, this final scrap value also enters into the calculation in its own right, since if the new machinery is put in, there is a cash inflow foregone. Generally, the amount is small and it is often ignored in these differential cost calculations.

3.2.2. Differential costs

Any cost or benefit which is not affected by the alternatives under consideration can be disregarded. The managing director's salary, for example, is unlikely to be altered whatever choice is made. It can, therefore, be ignored. Suppose that the alternatives under consideration are buying a part from outside or continuing to manufacture it on the premises. All benefits, all administrative, distribution and selling expenses, and all production costs, other than those directly associated with the manufacture of the part are unlikely to be affected by the decision. Consequently, there is no need to consider them.

Although we are only concerned with differential costs, it is often convenient in practise to put down *all* the costs under each of the alternatives to arrive at the net difference. This means that a lot of the expenses will be entered more than once. The advantage of this routine procedure is that no items of costs are likely to be overlooked. When attention is focused solely on differential items it is possible to overlook one item with disastrous results.

There are two types of costs which might seem at first sight to be differential costs, but in practise rarely are. These are:

1. Variable costs
2. Allocated costs

The term variable costs is short for 'costs directly variable with volume of production'. It is a classification of costs which is useful when considering likely changes in volume of production in the future. This is not the same as considering two alternative choices of action now. In certain circumstances, e.g., when one of the alternatives involves a change in output, then the variable costs may be differential costs. In general, they are not the same.

In general, when estimating differential costs, allocated costs, too, should be viewed with suspicion. Allocated costs are those overheads which are charged to a particular product, batch, department, or process on a *pro rata* basis. The usual methods of allocation are:

(*a*) By an oncost (that is a percentage addition) on a direct labour hour basis. This is the usual method for Government departments, Local Authorities, and nationalized bodies, and those firms in the private sector characterized by having a high labour content as part of their manufacturing process.

(*b*) By an oncost on a machine hour rate (this is the usual method in capital intensive organizations, and in particular in those sections of private organizations where 'machines dominate men').

(*c*) On a specific basis of allocation for each item of overhead expense (this is the traditional method advocated in books on costing—the main disadvantage is that it is unwieldy and expensive to operate).

Whatever method is used, it is unlikely that the amount of cost prorated to the part manufactured on the premises (to continue with the previous example) will be saved if the part is bought out. The total costs to the firm for rent, heat, and light are certain to remain unaltered by the decision. Although a part of this cost has been allocated to that department or section which manufactures the part, cessation of production will only mean that the remaining departments or sections will have to absorb more of the total costs.

It is comparatively easy to see that this is true in the case of some simple expense such as rent. Unless the freed floor space will actually be used for some additional revenue producing item (such as the manufacture of new products) or it can be rented out, there will be no change in total costs and benefits. It is not so easy to decide whether this same principle applies in the vexed case of labour saving. Most alternative choice calculations include figures for differential salaries or wages. Typically the main benefit from the introduction of more automated machinery will be the direct labour saved. There is a great tendency in such circumstances to work out the theoretical reduction in wages that should arise, and to use this figure in the calculation. The problem in real life is that getting rid of staff is not likely to foster good labour relations. What is much more likely to happen is that employees will be given other work until 'natural wastage', sufficient to absorb the surplus, has occurred. The true saving in wages is often much less than the calculated figure. Worse still, when jobs are 'found' to keep the supernumerary staff employed, it is often very difficult afterwards to revert back to the prior position. Put another way, a little bit more fat has been added, and cutting away fat is never easy. Sometimes executive staff who are made redundant as a result of some large scale business decision will be employed in new jobs in other departments in the company. It is very difficult to decide whether the new post gives a benefit to the company equal to the executive's salary or not. It may be that the manager of the other department has repeatedly pushed for an assistant manager to help him. If the redundant manager fills this post, is he going to produce the necessary real benefit? One thing is certain and that is the department got by before he arrived! As we shall see in chapter 8 it is hard to measure, let alone estimate in advance, the benefit from a manager's performance.

Wage and salary differentials need to be gross wages inclusive of tax, N.H.I. pension fund payments, and all fringe payments in so far as they are a cost saved to the company. The extra charge to the company over and above the gross wages is frequently very substantial. To simplify the calculations it is often convenient to arrive at an oncost figure which on average covers these extra payments, and then to apply this percentage to the gross wages in each case.

To summarize, in any particular problem of alternative choice decisions the costs and benefits that are relevant are just those which will be affected by taking one course of action rather than another at that point in time. The cost elements that are relevant vary, however, with the nature of the choice. A classic example of this, is in the decision as to whether it is cheaper to use a car or not. Background information available to help in this choice is as follows:

		Average per mile	
Variable costs:		(pence)	
Petrol, oil, lubricants		1·80	
Maintenance		1·30	
Tyres		0·45	
	Total	3·55	
		Annual	
Non-variable costs:		(£)	
Road Fund Licence		25	(£9·15 for 4 months)
Insurance		30	
Depreciation		200	
	Total	£255	

The prior assumption in each case is that there is no substantial difference in the convenience of going by car or train. The only problem is which is cheaper. How should one make the following decisions?

(*a*) Whether to take a trip up North by car or by train. The car is in your possession and already taxed.

(*b*) Whether to tax the car for the remaining four months of the year. At the end of the year, after the Motor Show when the new registration letter changes, you are proposing to buy a new car in any case. Should you leave it in your garage till then, or tax it for the remaining four months? (ignoring such factors as any higher resale value).

(*c*) You live in London and do not own a car but are considering whether to buy one, or whether to continue to use taxis and trains.

The costs which have to be taken into account in making the decisions vary for each of the above. For the first decision, i.e., whether to make a particular trip, granted that you have available a taxed car, the only costs that are relevant are the variable costs (3·55 pence per mile). For the second decision, i.e., whether to tax and run the car for the remaining four months, the Road Fund Licences and the insurances are additional costs which need to be taken into account. Of course the scale of the comparison, too, is larger than in the first decision, so that the total variable costs and total benefits will both be greater. In the final decision, i.e., whether to buy the car or not, all the costs are relevant.

3.3. Benefits and pricing considerations

So far we have restricted the decisions to a number of discreet alternatives relating to the relevant costs if one choice, rather than another, is made. Let us now consider the benefits, but still restrict our analysis to the conventional business case where the only benefit considered is the revenue from sales. In theory at any rate, there are an infinite number of possible revenues depending on the choice of the sales price. In practice, as we have noted elsewhere, one of two positions is likely to apply. First, a clear market price exists and there is no possibility of departing from it. This often arises when there is a market leader who sets the price, or—much the same thing—oligopolistic, quasi-monopolistic, cartel, or informal price fixing arrangements apply. However, these are not the only circumstances in which a fixed price policy affectively applies. In most commodity markets, for example, the price, though not fixed in the sense of remaining set at a certain figure, is fixed in the sense that it is determined by the market. From the point of view of any trader the price is fixed: he has no discretion. In such circumstances the aim of the business is restricted to selling as much as possible at the given price and for the lowest cost.

In many cases, however, price flexibility does apply. In such cases a variety of choices are available. Before we consider how to arrive at a decision rule we need first to ask the question, what is it that we are in business for? At the beginning of this chapter we suggested that many businesses (particularly, perhaps, family firms or high prestige industrial concerns) really exist as a projection or identification of the needs of the directors. Within this framework, however, the business is presumably directed with certain financial goals either consciously or unconsciously in mind.

It is strange how rarely this simple question as to the overall aim of a business is asked in practice, or if asked, answered! Since profits are regarded as the measure of financial success probably the implied answer is that the aim is to maximize profits, subject to reasonable security and preferably with overall long term expansion (or certainly no contraction). If we take it that this is so, the next question is how can profits be earned? The starting point is the realization that all business is determined by what we can sell. Any production not sold must be a dead loss. To arrive at the optimum level of sales, we have to remember that if we sell more units the total contribution is the additional revenue from the sales less the variable expenses (fixed expenses, as we have said *ad nauseam*, do not, by definition, alter, and so do not enter into the decision). Provided the costs of getting these extra sales does not exceed the contribution, we shall receive more profit. On this basis, we shall push up our scale of activity so long as the cost of obtaining extra sales does not exceed the contribution from those sales.

The position becomes a little more difficult in practice when we take into account price fluctuation, although it is true that the theory remains the same. Let us initially make the highly questionable supposition that for any particular price at which the produce is to be sold the corresponding volume of sales can be estimated. In that case the position will be along the lines shown in Fig. 3.1.

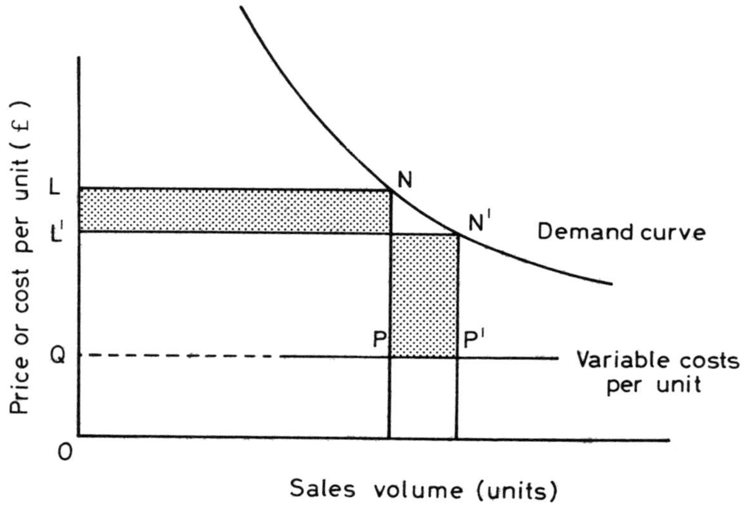

Figure 3.1.

NP is the unit contribution (sales price less variable costs per unit). The total contribution, i.e., unit contribution multiplied by volume, is represented by the rectangular area LNPQ. If price is reduced a little, and sales go up a little, the new total contribution will be represented by L'N'P'Q. The net gain in contribution will be the difference between the vertical and the horizontal shaded areas. So long as the vertical portion exceeds the horizontal, so long will price reduction pay.

3.4. Problems in assessing costs and benefits

All seems simple, in this, the best of all business worlds; however, there are many difficulties when we come to look at the problem from a decision-making point of view; some of these we have already touched on, but many remain. They are summarized here under three headings.

1. Constraints. Even if we allow that single figure estimates can be used for all the factors entering into the decision, severe problems arise when translating theory into practice. It is easy to say, for example, that production should be increased because the net revenue from the sales will substantially exceed the additional cost in overtime rates, etc. Easy, but quite pointless, if the raw materials needed to make the additional units, are not available. Dealing with constraints, in one form or another, is perhaps the principal problem in deciding which is the appropriate course of action to take in the deterministic business situation.

Constraints can be divided into:

(*a*) those primarily internal to the business or organization, such as might arise from, for example, the limited number of machines available, the shortage of skilled labour on the floor, in the draughtsmen's office, in the computer programming section, or the shortage of materials, power, etc.

(*b*) those primarily external to the business. Since any business is built around sales the most usual constraint for a profit oriented organization is the limit on sales set by the market. However, there are many other external restraints, some legislative, e.g., the siting of factories, shortage of skilled labour (here used in the sense that additional labour cannot be obtained because of a local or national shortage) or raw materials (due to import restrictions). For public sector organizations, external constraints are likely to be even more varied and powerful. A government department will be under strong political pressure to spend money in certain ways and in particular areas.

It is evident from a consideration of these lists that the dividing line between internal and external restraints is not clear-cut. One merges into the other. These problems are dealt with in chapter 4, in general by the use of mathematical programming techniques. Fortunately, the body of knowledge on this subject is fairly substantial.

2. Time. The costs of obtaining extra sales are not likely to coincide in time with the benefits from the additional revenue. Expenditure on a new machine which will dramatically cut costs, improve the product and so increase sales, will take place at the time of purchase, and generally in one lump sum. The traditional book-keeping method of dealing with this problem is to allocate the cost of the fixed asset over its life. This straight line depreciation method implies, amongst other things, that equal periods of time, whether at the beginning or end of the asset's life, are of equal value.

Obviously, this is not the case, and *ad hoc* book depreciation methods, or even the more clearly defined tax depreciation methods, are utterly irrelevant. For decision purposes, the DCF or PV approaches do take account of time correctly. These techniques and the whole problem of time are discussed at length in chapters 5 and 6.

3. Uncertainty. Once we accept the fact that for decision purposes we are looking into the future, and the future is always uncertain, it will be apparent that many of the figures which will be used in the analysis will be just the best estimates available. Sometimes these will be fairly firm figures, sometimes the possible variations from them will be thought to be substantial. In the latter case we must take account of the chance that these figures are relevant by some method such as, for example, assigning probabilities to them and working out the consequences. The probabilistic or stochastic approach—as this is called—will be dealt with in chapter 7, the summary chapter on decision making.

4. The quantitative background

4.1. Introduction

Much of this chapter is concerned with the analysis of the problem of constraints; that is, those limitations that the real world imposes on the operation of any organization, whether in the private or public sector. The basic mathematical technique for dealing with this problem is *linear programming*. Both linear programming and its counterpart, *regression analysis*, assume that problems of this nature can either be expressed in linear terms, or changed into linear terms by suitable transformations. The term linear, it should be noted, is used here and throughout as meaning that no higher terms in a variable than the first are used. For instance, if the total available stock of raw material is 650 lb and we are considering the quantity (x) of this raw material to use in our production process then,

$$x \leqslant 650$$

Note that no higher powers than the first (i.e. not x^2 or x^3 etc.) are used in this mathematical statement. In §4.5 on multiple regression analysis this question of linearity is considered more fully.

The analysis of constraints cannot be done without the use of a considerable amount of mathematics. Since mathematical techniques such as matrix algebra have to be introduced here, it seems appropriate to *develop and deal with all the mathematical techniques in this chapter*, even though some of them will not be required till a good deal later.

4.2. Linear programming (LP)

Let us consider two simple problems of constraints, one taken from the business world, and one from the public sector. The business example will be explored in depth and will provide a good introduction to linear programming.

4.2.1. A business linear programming example

A machine can turn out two different products M1 and M2. The machine can only be run for 40 hours a week, and only 27 lb of material is in stock and available for this week. The machine running time, material usage and profit for each of the products M1 and M2 is given in matrix* form as:

		Machine running time per unit (hours)	*Material usage (lb)*	*Profit per unit (£)*
Product:	M1	2	3	3
	M2	5	2	4

The problem is to find how many of each of the units should be produced to provide maximum profit.

Because this is a comparatively simple problem we can use a graphical solution based on traditional algebraic concepts. Later, we shall have to extend this so as to include matrix algebra. Fortunately, this basic solution provides a very clear guide as to how to approach the more general solution.

Let us call the number of units of M1 produced x_1, and the number of M2 units produced x_2.

Each unit of M1 takes 2 hours so that x_1 units will take $2x_1$ hours.
Each unit of M2 takes 5 hours so that x_2 units will take $5x_2$ hours.
Total number of hours $= 2x_1 + 5x_2$.
But the machine can only run for 40 hours.
Hence $2x_1 + 5x_2 \leqslant 40$ (ignoring any setup time).

Using a precisely similar approach we arrive at:
$3x_1 + 2x_2 \leqslant 27$, as the constraint for the material usage
and $3x_1 + 4x_2$ as the total profit which we wish to maximize.

In linear programming terminology this is usually referred to as the objective function, and given the symbol Z, so that

$$Z = 3x_1 + 4x_2$$

Finally, since 'minus' amounts of M1 and M2 cannot be produced, x_1 and x_2 cannot be negative, so that,

$$x_1 \geqslant 0 \text{ and } x_2 \geqslant 0$$

* The term matrix is here used in the restricted sense of a set of figures laid out in rectangular shape.

To sum up, the constraints are:

$$2x_1 + 5x_2 \leqslant 40$$
$$3x_1 + 2x_2 \leqslant 27$$
$$x_1 \geqslant 0 \textit{ and } x_2 \geqslant 0$$

The aim is to maximize the objective function:

$$Z = 3x_1 + 4x_2$$

4.2.2. A motorway linear programming example

The total motorway budget for both the North-West Region and South-East Region is £30 000 000 for the next financial year.

The S.E. is more heavily populated, and on a cost-benefit analysis basis the benefits due to a motorway are estimated to be £90 000 per mile. The N.W. is less populated and the benefits due to a motorway are £60 000 per mile.

The cost of building is greater in the S.E. than in the N.W. The cost of building in the S.E. is £1·25 million per mile, and the cost of building in the N.W. is £1 million per mile.

The construction industry in the N.W. has some slack, but cannot build more than 20 miles per year. In the S.E. building is limited to 15 miles per year.

The Minister is under political pressure not to invest in the S.E. more than $2\frac{1}{2}$ times as much as in the N.W.; but, because the N.W. needs development considerations, investment in the N.W. can be up to 4 times as much as in the S.E.

Let us call the number of miles in the S.E. x_1, and the number of miles in the N.W. x_2.

The constraints are:

$$1{\cdot}25x_1 + x_2 \leqslant 30 \qquad \text{(Building cost)}$$
$$x_1 \leqslant 15 \text{ and } x_2 \leqslant 20 \qquad \text{(Building capacity)}$$

and

$$\left.\begin{aligned} 1{\cdot}25x_1 &\leqslant 2{\cdot}5x_2 \\ x_2 &\leqslant 5x_1 \end{aligned}\right\} \qquad \text{(Political pressure)}$$

$$x_1 \geqslant 0 \quad x_2 \geqslant 0 \text{ (No `negative' motorways!)}$$

The aim is to maximize the annual benefits:

$$Z = 90\,000x_1 + 60\,000x_2$$

The layout of both these linear programming examples is similar. We shall confine our analysis to the business example. The treatment of the motorway example would follow on practically identical lines.

4.2.3. The analysis of the business linear programming example

Let us consider the first of the two constraints given by

$$2x_1+5x_2 \leqslant 40$$

We can easily draw the line

$$2x_1+5x_2 = 40$$

by putting $x_1 = 0$ to find where the line cuts the x_2 axis, and $x_2 = 0$, to find where it cuts the x_1 axis. The points are A (O, 8) and E (20, O), in Fig. 4.1.

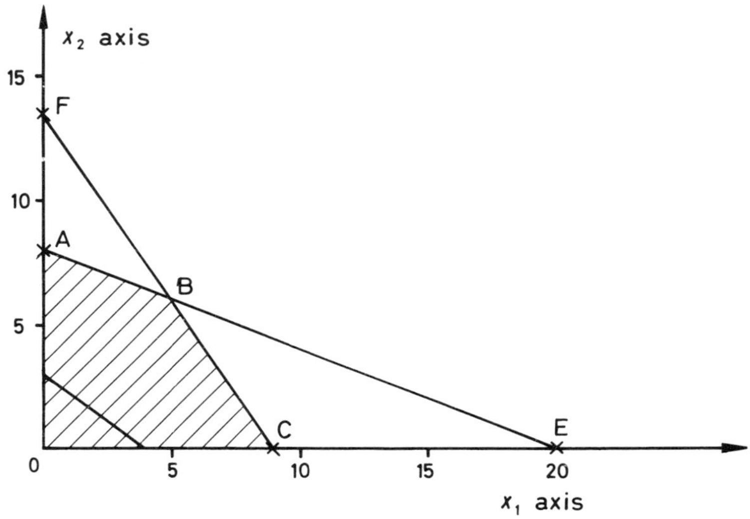

Figure 4.1.

What effect does putting $2x_1+5x_2$ equal to some number less than 40 have on this equation? By taking any suitable number (e.g., 30) it is easy to check that the new line will be parallel to AE, but nearer the origin O. It follows that the effect of the constraint $2x_1+5x_2 \leqslant 40$ is to restrict the solution to the area to the left of and below the line AE. Similar remarks apply to the second restraint, $3x_1+2x_2 \leqslant 27$, the effect of which is to confine the solution to the area to the left of and below the line FC ($3x_1+2x_2 = 27$). The constraints $x_1 \geqslant$ O, $x_2 \geqslant$ O clearly confine the solution to the quadrant shown, that is to the right of the vertical x_2 axis, and above the horizontal x_1 axis.

Taken altogether, these constraints, therefore, restrict the solution to the shaded area OABC.

Next, consider the objective function:

$$Z = 3x_1 + 4x_2$$

We wish to maximize the value of this function. If we put $3x_1 + 4x_2 = 12$ (say) this will give a line through the points (4, O) and (O, 3). Increasing the value will give a line parallel to this but to the right and above this line by an argument analagous to that used for the constraints. The problem, therefore, is to find what line can be drawn farthest from O parallel to this line which yet has a point within the shaded area. This, clearly, is the parallel line through the point B. Any line farther away from O will have no point on it which will satisfy the constraints. B is the point (5, 6) and, therefore maximum profit is obtained by producing 5 units of M1 and 6 units of M2. Putting these figures into the objective function, the value of this profit is $3 \times 5 + 4 \times 6 = £39$.

4.2.4. Conclusion

The most important thing to note from this simple analysis is that the maximum point occurs at B, a corner of the shaded area representing the constraints. Even if the slope of the objective function had been different it is obvious that the solution would have been at one of the corners of this convex set of points ABC.

This rule—that the maximum lies at a corner—is of great importance. As its application is quite general, it provides the basis for the standard mathematical technique used for solving problems with many constraints —the renowned Simplex method.

To express a 'corner' in mathematical terms we must first convert the constraint inequalities into equalities by inserting two 'slack' variables x_3 and x_4. The constraints will then read,

$$2x_1 + 5x_2 + x_3 = 40$$
$$3x_1 + 2x_2 + x_4 = 27$$

and $x_1 \geqslant 0$, $x_2 \geqslant 0$, $x_3 \geqslant 0$, $x_4 \geqslant 0$ (clearly x_3 and x_4 must be non-negative too). Let us now consider the significance of x_1, x_2, x_3 and x_4. If we put $x_3 = 0$ and then $x_4 = 0$ we have the lines AE and FC respectively. The lines $x_1 = 0$ and $x_2 = 0$ are obviously the vertical axis (OAF) and the horizontal axis (OCE) respectively. These four lines $x_1 = 0$, $x_2 = 0$, $x_3 = 0$, $x_4 = 0$ meet in six different points. Four, (O, A, B, and C) are the corners that we are concerned with: two, (E and F) lie outside and are not of practical interest.

We can easily programme a computer to put, first $x_1 = x_2 = 0$, then $x_2 = x_3 = 0$ and so on, and hence test each corner, working through all the combinations one after another. The Simplex method does indeed use this general approach, though it pursues a particular logical procedure in moving from one corner to another. The details of the Simplex approach are not especially important, but for the sake of completeness they are given in an appendix to this chapter. What the Simplex method does do is to provide a logical solution to the problem of maximizing a linear objective function:

$$Z = P_1 x_1 + P_2 x_2 + --- + P_n x_n$$

that is, finding those values of the variables x_1 x_2, etc., which make Z as large as possible.

The constraints, which are linear, too, and restrict the values of x_1 x_2, etc., are:

$$\begin{aligned}
a_{11} x_1 + a_{12} x_2 + & --- + a_{1n} x_n \leqslant c_1 \\
a_{21} x_1 + a_{22} x_2 + & --- + a_{2n} x_n \leqslant c_2 \\
- \quad - & \qquad\quad - \\
- \quad - & \qquad\quad - \\
a_{m1} x_1 + a_{m2} x_2 + & \qquad\; + a_{mn} x_n \leqslant c_m
\end{aligned}$$

All the coefficients, P_1 P_2 $---$ a_{11} a_{12} $\cdots$ c_1 c_2, etc., throughout, are fixed constants.

Programmes based on the Simplex approach are readily available and provide comparatively quick and easy answers to complex problems of this nature.

4.3. Integer programming

At this stage the reader (if he is still with us!) may well feel that the theory of linear programming, though absolutely fascinating, is indeed one of those things in life of which one can say 'enough is enough'. Now, surely is the time to press on and deal with some of the important applications of the technique. However, there is a rather important problem that we have not yet dealt with which may arise when the answers given by standard linear programming techniques are not integers (i.e., whole numbers). In our graphical example the optimal solution was $x_1 = 5$, $x_2 = 6$. Had the amount of metal available been $27\frac{1}{2}$ lb rather than 27, it is easy to see (from the Fig. 4.1) that the line CF would have been very slightly farther away from the origin than the old position of CF (though still parallel to it). In that case, the optimal solution would have been just over 5 for x_1, and just under 6 for x_2. But this may well be a ridiculous answer. After all, what use is it producing *nearly* 6 of M2, if sales are made, as no doubt they are, in whole units. If the situation is such that only integer solutions are useful, then our technique has apparently let us down. Certainly in many linear programming problems only integer solutions are meaningful. For instance, the problem may be to find what mix of planes and tankers it is best to buy to transport raw materials from subsidiaries overseas, having regard to flexibility and least cost requirements. Fed with our linear programme the computer might print out:

Boeing	0·85
Tankers	16·29

Just try buying and using 0·85 of a Boeing!

Clearly for some linear programming problems we need to refine our technique so that only integer solutions will be considered. This refinement is called integer programming. One such technique (the 'cutting plane') has four stages.

1. If in any particular constraint equation all the a_{ij}'s and c_j's (using a similar notation) are not integers, multiply through by the smallest positive integer that will make all the coefficients integers. If this is done before the slack variable is added, then this guarantees that all coefficients, including the slack variable, will be integers.
2. Find the optimal solution of the new set of equations in the normal way. Frequently, the Simplex technique will give an integer solution directly. If not:
3. Write any non-integer solution x_1 (say) as $I+F$ where I is the integer part of the solution and F is the fractional part.
4. Substituting this value for x_1 in the original equations, and making use of the fact that F is a fraction will give rise to an additional constraint. This can now be added to the original restraints and the problem properly solved by the basic Simplex approach. Each non-integer solution will have to be dealt with this way.

One final problem at least needs to be mentioned, though it is really only an extension of the main integer problem (and is dealt with as such), which is that in some applications of linear programming the only acceptable solutions are either 0 or 1.

4.4. Applications of linear programming

Almost all deterministic problems in business decision making can be expressed in linear terms. To recapitulate, we mean by this that they can be expressed as a series of equations (or inequalities, which will then be converted into equations by adding slack variables), in which higher powers of the variable than the first are absent. More specifically, if x_1 x_2 x_3, etc., are the variables and a_{11} a_{12}, etc., are the constants, then the terms in the equation will be of the form $a_{11}x_1$, $a_{12}x_2$, etc., but not $a_{11}x_1^2$ or $a_{11}x_1^3$ or even $a_{11}x_1x_2$.

The requirement is usually to maximize or minimize a certain function, expressed as a linear equation, subject to a series of linear restraints. As we have seen the solution by a computer program based on the Simplex routine is quick and simple. Although the actual calculations would be long and tedious if done manually, they are reiterative. In other words, they are eminently suitable to the way a computer works.

Typical uses of linear programming for business decision making include:

1. Network analysis, e.g., Critical Path Analysis (CPA), Programme Evaluation and Review Technique (PERT), PERT/COST. Line of Balance (LOB), etc.
2. Transportation problems, e.g., routing goods from factories to warehouses. In general, the optimum location and use of stores, warehouses, factories, cash and carry depots, refineries, etc.
3. Assignment problems, i.e., least cost assignment of men to jobs, or jobs to machines.
4. Mix and utilization problems. How to fit or cut pieces of a fixed size. How to mix materials for production at minimum cost. How to blend chemicals of various types or grades to achieve maximum output at minimum cost. How to allocate staff, cash, materials, machines, to factory depots and sites. How to plan forward, using all these resources.
5. Stochastic problems, i.e., how to take into account all the foregoing factors when the outcome is not regarded as precisely determined, although some probability or likelihood figure can be estimated for each.

It is not intended to go into these applications in very great detail. They do form, however, a most important part of the decision-making process in a business and consequently it is worthwhile spending some time on the more important uses.

4.4.1. Network models

In all business situations there are a number of different activities that have to be undertaken to arrive at a successful conclusion. Sometimes these activities are in series, that is, one must follow after another. To produce this paragraph for example, I must first pick up my pen and then write it. Diagrammatically,

Activity	Description	Time required
A	Pick up pen	3 seconds
B	Write	40 seconds (say!)

On the other hand, many business activities can be done in parallel. For instance, the body and the engine of a car can both be built at the same time. Most complex business operations consist of some activities in series and some in parallel. Let us consider the production of a mobile anti-pollution spray unit, each unit of which consists essentially of a large tank and a spray section. Both parts are purchased from outside suppliers, and both require modification before the spray section is attached to the tank. The assembled spray/tank section will then have to be lowered on to the chassis which will itself have had to undergo substantial modification. Activities and times required for completion are:

Activity	*Nodes*	*Description*	*Time required (days)*
A	1–2	Modify spray	4
B	1–3	Modify tank	10
C	1–4	Modify chassis	14
D	2–3	Assemble spray to tank	5
E	3–4	Assemble spray/tank to chassis	6
F	4–5	Paint	2

The spray can be assembled to the tank whilst the tank is being modified; similarly for the spray/tank to chassis.

The nodes have been added on the principle that an activity begins and ends at a node, and nodes have been numbered in accordance with the rule that each activity shall terminate at a node with a higher number than it started with.

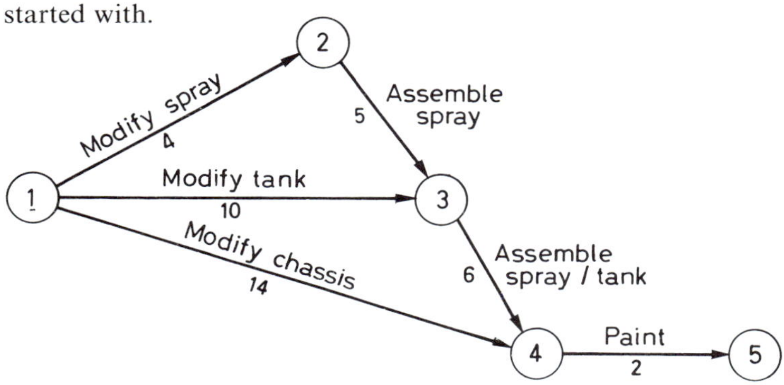

There are three paths from start to finish; they are:

Nodes 1 – 2 – 3 – 4 – 5 – 17 days in all.

Nodes 1 – 3 – 4 – 5 – 18 days in all.

Nodes 1 – 4 – 5 – 16 days in all.

Since all these paths have to be travelled the total time that the production will take is determined by the length of the *longest* one. This is the path (1 – 3 – 4 – 5), taking 18 days in all. It is called the critical path.

In our example it was easy to find this route just by looking at the diagram. In any major construction problem there may well be hundreds of activities, and this simple approach will not suffice. Let us look at this as a linear programming problem. The times from one node to another in matrix form are:

		To node 1	2	3	4	5
	1	0	4	10	14	x
	2	0	0	5	x	x
From node	3	0	0	0	6	x
	4	0	0	0	0	2
	5	0	0	0	0	0

As a consequence of our principle of numbering nodes all elements below and to the left of the principal diagonal are obviously zero. Such a matrix is usually referred to as upper triangular. All elements on the principal diagonal of this matrix are zero too. Known activity times are entered as such in the matrix. Unknown activity times are represented by x's.

Clearly we wish to find the maximum value of

$$Z = 4x_{12}+10x_{13}+14x_{14}+5x_{23}+6x_{34}+2x_{45}$$

using the usual matrix notation for the numbering of the elements.

Subject to the restraints:

$$\begin{array}{lr}
x_{12}+x_{13}+x_{14} = 1 & \text{(Node 1)}\\
-x_{12}+x_{23} = 0 & \text{(Node 2)}\\
-x_{13}-x_{23}+x_{34} = 0 & \text{(Node 3)}\\
-x_{14}-x_{34}+x_{45} = 0 & \text{(Node 4)}\\
-x_{45} = -1 & \text{(Node 5)}
\end{array}$$

and $x_{12} \geqslant 0$, $x_{13} \geqslant 0$, $x_{14} \geqslant 0$, $x_{23} \geqslant 0$, $x_{34} \geqslant 0$, $x_{45} \geqslant 0$.

The restraints are simply explained. Beginning with the source (Node 1), one of the paths represented by x_{12} x_{13} x_{14} must be taken. One of these must be 1, the others must then be zero. Hence the restraint that altogether they must add up to 1. For node 2, if x_{12} is 1, then x_{23} must be 1, if, on the other hand, one of the other two paths from the source is chosen so that x_{12} is zero, then x_{23} must be zero. Hence the restraint. Similar explanations apply for all the other nodes.

We have now reduced the problem to linear programming form so that it can be solved by a computer programme based on the Simplex method.

The importance of determining the critical path is obvious once it is realized that reducing the time of any activity which is on this route will reduce the total production time. The corollary of this is that effort spent in reducing time on activities not on the critical path is, prima facie, time wasted. Reverting to the spray unit example, it is pointless to pay men engaged on the chassis overtime rates to get their modification through rapidly, as this activity is not on the critical path. On the other hand a delay of more than two days on this activity will affect total production time. This permissible delay is referred to as slack, and most computer programmes for critical path analysis print out the slack for each activity. Many sophisticated critical path programmes indeed allow for a number of other factors, and it is here that the real benefit of programming is felt in practise. Such programmes show:

1. The incremental costs of a crash programme to shorten the time of an activity on the critical path. The effect of this shortening on the total network is also shown, i.e., the throwing up of the next critical path, the cost of shortening this path, and so on. The final result of this analysis is the production of a time/cost trade off curve indicating how much production completion times can be reduced against the corresponding cost.
2. Multiple time estimates. So far the time for each activity has been regarded as fixed. There are two possible approaches here; one is to assess both the most optimistic time and the most pessimistic time and feed these into the computer together with the most likely time for the activity. The other is to feed in the most likely time together with the standard deviation of the time for each activity.
3. In some jobs (e.g., construction) where the investment is heavy, time is money. We need therefore to associate with each activity its cost. A difference in the time when an activity is started or finished will not affect the final time when the whole project is completed (unless the activity lies on the critical path) but may affect the budget schedule. The technique of PERT/COST takes this factor into account.

LOB. CPA networks were originally designed for one off projects. In a factory, batch or continuous production is very often the rule. The corresponding technique is LOB (Line of Balance). The thinking behind LOB is simple. Suppose we need to have a stated number of units (part of a batch or a continuous production run perhaps) ready by a certain date for a sale or shipment. Suppose, further, that in the last stage of all, each unit has to be given a series of coats of paint. This takes perhaps a week. One week, therefore, before the sale or shipment date we need to have this stated number of units assembled, ready for painting. By checking on the cumulative number of units which have arrived at this point (called a control point) we shall have a measure of how well the actual production of today, at this control point, compares with the target number. If our production is properly balanced then the actual number of units will line up with the scheduled production (LOB) at this point.

Working backwards we arrive at a series of control points. At each control point we can compare the number of units that should be ready with the number that actually are at any moment in time. LOB is an eminently suitable technique for computerization. The results will generally be presented in the form of a table showing the scheduled production against the actual production for each control point. A visual presentation in the form of a vertical bar chart, however, shows even more clearly where production is falling behind schedule. Figure 4.2 indicates the form of a typical LOB bar chart.

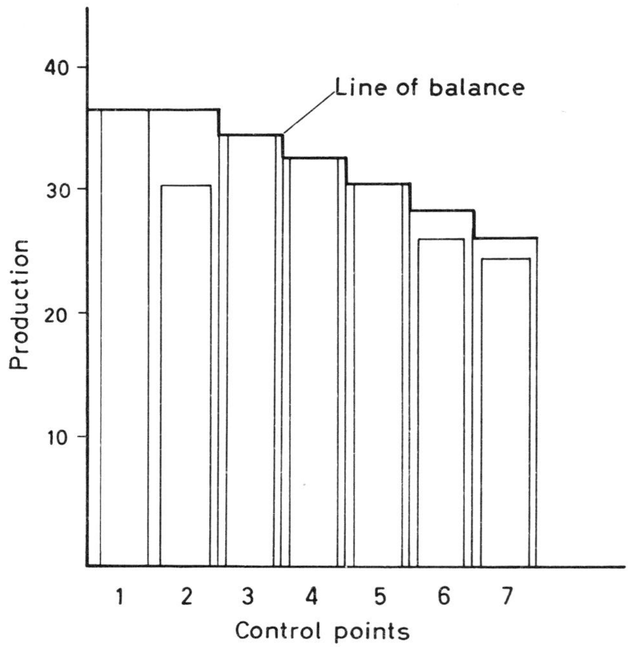

Figure 4.2.

Any network analysis needs to be updated. At frequent intervals the date or time when activities are actually completed, or control points are reached, should be fed into the computer. The print out will give a new critical path together with all the associated information based on the new situation.

4.4.2. Transportation problems

In a sense transportation problems can be considered as special cases of the more general allocation or assignment problems. However, they provided one of the earliest applications of linear programming, and they are still one of the most important. The common characteristic of all these types of problems is that all the units available must be assigned. Thus if we are transporting 65 identical container units from three ports to five delivery points we must not assign more or less than the 65 units. Suppose the transportation costs for each route are:

		Delivery points				
		1	2	3	4	5
	1	2	3	5	7	5
Ports	2	4	2	2	4	7
	3	8	3	7	6	4

The initial and final depositions of the loads are:

	Ports		*Delivery points*	
	1	16	1	15
	2	29	2	20
	3	20	3	13
			4	12
			5	5
Totals:		65		65

If x_{ij} represents the number of units going from port (i) to delivery point (j), then we wish to minimize the total cost, (Z) say, where

$$Z = 2x_{11}+3x_{12}+5x_{13}+7x_{14}+5x_{15}+4x_{21}+2x_{22}+2x_{23}+4x_{24}+ 7x_{25}+8x_{31}+3x_{32}+7x_{33}+6x_{34}+4x_{35}$$

Subject to the restraints:

$$x_{11}+x_{12}+x_{13}+x_{14}+x_{15} = 16 \text{ (the units from port 1)}$$
$$x_{21}+x_{22}+x_{23}+x_{24}+x_{25} = 29 \text{ (the units from port 2)}$$
$$x_{31}+x_{32}+x_{33}+x_{34}+x_{35} = 20 \text{ (the units from port 3)}$$

and $$x_{11}+x_{21}+x_{31} = 15 \text{ (the units to delivery point 1)}$$

and similarly for delivery points 2, 3, 4, and 5.

4.4.3. Assignment problems

These problems typically involve the least cost allocation of men to jobs, or men to machines, or machines to jobs. Taking the last case the supposition is that we have the same number of machines to do the work as there are jobs available, but that they do this work with varying degrees of efficiency. The more efficiently the job is done the lower the cost to the firm. Taking a very simple case with three jobs and three machines the respective costs might be:

		Jobs 1	2	3
	1	7	12	15
Machines	2	13	8	18
	3	9	4	10

The least cost solution is one which minimizes the objective function

$$Z = 7x_{11}+12x_{12}+15x_{13}+13x_{21}+8x_{22}+18x_{23}+9x_{31}+4x_{32}+10x_{33}$$

The constraints are:

$$\left.\begin{aligned} x_{11}+x_{12}+x_{13} &= 1\\ x_{21}+x_{22}+x_{23} &= 1\\ x_{31}+x_{32}+x_{33} &= 1 \end{aligned}\right\}\text{ Each machine can be used once and once only.}$$

$$\left.\begin{aligned} x_{11}+x_{21}+x_{31} &= 1\\ x_{12}+x_{22}+x_{32} &= 1\\ x_{13}+x_{23}+x_{33} &= 1 \end{aligned}\right\}\text{ Each job needs to be done once and once only.}$$

(all x_{11}, x_{12}, x_{23}, etc., must be 0 or 1).

4.5. Regression analysis—the counterpart of linear programming

In the business linear programming example (§4.2.1 and §4.2.3), the objective function Z (the profit) was given in terms of x_1 and x_2, the number of units of M1 and M2 produced respectively by the equation

$$Z = 3x_1+4x_2$$

There was no problem in arriving at this expression for the profit in terms of the variables x_1 x_2. The argument, it will be remembered, was on these lines. Given that the profit per unit of M1 is £3, the profit for x_1 of

M will be $3x_1$. Similarly, the profit for x_2 of M is $4x_2$, and the total profit is therefore $3x_1 + 4x_2$.

It is not always so easy to arrive directly at a relationship between variables such as x_1 x_2, called independent variables, and a variable (or variables) such as Z called the dependent or response variable. This may be because any possible theoretical relationship is too difficult to arrive at. An extremely simple example of this would be the relationship between the value of a current (I) and the drop in voltage (V) when it passed through a constant resistance (R). If Ohm's law ($V = RI$) were *not* known, a number of experimental observations of values of I and R would then seem to indicate this precise relationship, but not prove it. On the other hand, it may be that there is no precise linear relationship, and yet there is some sort of correlation between the variables. One example of this would be the relationship between the height and weight of individuals. Though there is no unique or specific relationship between the height and weight of a particular person, it is obviously true that, in general, the greater the height of a person the greater his weight.

Sometimes we just suspect that there may be a linear relationship, and finding the regression line is then secondary to the aim of seeing how closely the actual position of the variables fits this line. The regression line is often called the line of best fit, or sometimes the least squares line, after the method of finding it. Further simple examples of the use of regression analysis to test a suspected linear correlation between factors would be in checking whether the belief that there is a relationship between the hours of sleep that animals require, and their intelligence, has a scientific basis or not, or to check on the correlation between artistic achievement in men and physical/sensual deprivation.

Generally, however, we shall be concerned with the first of the two aims of regression analysis. We take it as pretty certain that there is some linear relationship between the variables, and the problem is just that of finding the precise form that the equation should take. The second aim, the problem of how accurately this regression line fits the facts, and hence whether the linear relationship assumption is justified or not and indeed which variables should enter the regression equation, is not so relevant here, though it is of great importance in much statistical work.

Reverting to the business situation, let us consider how total cost might alter with variations in volume of output. At this stage we will assume that there is only one type of product made. Historical data will give us a series of values for total cost (Y) against the corresponding production (X). We take it as certain that cost varies in some way with production. If we believe the relationship is linear it will be of the form $Y = B_0 + B_1 X$. For any individual value for X the corresponding value for Y will fall off the regression line by a *residual* small amount E (say). Hence in each case

$$Y = B_0 + B_1 X + E$$

If all the E's are small we shall have a good fit, and our mathematical model of the relationship between X and Y, i.e., the regression line, can be regarded as satisfactorily representing the true life situation.

Suppose that we have n sets of past results $(X_1\ Y_1)\ (X_2\ Y_2) --- (X_n\ Y_n)$ giving the production and the corresponding cost for the last n periods. For each value (i say) we can write,

$$Y_i = B_0 + B_1 X_i + E_i \text{ (all values of } i \text{ from 1 to } n)$$

Hence the deviation, $E_i = Y_i - B_0 - B_1 X_i$, and clearly in order to have our regression line as good a fit as possible we wish to arrange for the E_i's to be as small as possible.

But how precisely shall we do this? Shall we arrange for the average value of the E_i's, i.e., $\sum E_i/n$ to be as small as possible? This might seem the simplest solution, but unfortunately a large negative E_i would just cancel out a large positive E_i and so would not contribute its real weight. One way to deal with this is to use the square of each deviation. This neatly gets over the difficulty of the minus sign, and also gives extra weight to large individual deviations. The squares of deviations is called the variance, and it is the measure of dispersion most used in statistical analysis. The square root of the variance is called the standard deviation. On this basis we wish to minimize S (say) where

$$S = \sum E_i^2 = \sum (Y_i - B_0 - B_1 X_i)^2$$

More precisely, we wish to find those values (b_0 and b_1, say) for B_0 and B_1 which will make S a minimum. S can therefore be regarded as a function of the parameters B_0 and B_1. To find the minimum we differentiate partially, first with respect to B_0, and then to B_1 and put the results equal to 0. Thus,

$$\frac{\partial S}{\partial B_0} = -2 \sum (Y_i - B_0 - B_1 X_i)$$

$$\frac{\partial S}{\partial B_1} = -2 \sum X_i (Y_i - B_0 - B_1 X_i)$$

For those whose calculus is rusty this involves two steps in principle:

First, $$\frac{\partial S}{\partial B} = \frac{\partial S}{\partial Z} \cdot \frac{\partial Z}{\partial B}$$

where $Z = Y_i - B_0 - B_1 X_i$ for B equal to B_0 and then B_1, and, as $S = Z^2$,

then $$\frac{\partial S}{\partial Z} = 2Z$$

Second,
$$\frac{\partial Z}{\partial B_0} = -1$$
$$\frac{\partial Z}{\partial B_1} = -X_i$$

Combining these two gives the equations above. Putting these each equal to 0, the values for b_0 and b_1 satisfy:

$$\sum (Y_i - b_0 - b_1 X_i) = 0$$
$$\sum X_i(Y_i - b_0 - b_1 X_i) = 0$$

These reduce to

$$\sum Y_i - n b_0 - b_1 \sum X_i = 0$$
$$\sum X_i Y_i - b_0 \sum X_i - b_1 \sum X_i^2 = 0$$

That is,

$$\left.\begin{aligned} b_0 n + b_1 \sum X_i &= \sum Y_i \\ b_0 \sum X_i + b_1 \sum X_i^2 &= \sum X_i Y_i \end{aligned}\right\} \quad (4.1)$$

These are a pair of simultaneous equations which we can solve for $b_0\, b_1$. They are often referred to as the normal equations.

At this stage an example may be helpful, though we still need to assume that only one type of product is made. Let us suppose that the figures for the last eight quarters for the volume of production (X) of these units, and the cost (Y) in £'s, are as follows:

Quarter	X	Y	X^2(*thousands*)	XY(*millions*)
1	932	24 620	868·6	22·95
2	962	24 010	925·4	23·10
3	1 024	25 340	1 048·0	25·95
4	1 115	25 320	1 243·0	28·22
5	1 291	26 830	1 666·0	34·63
6	1 230	26 420	1 513·0	32·49
7	1 206	25 670	1 455·0	30·95
8	1 470	27 310	2 161·0	40·15
	$\sum X = 9\,230$	$\sum Y = 205\,520$	$\sum X^2 = 10\,880{\cdot}0$	$\sum XY = 238{\cdot}44$

X^2 and XY have been worked out for each of the quarters, and the totals of all these columns ($\sum X$, $\sum Y$, $\sum X^2$ and $\sum XY$) are the figures we require. Our normal equations are therefore:

$$b_0 \times 8 + b_1 \times 9230 = 205\,520$$
$$b_0 \times 9230 + b_1 \times 10\,880\,000 = 238\,440\,000$$

To solve these simultaneous equations, multiply the first by 9230 and the second by 8 and subtract. This gives,

$$b_1 = 5{\cdot}68$$

and substituting in either equation gives

$$b_0 = 19\,120$$

The equation to the regression line is therefore:

$$Y = 19\,120 + 5{\cdot}68\ X$$

and this line, together with points representing the figures for the last eight quarters, is shown in Fig. 4.3. This particular regression line could probably have been drawn pretty accurately by eye.

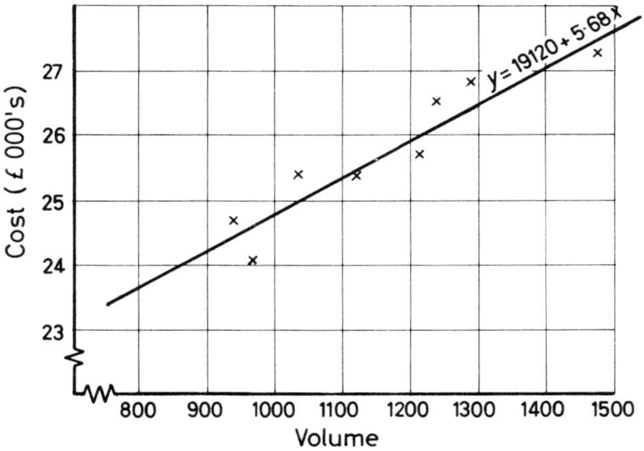

Figure 4.3.

The graphical solution is useful when we have only one independent variable (X) to compare with the dependent variable (Y). On this basis we would need to use three-dimensional geometry if we had two independent variables X_1, X_2, and n-dimensional geometry for the general case. Clearly we would like a more powerful technique.

We therefore revert to the basic equation $Y_i = B_0 + B_1\ X_i + E_i$, which holds good for all values of i from 1 to n. We can write these as:

$$Y_1 = B_0 + B_1\ X_1 + E_1$$
$$Y_2 = B_0 + B_1\ X_2 + E_2$$
$$Y_3 = B_0 + B_1\ X_3 + E_3$$

— —

— —

$$Y_n = B_0 + B_1\ X_n + E_n$$

Changing to matrix notation, we call Y the column vector of the values of the dependent variable, X the matrix of the independent variables, B the column vector of the parameters, and E the column vector of the individual errors E. That is:

$$Y = \begin{bmatrix} Y_1 \\ Y_2 \\ Y_3 \\ - \\ - \\ Y_n \end{bmatrix} \quad X = \begin{bmatrix} 1 & X_1 \\ 1 & X_2 \\ 1 & X_3 \\ - & - \\ - & - \\ 1 & X_n \end{bmatrix} \quad B = \begin{bmatrix} B_0 \\ B_1 \end{bmatrix} \quad E = \begin{bmatrix} E_1 \\ E_2 \\ E_3 \\ - \\ - \\ E_n \end{bmatrix}$$

and the fact that our basic equation holds good for all the n values can be written as:

$$Y = XB+E$$

This follows since the matrix multiplication XB gives a column vector with the values $B_0+B_1 X_1$, $B_0+B_1 X_2$, etc., etc., and adding E gives the set of right-hand values of our basic equation, and finally if the two matrices (Y) and $(XB+E)$ are written down as equal, this means that all the corresponding elements are equal.

The transpose of the column vector E will be a row vector E' such that

$$E' = [E_1\ E_2\ E_3 --- E_n]$$

The multiplication

$$E'E = [E_1\ E_2\ E_3 --- E_n] \begin{bmatrix} E_1 \\ E_2 \\ E_3 \\ - \\ - \\ E_n \end{bmatrix} = [E_1^2+E_2^2+E_3^2+ --- E_n^2]$$

Similarly,

$$Y'Y = [Y_1^2+Y_2^2+Y_3^2+ --- Y_n^2]$$

and

$$X'X = \begin{bmatrix} 1 & 1 & 1 & --- & 1 \\ X_1 & X_2 & X_3 & --- & X_n \end{bmatrix} \begin{bmatrix} 1 & X_1 \\ 1 & X_2 \\ 1 & X_3 \\ - & - \\ - & - \\ 1 & X_n \end{bmatrix} \quad \begin{bmatrix} n & \sum X \\ \sum X & \sum X^2 \end{bmatrix}$$

$$X'Y = \begin{bmatrix} 1 & 1 & 1 & --- & 1 \\ X_1 & X_2 & X_3 & --- & X_n \end{bmatrix} \begin{bmatrix} Y_1 \\ Y_2 \\ Y_3 \\ - \\ - \\ Y_n \end{bmatrix} = \begin{bmatrix} \sum Y \\ \sum XY \end{bmatrix}$$

If we postmultiply $X'X$ by the column vector

$$b = \begin{bmatrix} b_0 \\ b_1 \end{bmatrix}$$

we have the left-hand side of the two normal equations (4.1). These normal equations can therefore be written in matrix form as:

$$X'Xb = X'Y$$

giving

$$b = (X'X)^{-1}X'Y$$

We now have the layout in quite general form, so that we can extend the problem from the present position, where we have only one independent variable X, to the general regression situation where we have any number (p, say) of independent variables. Specifically,

$$Y = XB + E$$

where

Y is a $(n \times 1)$ column vector of n results;

X is an $(n \times p)$ matrix whose elements are the values of the p independent variables, each for n different results;

B is a $(p \times 1)$ column vector of the parameters—the values of which we wish to find;

and E is a $(n \times 1)$ column vector of errors.

The solution is the same, i.e., the values for B are given by

$$b = (X'X)^{-1}X'Y$$

This is the matrix solution to the multiple regression problem. Since we know* a computer method for matrix inversion this is the best method to use. When the number of parameters is small, say up to three, the alternative approach by partial differentiation can be used. We have already seen one example of this in the calculation earlier in the section when we had only one variable (X) and two parameters B_0 and B_1. We now consider the case where there are two independent variables X_1 X_2 and three parameters B_0 B_1 B_2. The basic algebraic equation will be

$$Y = B_0 + B_1X_1 + B_2X_2 + E$$

* See appendix on 'Introduction to Matrix Algebra'.

The matrix solution for the parameters will be given by

$$b = (X' X)^{-1} X' Y$$

Alternatively, we can write

$$S = \sum E^2 = \sum (Y_i - B_0 - B_1 X_{1i} - B_2 X_{2i})^2$$

and differentiate partially with respect to B_0 B_1 and B_2 giving the algebraic form of the normal equations

$$\begin{aligned} b_0 + b_1 \sum X_{1i} + b_2 \sum X_{2i} &= \sum Y_i \\ b_0 \sum X_{1i} + b_1 \sum X_{1i}^2 + b_2 \sum X_{1i} X_{2i} &= \sum X_{1i} Y_i \\ b_0 \sum X_{2i} + b_1 \sum X_{2i} X_{1i} + b_2 \sum X_{2i}^2 &= \sum X_{2i} Y_i \end{aligned}$$

Solving these simultaneous equations will give the required values of b_0 b_1 b_2 for the parameters B_1 B_2 B_3.

As an example of this three parameter problem, suppose the total costs (Y) in (£1000's) corresponding to the volume of production of X_1 units of one product and X_2 units of another product for the last nine periods are given by

Y	X_1	X_2
200	100	100
206	104	99
207	106	110
220	111	126
210	111	113
216	115	103
223	120	102
233	124	103
237	126	98

Working out the values for $\sum X_1 \sum Y \sum X_1 Y \sum X_2 Y$, etc., on the same lines as in the earlier example and putting these values in the normal equations above, and then solving for the parameters gives

$$b_0 = 50{\cdot}6587$$
$$b_1 = 1{\cdot}3642$$
$$b_2 = 0{\cdot}1139$$

so that the equation to the regression line is

$$Y = 50{\cdot}6587 + 1{\cdot}3642 X_1 + 0{\cdot}1139 X_2$$

For problems with more than two independent variables the matrix inversion technique is recommended. It follows that, when quite a large number of different goods are produced in a factory, establishing the regression line which represents the cost elements of each product, really means the use of a computer and one of the standard matrix inversion programmes.

4.5.1. Extensions of the regression model

We have argued that in the business situation it often seems intuitively obvious that the model can be represented by an equation which is linear in the independent variables. In our product cost example if x units of M1 are produced and the variable cost per unit is a, then total cost will be of the form $ax+c$, where c is a constant. Most arguments justifying a linear form are roughly analogous to this. Sometimes, however, the linear assumption is clearly not justified. For instance in a closed market situation where the total sales revenue obtainable for a product is theoretically a constant sum c (say, regardless of the quantity sold), then the relationship between x, the unit price, and y the quantity sold is given by $xy = c$ or $y = c/x$. For another example consider the rate of production of a new item x months after the beginning of a production run. Frequently it is found to be fairly accurately described by the equation

$$y = A(1-e^{-bx})$$

where A and b are constants. This curve is called the learning curve, and is dealt with in the chapter on training.

Neither of these equations are linear in x, and consequently regression analysis would, prima facie, not appear to be a technique capable of dealing with them. However, if we write $Z = 1/x$, i.e. we use the reciprocal of x as the independent variable, we have the equation $y = cZ$ for our closed market model. This is linear in Z and therefore regression analysis can be used.

In the second case, if we write $y_1 = \{(A-y)/A\}$ so that $y_1 = e^{-bx}$, take logarithms of both sides, so that $\log y_1 = -bx$, and finally write y_2 for $\log y_1$, we have $y_2 = -bx$. This, too, is now in linear form. Reverting to the original variables, the learning curve is $\log \{(A-y)/A\} = -bx$. This means that when working out the regression line the columns for the independent variable (X) will show the individual values of x, but the columns for the dependent variable will show the individual values of $\log \{(A-y)/A\}$.

In scientific models it is not uncommon for the relationship to be a polynomial in one independent variable. That is, expressed as an equation of order n,

$$y = B_0+B_1 x+B_2 x^2+ --- B_n x^n$$

Such models are 'intrinsically linear' models—using this term in the sense that they can be expressed in linear terms by suitable transformations. All we have to do is write:

$$Z_1 = x, Z_2 = x^2, Z_3 = x^3 --- Z_n = x^n,$$

and the equation is transformed into

$$y = B_0 + B_1 Z_1 + B_2 Z_2 + B_3 Z_3 + --- B_n Z_n$$

which is linear in the variables $Z_1 Z_2 Z_3 --- Z_n$. It is therefore in a suitable form for dealing with by regression analysis.

The special case of the second order model:

$$y = B_0 + B_1 x + B_2 x^2$$

will be transformed into:

$$y = B_0 + B_1 Z_1 + B_2 Z_2$$

which is a linear model with two independent variables.

This particular model has many applications in the field of science. One typical example would be when a ball is thrown in the air. Ignoring the drag effect of the air's resistance, the vertical height (y) at any time (t) is given by the equation $y = ut - \frac{1}{2} gt^2$ where u is the initial vertical velocity and g is the gravitational constant. Management models are not quite so common, though one occurs when we look at the relationship between volume of production (y) from a factory, and the size of the workforce (x). In some industrial situations the equation $y = B_0 + B_1 x + B_2 x^2$, where B_0 B_1 and B_2 are positive constants, and B_2 is fairly small, has been found to represent the relationship fairly exactly.

4.5.2. Dummy variables

Sometimes data may arise from several sources, for example they may come from various factories, machines and operators or task forces all of whom are doing much the same thing. If we wish to use the information available from all these sources in determining the regression line we really should allow for possible inate differences as between these sources. This can be done by the introduction of dummy variables which are included to reflect these differences between one source and another. Again reverting to our basic example of the relationship between the cost (y) and the output of two (say) basic products (X_3 X_4), both of which are produced at three separate factories, we need to introduce two dummy variables X_1 and X_2 to reflect the differences that the data from any two of the plants may have when compared with the data from the third plant.

The basic equation will be

$$Y = B_0 + B_1 X_1 + B_2 X_2 + B_3 X_3 + B_4 X_4$$

and X_1 and X_2 will be used for plant identification for individual data readings in accordance with this simple rule:

X_1	X_2	
1	0	for data from plant No. 1
0	1	,, ,, ,, ,, No. 2
0	0	,, ,, ,, ,, No. 3

The other data readings for X_3 and X_4 will be entered in the usual way. We now have a series of data readings for four independent variables (X_1 X_2 X_3 X_4) and so the regression line can be determined.

Dummy variables can also be used when there is a once and for all basic change in the structure. For instance, in the example above, all the data may have come from one plant over a period of time. At some stage, however, there may have been some substantial change or improvement in the operation of the plant, due perhaps to the introduction of some more sophisticated machinery in one section. To allow for the effect of this, one dummy variable will need to be used which will have a value of 0 for periods before the change, and 1 for periods after the change.

4.5.3. Problems and limitations of regression analysis

It must be obvious that regression analysis is an extremely powerful tool for producing models in all sorts of situations varying from the simple one product business to macro models for the national economy. The management uses are many and there will be some further discussion of these in the chapter on the measurement of management. The great advantage of all these models, whether management, scientific or economic, is that once their equation or form has been established all the standard tools of mathematical analysis can be used. In particular, forecasts into the future can be made with far increased accuracy and confidence. Regression analysis however, like all sophisticated techniques, has its drawbacks and limitations. We have already noted that in general terms regression analysis can be applied either when a linear relationship between the dependent variable and the independent variables seems intuitively obvious, or when it is surmised that a linear relationship may adequately reflect the situation. In both cases, but particularly in the latter, we need really to show that the degree of fit of the regression line to the observed data is reasonably close. The regression line is that line which minimizes the squares of the deviations of the data from it (i.e., it minimizes $\sum E^2$). Any set of data will have a regression line, but unless the relationship is intrinsically linear this line is little other than a statistical curiosity.

Statistical techniques however do exist which relate the size of the residuals to the data and hence determine if there is any significance to the linear assumption.

Since our whole approach has been based on trying to minimize the value of $\sum E^2$, the standard deviation of the residuals is probably the most appropriate measure of all to use. However, there are several such tests—significance tests—as they are called. One simple approach to the problem is, having found the regression line, to apply this model to the determination of the value of the dependent variable for the next few sets of data of the independent variables, and see how closely it gives the actual observed data for the dependent variable. In other words, to test our linear assumption and see if it works.

When the data for the independent variables consist of sets of observations over a period of time, there is a particular problem. Because of the trend effect of time (basically due to inflation), there is a correlation between these successive data. This correlation is usually referred to as autocorrelation. In our example of the relationship between the costs and the volume of production of one or more products, it may well be that gradually rising total cost figures reflect nothing more than the effect of inflation on costs. Such increases in both sets of figures do not result from any intrinsic linear relationship between the variables, but simply show that costs rise with price inflation. This phenomenon is often referred to as 'drift'. The best way to deal with this situation is to reduce all costs to a common basic figure, i.e., to reduce them by the amount of inflation. Any correlation between the revised cost figures and the production figures is then likely to be genuine.

Where there are trends or periodic movements in significant variables that are omitted from the regression equations, the residuals may be autocorrelated. One way of dealing with this is to introduce time as one of the independent variables. For dealing with quarterly seasonal variations the best method is to use three dummy variables (000, 100, 010, 001 for the quarters).

Sometimes there is an intrinsic correlation between the dependent variables so that they are not truly independent of each other. This is referred to as multicollinearity. In the business situation multicollinearity is by no means an unknown phenomenon. In determining variable costs of genuinely separate products it is, however, not likely to occur. It could arise if we were making a particular product and its container and tried to cost each as a separate independent variable. Clearly a product and its container are linked by volume of output.

4.6. Markov chains

Sometimes the outcome of an event is dependent solely on the preceding situation. In mathematical terms the probability that an event will or will not take place is determined by the preceding event. The term Markov process—or Markov 'chain', when we have a series of events each dependent on its predecessor—is applied to such situations.

Examples of the Markov process abound. One classic business application is in brand switching. The supposition here is that within the next time period there is a known probability that consumers will switch from one brand to another. The problem is to determine the final market share if this process continues. For example:

A certain industrial connurbation has, we suppose, two main dairies (X and Y) who for practical purposes supply all the milk in the city area. There is a third group of small independent retailers, but their share of the market is small. Moreover, their customers remain with them, and therefore provide a separate constant section which can be excluded from the analysis.

Customers do switch from one of the two main suppliers to the other for various reasons. The probability of a switch or a retention over a three month period can be estimated fairly accurately from past data. In matrix form they are shown as:

		To	
		X	Y
From	X	0·90	0·10
	Y	0·05	0·95

Clearly users of milk Y have a high brand loyalty. The chance that a customer of Y will remain a customer at the end of three months is 0·95. In other words there is a 95 per cent chance that he will still be with Y.

The probable market share at the end of the next quarter, assuming that the same probabilities apply, is easy to calculate. If the present market share for X and Y is given by the row vector,

$$\begin{matrix} X & Y \\ [0{\cdot}6 & 0{\cdot}4] \end{matrix} \text{ then the product,}$$

$$[0{\cdot}6 \quad 0{\cdot}4]\begin{bmatrix} 0{\cdot}90 & 0{\cdot}10 \\ 0{\cdot}05 & 0{\cdot}95 \end{bmatrix} = [(0{\cdot}6\times 0{\cdot}9+0{\cdot}4\times 0{\cdot}05 \quad 0{\cdot}6\times 0{\cdot}1+0{\cdot}4\times 0{\cdot}95)]$$

$$= [0{\cdot}56 \quad 0{\cdot}44] \text{ gives the market share after one quarter.}$$

X's market share, for instance, is made up of those who started with X and have not changed ($0{\cdot}6\times 0{\cdot}9$) and those who started with Y and changed to X ($0{\cdot}4\times 0{\cdot}05$). Similarly for Y.

The matrix

$$\begin{bmatrix} 0{\cdot}90 & 0{\cdot}10 \\ 0{\cdot}05 & 0{\cdot}95 \end{bmatrix}$$

is usually called a transition matrix. If we refer to this as matrix A, for short, then the market share after one quarter can be written as

$$[0{\cdot}6 \quad 0{\cdot}4]\, A$$

Assuming that the same probabilities apply to the second quarter the market share at the end of six months will be

$$[0{\cdot}6 \quad 0{\cdot}4]\, AA = [0{\cdot}6 \quad 0{\cdot}4]\, A^2$$

and the market share at the end of three quarters, four quarters or, in general, n quarters will be, by analogous reasoning,

$$[0{\cdot}6 \quad 0{\cdot}4]\, A^3$$

$$[0{\cdot}6 \quad 0{\cdot}4]\, A^4$$

and

$$[0{\cdot}6 \quad 0{\cdot}4]\, A^n$$

Working out the market shares for the third and fourth quarters and putting them down together with the current (C) market share in, we have the results shown in Table 4.1.

Table 4.1

Quarter	X	Y
C	0·600	0·400
1	0·560	0·440
2	0·526	0·474
3	0·497 1	0·502 9
4	0·472 535	0·527 465

From this table, as it stands, it is not too easy to see any clear trend or pattern emerging. Plotting the results on graph paper (Fig. 4.4), and carrying on the curves by eye, does seem to indicate that the figures for the market share of both X and Y become more fixed and stable the further we go into the future. Y is obviously tending to settle down in some position well into the top half of the market share, with X in the lower half. If we suppose that these final fixed shares are p and q, it follows that

$$[0{\cdot}6 \quad 0{\cdot}4]\, A^n \rightarrow [p \quad q] \tag{4.2}$$

when n tends to infinity, and also

$$[p \quad q]\, A = [p \quad q] \tag{4.3}$$

since, once we have arrived at the final stable state, a further transition must, by definition, leave the market share unchanged.

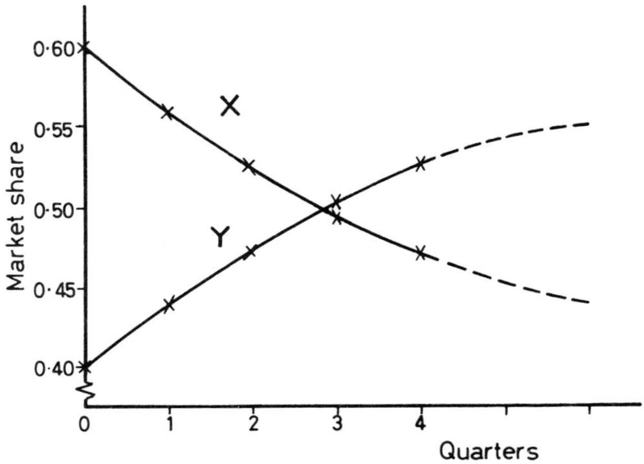

Figure 4.4.

The second equation, i.e., (4.3), in full is

$$[p \quad q]\begin{bmatrix} 0{\cdot}9 & 0{\cdot}1 \\ 0{\cdot}05 & 0{\cdot}95 \end{bmatrix} = [p \quad q]$$

Multiplying out, this gives

$$0{\cdot}9p + 0{\cdot}05q = p$$

and

$$0{\cdot}1p + 0{\cdot}95q = q$$

We cannot solve these equations for p and q as they stand. All we can get is the ratio p/q. However since p and q together take up the full market share, we also have $p+q = 1$. Using this in combination with either of the preceding equations to solve for p and q, we get

$$p = \tfrac{1}{3}$$
$$q = \tfrac{2}{3}$$

Final market shares are therefore $\frac{1}{3}$ for X and $\frac{2}{3}$ for Y.

It will be noted that in the calculation of these market shares we only used eq. (4.3). The original market share figures of 0·6 and 0·4 did not enter into it at all. It follows that final market shares depend only on the transition probabilities. The original market shares are irrelevant, and whatever they may have been, the final market shares reached will be the same. Naturally, it will take a little longer to get to near the final market shares if the initial shares are way out of line with these. The end result, however, will always be the same.

Although we have not calculated the value of A^n as $n \to \alpha$ in the first equation, it is easy to check and confirm that the equal row matrix,

$$\begin{bmatrix} \frac{1}{3} & \frac{2}{3} \\ \frac{1}{3} & \frac{2}{3} \end{bmatrix}$$

fits in easily enough. Indeed this is one example of a more general rule, which we quote just for interest, and which says that if A is a regular transition matrix (i.e., A and all its powers have only positive elements) then the value of A^n as $n \to \alpha$ is a matrix with positive elements and all rows equal.

4.6.1. Limitations of the simple Markov process

One obvious limitation of the Markov chain process is that in the business world probabilities are unlikely to remain the same far into the future. Against this it can be argued that the future is inherently uncertain, and the best available guide to it is the present position, and it is this continuance of the present probability that is implied in the Markov process.

The advantages of the Markov process are substantial. Obviously it is of interest to a marketing director to know which way a market share is going. Unless he is given this information he will not really be in a position to calculate whether it is worth while undertaking or altering any advertising campaign.

Non-business applications of the Markov process are particularly interesting. For instance if we arbitrarily divide society into three money classes, i.e., rich, medium, and poor, we can determine a transition matrix giving the probability of a person born in one class ending up in the same class or moving to another. We can then determine the distribution of the population after a given period of time and also the ultimate distribution of the population between classes, assuming that the probabilities remain constant over time. Social mobility within a village has been analysed by this process. Indeed the future of this process is probably in the analysis of ecologically closed systems with particular reference to self-supporting life systems suitable for outer space.

4.6.2. Absorbing Markov chains

One particular type of Markov model is of special interest both in its business and social applications. This occurs when the possible final outcomes from the process are limited to two in number. For example:

Hospital

Patients may stay one, two, three, or even more months, but in the long run they either leave or they die.

School or college

Students pass from one year or grade to another. These are stages in the process. At each stage the student will normally proceed to the next stage, but he may, if he is very bright, jump two stages. On the other hand, if he has done badly he may stay in the same class or even, conceivably, go back a grade. At any time he may leave the place, and this is one of the two possible final outcomes. The other is that he passes his course successfully.

Production process

At any stage in the factory process the product . either be passed on to the next machine, process or department, presumably after some sort of testing. This will be the normal step. However, the result of the test may be unsatisfactory, and the product may have to be reprocessed, or even sent back for work at an earlier stage. At any time the product may be scrapped. The normal outcome on the other hand is that it will complete the whole process satisfactorily.
These are the only two possible outcomes:

Stock

An item in stock is there to be sold. It may stay for one, two, three, or even more months. It may be reduced in price. In the long run it will either be sold, or it will be declared obsolete.

Accounts receivable

Debtors are usually classified by the age of the debt. An account which is say two months old may either be paid, become a three months old debt—i.e., pass into the next age class—or possibly be declared a bad debt. In the long run all debts will either be paid or regarded officially as a bad debt.

We have quoted two social and three business examples of Markov process, all of which have this special feature in common. In each case, although there are several stages in the process, and several possible outcomes at each stage, there are, nevertheless, only two possible eventual outcomes. These final outcomes, one of which must always be reached in the long run, are called absorbing states.

In a rather general sense almost all social or business processes can be seen as absorbing Markov processes. Every child is born single and goes from one age group to another. The only possible outcomes are death or marriage. All fixed assets, indeed all investments of a business, grow older by stages. The only possible outcomes are sale or scrap.

In order to analyse absorbing Markov chains let us take the case where there are two transient states 1 and 2 and two absorbing states S and F, standing, perhaps, for 'success' or 'failure'. The calculation or assessment of the expected probabilities of proceeding from one state to another will presumably have been based mainly on past experience. Suppose they are:

	S	F	1	2
S	1	0	0	0
F	0	1	0	0
1	b_{11}	b_{12}	a_{11}	a_{12}
2	b_{21}	b_{22}	a_{21}	a_{22}

Since S and F are absorbing states the probability of proceeding from either of them to any other state is nil. Conversely, the probability of remaining in the same absorbing state is necessarily 1.

Let us concentrate on the probability of ending up in state S. The simplest approach is to list the ways that this can be done, and then add up all their probabilities. If the initial shares or quantities in states 1 and 2 are, say, x and y respectively, then the likelihood of them finishing up in S after one step is

$$[x \quad y]\begin{bmatrix} b_{11} \\ b_{21} \end{bmatrix}$$

This is because the chance of going straight from 1 to S is b_{11}, so that the share or quantity will be $x\,b_{11}$. From 2 to S it will be $y\,b_{21}$, and the total is therefore $x\,b_{11}+y\,b_{21}$.

The likelihood of going to S in two steps is a little more complicated. The possible ways are

$$\begin{aligned} &1 - 1 - S, \text{ i.e., } x\,a_{11}\,b_{11} \\ &1 - 2 - S, \text{ i.e., } x\,a_{12}\,b_{21} \\ &2 - 1 - S, \text{ i.e., } y\,a_{21}\,b_{11} \\ &2 - 2 - S, \text{ i.e., } y\,a_{22}\,b_{21} \end{aligned}$$

The total of these is

$$[x \quad y]\begin{bmatrix} a_{11} & a_{12} \\ a_{21} & a_{22} \end{bmatrix}\begin{bmatrix} b_{11} \\ b_{21} \end{bmatrix}$$

The likelihood of going in exactly three steps follows the same pattern, that is

$$[x \quad y]\begin{bmatrix} a_{11} & a_{12} \\ a_{21} & a_{22} \end{bmatrix}^2\begin{bmatrix} b_{11} \\ b_{21} \end{bmatrix}$$

and the likelihood of going to S in n steps is

$$[x \quad y]\,A^{n-1}\begin{bmatrix} b_{11} \\ b_{21} \end{bmatrix}$$

where

$$A = \begin{bmatrix} a_{11} & a_{12} \\ a_{21} & a_{22} \end{bmatrix}$$

Similarly, the likelihood of going to F after exactly n steps is

$$[x \quad y]\, A^{n-1} \begin{bmatrix} b_{12} \\ b_{22} \end{bmatrix}$$

Since S and F are absorbing states, once one has arrived at either of these states there is no coming out again. Hence the likelihood of being in S after n steps is the sum of the likelihood of getting there in one step, or in two steps, or in any number of steps up to n steps.

Hence, the likelihood of being at S after n steps is

$$[x \quad y] \begin{bmatrix} b_{11} \\ b_{21} \end{bmatrix} + [x \quad y]\, A \begin{bmatrix} b_{11} \\ b_{21} \end{bmatrix} + \\ + [x \quad y]\, A^2 \begin{bmatrix} b_{11} \\ b_{21} \end{bmatrix} + --- + [x \quad y]\, A^{n-1} \begin{bmatrix} b_{11} \\ b_{21} \end{bmatrix}$$

i.e.,

$$[x \quad y]\, [I + A + A^2 --- A^{n-1}] \begin{bmatrix} b_{11} \\ b_{21} \end{bmatrix}$$

where I, the identity matrix, has been introduced to preserve the general layout.

Now the sum to infinity of a geometric series $1 + x + x^2 + ---$ is $1/(1-x)$ or $(1-x)^{-1}$, provided $x < 1$.

By analagous reasoning we may infer that the sum to infinity of the above series of powers of matrices is

$$[x \quad y]\, [I - A]^{-1} \begin{bmatrix} b_{11} \\ b_{21} \end{bmatrix}$$

where $[I-A]^{-1}$ is the inverse of the matrix $[I-A]$.

Hence, the final probability of ending up in the absorbing state S is

$$[x \quad y]\, [I - A]^{-1} \begin{bmatrix} b_{11} \\ b_{21} \end{bmatrix}$$

and of ending up in the absorbing state F is

$$[x \quad y]\, [I - A]^{-1} \begin{bmatrix} b_{12} \\ b_{22} \end{bmatrix}$$

The matrix $[I-A]^{-1}$ is often referred to as the fundamental matrix of an absorbing Markov chain.

We have now arrived at our answer. The product matrices above show the amounts of x and y, (i.e., the amounts currently in the transient states 1 and 2) which will eventually finish up in the absorbing states S and F.

Two further points need to be made. First, when the transient states are states of time, as in the ageing of debtors, then, since time cannot go backwards, probabilities such as a_{21} in our example, must be nil. This proviso does not of course hold generally; for example it is not applicable to the production process.

Second, the approach which we have described is quite general. Although we used only two transient states we could have used the same format and extended the transient states to any number, n say.

The layout will still be of the form (sometimes referred to as canonical)

$$\left[\begin{array}{c|c} I & O \\ \hline B & A \end{array}\right]$$

where I and O are the identity and null matrices, and A and B are respectively.

$$\begin{bmatrix} a_{11} & a_{12} & --- & a_{1n} \\ a_{21} & a_{22} & --- & a_{2n} \\ - & - & & - \\ - & - & & - \\ a_{n1} & a_{n2} & & a_{nn} \end{bmatrix}$$

and

$$\begin{bmatrix} b_{11} & b_{12} \\ b_{21} & b_{22} \\ - & - \\ - & - \\ b_{n1} & b_{n2} \end{bmatrix}$$

4.7. Input-output analysis

For the purpose of this analysis it is assumed that the corporate body can be split up into a number of separate sectors each supplying goods or services to other sectors. In a homogeneous business corporation the sectors will be those of factories or departments within a factory. Partly manufactured goods will go from one department or factory to another. Valuing these goods, i.e., putting a transfer price on them, is difficult; it is, however, essential if we wish to measure one department's output accurately with a view to assessing the performance of the manager in charge (see chapter 8).

Not all the sectors will be factory departments producing physical goods. Service departments, such as the management services department, will supply services, probably to all the line departments.

In a conglomerate, or large business corporation, each product group can be considered as a separate sector or division. Indeed the term division is commonly applied to such large but separate parts of the corporate entity. In these cases, though some of the goods produced may go to other divisions, the main output will be in sales made outside the corporation. In terminology analogous to that used by economists, we can say that these sales go to the final demand sector. Generally, it is only necessary to consider a complete business division in this sense when we are concerned to measure the output of the division as a whole and, arising from that, the efficiency of the divisional director.

The more usual business situation is that of a single organization, with a number of separate departments, each taking part in the overall production process. Typically, there will be a standard flow pattern for the manufacture of goods from one department to the next in line and so on. Sometimes, however, goods will be reprocessed, and sometimes goods will miss out on some departments. We need to take account of all these possibilities.

In money terms let us call:

The total output of department i	X_i
The output of department i to department j	X_{ij}
The output of department i to final demand (i.e., 'sold' outside the business)	Y_i

It follows that

$$\sum Y_i = \text{Total business sales}$$

and

$$X_i = \sum_{j=1}^{n} X_{ij} + Y_i \tag{4.4}$$

for all i from 1 to n, where n is the number of departments.

Now if (and only if) the demand that department j makes of department i depends on (i.e., is directly variable with) department j's output, then

$$X_{ij} = a_{ij} X_j \tag{4.5}$$

where a_{ij} is constant for a given i and j. Moreover, since value has presumably been added in department j

$$a_{ij} \leqslant 1$$

Equation (4.4) can be rewritten as

$$X_i - \sum X_{ij} = Y_i$$

Putting in the values for X_{ij} from eq. (4.5) gives

$$X_i - \sum a_{ij} X_j = Y_i$$

where j varies from 1 to n.

Now this is true for all values of i from 1 to n, that is, in detail

$$\begin{array}{l} X_1 - a_{11} X_1 - a_{12} X_2 - a_{13} X_3 --- a_{1n} X_n = Y_1 \\ X_2 - a_{21} X_1 - a_{22} X_2 - a_{23} X_3 --- a_{2n} X_n = Y_2 \\ \quad - \quad - \quad - \quad - \\ \quad - \quad - \quad - \quad - \\ X_n - a_{n1} X_1 - a_{n2} X_2 - a_{n3} X_3 --- a_{nn} X_n = Y_n \end{array}$$

Grouping up the X_1's in the first equation, the X_2's in the second and so on, these equations in matrix form, are

$$\begin{bmatrix} 1-a_{11} & -a_{12} & -a_{13} --- & -a_{1n} \\ -a_{21} & 1-a_{22} & -a_{23} --- & -a_{2n} \\ - & & - & - \\ - & & - & - \\ -a_{n1} & -a_{n2} & -a_{n3} --- & 1-a_{nn} \end{bmatrix} \begin{bmatrix} X_1 \\ X_2 \\ - \\ - \\ X_n \end{bmatrix} = \begin{bmatrix} Y_1 \\ Y_2 \\ - \\ - \\ Y_n \end{bmatrix}$$

If we call the matrix of input-output coefficients A, so that:

$$A = \begin{bmatrix} a_{11} & a_{12} & a_{13} --- & a_{1n} \\ a_{21} & a_{22} & a_{23} --- & a_{2n} \\ - & - & - & - \\ - & - & - & - \\ a_{n1} & a_{n2} & a_{n3} --- & a_{nn} \end{bmatrix}$$

then the matrix on the left is:

$$I - A$$

where I is the indentity matrix of order n.

If we call the column vector of total outputs X, and the column vector of outputs to final demand (i.e., 'sales') Y, then:

$$(I - A)\, X = Y$$

giving

$$X = (I - A)^{-1}\, Y$$

assuming the inverse of $(I - A)$ exists.

This inverse, $(I - A)^{-1}$, will be some matrix B (say) where

$$B = \begin{bmatrix} b_{11} & b_{12} & b_{13} & -- b_{1n} \\ b_{21} & b_{22} & b_{23} & -- b_{2n} \\ - & - & & -- - \\ - & - & & -- - \\ b_{n1} & b_{n2} & b_{n3} & -- b_{nn} \end{bmatrix}$$

and we have

$$X = B\, Y$$

This gives each department's output in terms of the sales (final demand) of the various departments. For instance the output of the first department, i.e., X_1, is

$$X_1 = b_{11} Y_1 + b_{12} Y_2 + b_{13} Y_3 + --- b_{1n} Y_n$$

and similarly for all the other departments.

Since sales are clearly determined in money terms, it follows that we have measured the output of a department in these terms and this is the main conclusion at which we wished to arrive. There are, however, two further steps in input-output analysis which are of general interest.

First, the matrix $X - Y$ gives directly that output of each department which goes to other departments as part of the production process, rather than to final demand.

Second, we can easily arrive at the marginal effect of having to produce one extra unit of final demand. For if:

$$X = (I - A)^{-1} Y$$

then

$$\Delta X = (I - A)^{-1} \Delta Y$$

where ΔX and ΔY are the respective increases.

Hence, corresponding to the need to produce, say, one extra unit of department n's for sale, the extra outputs required by the individual departments will be given by putting $\Delta Y = Y_n = 1$ (and $Y_1 = Y_2 = \ldots. Y_{n-1} = 0$), in the matrix above.

There are some substantial criticisms that can be made of the application of input-output analysis to the sections or department of a business. In particular, while inter-line department transactions will most likely be in accordance with a constant input-output coefficient, it is unlikely that the output from a service department, such as the Head Office, to a line department will be directly variable with the output of that line department. Input-output analysis is only realistic when confined to the manufacturing departments of a business organization.

Appendix on the Simplex method

The Simplex approach

Let us start off with the business example, but since we wish to arrive at the general rule, we re-write the equations as:

$$Z = P_1 x_1 + P_2 x_2 + P_3 x_3 + P_4 x_4 \text{ (where } P_3 = P_4 = 0)$$

subject to

$$\left.\begin{aligned} a_{11} x_1 + a_{12} x_2 + I.x_3 + 0.x_4 &= c_1 \\ a_{21} x_1 + a_{22} x_2 + 0.x_3 + I.x_4 &= c_2 \\ x_1 \geqslant 0 \quad x_2 \geqslant 0 \quad x_3 \geqslant 0 \quad x_4 &\geqslant 0 \end{aligned}\right\} \tag{4.6}$$

and (the last line above)

In the example we could start with the origin O (x_1 = O, x_2 = O). Since this gives zero profit, any other corner will give a higher profit. The Simplex plan is simply that we shall move from O to whichever of the adjacent corners A or C gives the greater increase of profit, and then that this same principle shall be applied in moving from corner A or C to the next corner, and so on. In our business example it is true that we could easily test all the corners as there are so few. However, when there are many constraints the logical 'profit maximizing' approach will usually be very much shorter.

We start, therefore, with the basic feasible solution $x_1 = x_2 = 0$ giving $Z = 0$. It follows that $x_3 = c_1$ and $x_4 = c_2$.

If we move to other corners (or indeed to any points within the prescribed area) we shall have other values for $x_1\ x_2\ x_3\ x_4$ which will satisfy eqs. (4.6). Successive new positions will be indicated by dashes, thus $x'_1\ x'_2\ x'_3\ x'_4$, then $x''_1\ x''_2\ x''_3\ x''_4$ and so on. The corresponding new values for the objective function will be denoted by Z', Z'', etc.

Along which line shall we move to arrive at the most suitable corner? There are two possible choices. Let us suppose, first, that x_2 remains stationary at zero so that $x'_2 = 0$, and that x_1 is increased by some Δ units, so that $x'_1 = \Delta$.

Then from eq. (4.6) above,

$$x'_3 = c_1 - a_{11}\,\Delta = x_3 - a_{11}\,\Delta$$

and

$$x'_4 = c_2 - a_{21}\,\Delta = x_4 - a_{21}\,\Delta$$

In that case,

$$\begin{aligned} Z' - Z &= P_1\Delta + P_2\,0 + P_3\,(x_3 - a_{11}\,\Delta) + P_4\,(x_4 - a_{21}\,\Delta) \\ &\quad - (P_1\,0 + P_2\,0 + P_3\,x_3 + P_4\,x_4) \\ &= \Delta\,(P_1 - a_{11}\,P_3 - a_{21}\,P_4) = \Delta\,S_1 \text{ (say)} \end{aligned}$$

Suppose next that Δ units are added to x_2 so that $x'_2 = \Delta$, $x'_1 = 0$. Then from eq. (4.6) above,

$$\left.\begin{aligned} x'_3 &= c_1 - a_{12}\,\Delta = x_3 - a_{12}\,\Delta \\ x'_4 &= c_2 - a_{22}\,\Delta = x_4 - a_{22}\,\Delta \end{aligned}\right\} \tag{4.7}$$

And,

$$\begin{aligned} Z' - Z &= P_1\,0 + P_2\,\Delta + P_3\,(x_3 - a_{12}\,\Delta) + P_4\,(x_4 - a_{22}\,\Delta) \\ &\quad -(P_1\,0 + P_2\,0 + P_3\,x_3 + P_4\,x_4) \\ &= \Delta\,(P_2 - a_{12}\,P_3 - a_{22}\,P_4) = \Delta\,S_2\text{ (say)} \end{aligned}$$

The factors in brackets (S_1 and S_2) are known as the Simplex criteria. Since the gain from including one unit of x_1 is S_1, then omitting one unit will result in a loss of S_1. Consequently, S_1 and S_2 can be interpreted as being the opportunity cost of omitting units of x_1 x_2 respectively.

Clearly, if S_1 and S_2 are both negative or zero, no gain from increasing x_1 and x_2 can be obtained. In that case we would already have arrived at the optimum. However, in this first case both S_1 and S_2 are easy to determine—as P_3 and P_4 are both equal to 0—so that they reduce to P_1 and P_2 respectively. Generally, however, as we proceed from one solution to another things will not be as simple as all this, and we need a more general expression for the Simplex criterion.

Consider then the matrix:

$$\begin{bmatrix} P_1 \\ P_2 \\ P_3 \\ P_4 \end{bmatrix} - \begin{bmatrix} a_{11} & a_{21} \\ a_{12} & a_{22} \\ 1 & 0 \\ 0 & 1 \end{bmatrix} \begin{bmatrix} P_3 \\ P_4 \end{bmatrix}, \text{ i.e., } \begin{bmatrix} P_1 & -a_{11}\,P_3 & -a_{21}\,P_4 \\ P_2 & -a_{12}\,P_3 & -a_{22}\,P_4 \\ P_3 & -\quad P_3 & +\quad O \\ P_4 & -\quad O & -\quad P_4 \end{bmatrix}$$

This gives the Simplex criteria worked out on the basic matrices of

$\begin{bmatrix} P_1 \\ P_2 \\ P_3 \\ P_4 \end{bmatrix}$ i.e., the transpose of all the coefficients in the objective function and $\begin{bmatrix} a_{11} & a_{21} \\ a_{12} & a_{22} \\ 1 & 0 \\ 0 & 1 \end{bmatrix}$ i.e., the transpose of all the coefficients in the constraint equations (4.6)

and $\begin{bmatrix} P_3 \\ P_4 \end{bmatrix}$ is the vector of the coefficients of the variables (i.e., x_3, x_4) currently in the solution. (Remember $x_1 = x_2 = 0$.)

This is the general* statement of the Simplex criterion and can be used again and again as we proceed from one corner to the next.

Let us assume that $P_2 > P_1$ so that the largest increment in Z would seem to come from increasing x_2.

By how much can we increase x_2? The limits are given by eq. (4.7) for it must be remembered that $x_3\,x_4$ too, must be non-negative.

The increase that is possible is the smaller of

$$\frac{c_1}{a_{12}} \text{ and } \frac{c_2}{a_{22}}$$

whichever makes x'_3 or x'_4 negative first.

Let us assume it is

$$\Delta = \frac{c_1}{a_{12}}, x'_3 = 0$$

* 'General', moreover, in the sense that the matrices permit of an obvious enlargement to cover any number of variables and constraints.

In that case, from (4.7),

$$x_4' = c_2 - a_{22}\frac{c_1}{a_{12}}$$

We have now arrived at the first solution, which is,

$$x_1' = 0 \quad x_2' = \frac{c_1}{a_{12}} \quad x_3' = 0 \quad \text{and} \quad x_4' = c_2 - a_{22}\frac{c_1}{a_{12}}$$

The last expression seems a little complicated but is easy to see how it can be arrived at in general terms.

Consider the augmented matrix,

$$\begin{array}{c} \\ \\ \end{array}\begin{matrix} & x_1 & x_2 & x_3 & x_4 \end{matrix}$$
$$\left[\begin{array}{c|cccc} c_1 & a_{11} & a_{12} & 1 & 0 \\ c_2 & a_{21} & a_{22} & 0 & 1 \end{array}\right] \begin{array}{l} --- R_1 \\ --- R_2 \end{array}\Big\} \text{ arrived at directly from equations (4.6)}$$

We have supposed that the maximum increase we can get is by increasing x_2. Clearly we have to divide c_1 and c_2 respectively by the coefficients of x_1 x_2 and choose the lesser of these. We have assumed that $x_2' = \dfrac{c_1}{a_{12}}$ is the lesser, and to arrive at the value for x_4' we have to apply the transformation,

$$\left[\begin{array}{c|cccc} \dfrac{c_1}{a_{12}} & \dfrac{a_{11}}{a_{12}} & 1 & \dfrac{1}{a_{12}} & 0 \\ c_2 - a_{22}\dfrac{c_1}{a_{12}} & a_{21} - a_{22}\dfrac{a_{11}}{a_{22}} & 0 & -\dfrac{a_{22}}{a_{12}} & 1 \end{array}\right] \begin{array}{l} --- R_1' = \dfrac{1}{a_{12}}R_1 \\ --- R_2' = R_2 - a_{22}R_1' \end{array}$$

and then the values for x_2' and x_4' are those shown on the left.

We have now arrived at a new solution x_1' x_2' x_3' x_4' by quite general methods which we can apply again to arrive at the next solution x_1'' x_2'' x_3'' x_4'' and so on until we arrive at the required optimum.

There will be no doubt as to when we have arrived at the optimum position because then (and only then) will all the Simplex criteria be negative. No movement to any other corner, or indeed to anywhere within the bounded area, will give any increase in profits.

The application of the Simplex method to the business linear:

PROGRAMMING EXAMPLE

Using the Simplex method to solve our simple two variable machine problem is rather like using a power press to crush a nut. However, many of the human problems in linear programming involve around two hundred rather than two variables and for them a power press is necessary. We are really concerned to understand a technique which *can* be applied to two hundred variable problems. The actual application in such a case is long and tedious and can safely be left to a properly programmed computer.

In our machine problem the first Simplex criterion is given by

$$\begin{bmatrix} P_1 \\ P_2 \\ P_3 \\ P_4 \end{bmatrix} - \begin{bmatrix} a_{11} & a_{21} \\ a_{12} & a_{22} \\ 1 & 0 \\ 0 & 1 \end{bmatrix}\begin{bmatrix} P_3 \\ P_4 \end{bmatrix} = \begin{bmatrix} 3 \\ 4 \\ 0 \\ 0 \end{bmatrix} - \begin{bmatrix} 2 & 3 \\ 5 & 2 \\ 1 & 0 \\ 0 & 1 \end{bmatrix}\begin{bmatrix} 0 \\ 0 \end{bmatrix} = \begin{bmatrix} 3 \\ 4 \\ 0 \\ 0 \end{bmatrix}$$

Since 4 is greater than 3 the largest increment would seem to come from increasing x_2.

To determine the amount of x_2 we have to divide the elements of b by the corresponding element in the x_2 vector in the augmented matrix.

$$\begin{array}{c|cccc} & x_1 & x_2 & x_3 & x_4 \\ 40 & 2 & 5 & 1 & 0 \\ 27 & 3 & 2 & 0 & 1 \end{array}$$

i.e., the lesser of

$$\frac{c_1}{a_{12}} = \frac{40}{5} \quad \text{or} \quad \frac{c_2}{a_{22}} = \frac{27}{2}$$

Since $x_2 = (40/5)$ is indeed the smaller of the two, this means that $x_3' = 0$, and

$$x_4' = 27-2\times 8 = 27-16 = 11 \text{ (from 4.7)},$$

x_1', of course, $= 0$.

This improved solution is obtained by transforming the matrix to give,

$$\left[\begin{array}{c|cccc} 8 & \frac{2}{5} & 1 & \frac{1}{5} & 0 \\ 11 & 2\frac{1}{5} & 0 & -\frac{2}{5} & 1 \end{array}\right] \begin{array}{l} --- \ R_1' = \frac{1}{5}R_1 \\ --- \ R_2' = R_2-2R_1' \end{array}$$

This new solution is $x_2' = 8 \quad x_4' = 11$ and this corresponds to the point A (0, 8) in the graphical solution.

The value of Z for this solution is

$$Z' = 3\times 0+4\times 8 = 32$$

(which is certainly better—as it should be—than the first value of zero).

We now repeat the process and check the value of

$$\begin{bmatrix} 3 \\ 4 \\ 0 \\ 0 \end{bmatrix} - \begin{bmatrix} \frac{2}{5} & 2\frac{1}{5} \\ 1 & 0 \\ \frac{1}{5} & -\frac{2}{5} \\ 0 & 1 \end{bmatrix} \begin{bmatrix} 4 \\ 0 \end{bmatrix}^*$$

i.e.

$$= \begin{bmatrix} 3 \\ 4 \\ 0 \\ 0 \end{bmatrix} - \begin{bmatrix} 1\frac{3}{5} \\ 4 \\ \frac{4}{5} \\ 0 \end{bmatrix} = \begin{bmatrix} 1\frac{2}{5} \\ 0 \\ -\frac{4}{5} \\ 0 \end{bmatrix}$$

The greatest (indeed the only) profit increase can be obtained by introducing x_1.

To determine the amount of x_1 we have to divide the elements of C by the corresponding element in the x_1 vector in the new augmented matrix

$$\left[\begin{array}{c|cccc} 8 & \frac{2}{5} & 1 & \frac{1}{5} & 0 \\ 11 & 2\frac{1}{5} & 0 & -\frac{2}{5} & 1 \end{array}\right] \begin{array}{l} --- \ R_1' \\ --- \ R_2' \end{array}$$

i.e., the lesser of $\frac{8}{\frac{2}{5}} = 20$ and $\frac{11}{2\frac{1}{5}} = \frac{45}{11} = 5.$

Since $x_1'' = 5$ is the smaller of the two, then $x_3'' = 0$, and the improved solution is obtained by transforming the matrix,

$$\left[\begin{array}{c|cccc} 6 & 0 & 1 & \frac{13}{55} & -\frac{2}{11} \\ 5 & 1 & 0 & -\frac{2}{11} & \frac{5}{11} \end{array}\right] \begin{array}{l} --- \ R_1'' = R_1'-\frac{2}{5}R_2'' \\ --- \ R_2'' = R_2'/2\frac{1}{5} \end{array}$$

The new solution is $x_1'' = 5 \quad x_2'' = 6 \quad x_3'' = 0 \quad x_4'' = 0$, and corresponds to the point B (5, 6) in the graphical solution.

* Since the variables currently in the solution are x_2' and x_4'.

We know that this is the optimum, but we can check it by finding the value of

$$\begin{bmatrix}3\\4\\0\\0\end{bmatrix}-\begin{bmatrix}0 & 1\\1 & 0\\\frac{13}{55} & -\frac{2}{11}\\-\frac{2}{11} & \frac{5}{11}\end{bmatrix}\begin{bmatrix}4\\3\end{bmatrix}$$

$$=\begin{bmatrix}3\\4\\0\\0\end{bmatrix}-\begin{bmatrix}3\\4\\\frac{22}{55}\\\frac{7}{11}\end{bmatrix}=\begin{bmatrix}0\\0\\-\frac{22}{55}\\-\frac{7}{11}\end{bmatrix}$$

All the elements of this column vector are nil or negative so no profit increase is possible.

Appendix on regression analysis: computer program*

We have shown that the problem of fitting a regression equation can be handled through the use of matrices. This approach is important, because if we wish to fit any linear model by least squares, the necessary calculations follow a common procedure, regardless of the number of independent variables being considered. The amount of calculation involved, however, grows very rapidly as the number of parameters to be estimated is increased. Thus, while the formulae are easy to remember and apply, the use of a computer is necessary in many cases. A suitable FORTRAN IV regression analysis program is shown in Fig. 4.5 and some details of the main features of the program are given below.

General description
The program is designed to handle up to twenty independent variables and two-hundred observations. All the computations are based on the formulae given in the previous sections. As an extension to these formulae the program also makes provision for calculating the Durbin–Watson statistic. This statistic measures the degree of autocorrelation in the regression residuals. It is defined as:

$$\frac{\sum_{t=2}^{n}(E_t - E_{t-1})^2}{\sum_{t=1}^{n} E_t^2}$$

where $E_t(t = 1, \ldots . n)$ denote the residuals from a fitted least squares regression. Exact significance levels for this statistic are not available, but Durbin and Watson have provided tables which tabulate its upper and lower bounds for various numbers of observations and numbers of independent variables.

1. The data cards must be preceded by a problem definition card. This card holds information on the number of regression coefficients to be estimated, M (equal to the number of variables in the problem, including the dependent variable), the number of observations, N, and whether or not a calculation and print-out is required of the Durbin–Watson statistic and the regression residuals. The value of M is punched in columns 1–2 of the problem definition card (right-

* This appendix has been taken with permission from: Hirst, M., *Building and Operating a Forecasting Model: The Regression Analysis Approach.* Mimeographed 1970.

```
C     MULTIPLE REGRESSION ANALYSIS PROGRAM. M. HIRST 1969.
C     DIMENSION ARRAYS. READ NUMBER OF VARIABLES M.
C     READ NUMBER OF OBSERVATIONS N. READ TYPE OF DATA. READ DATA.
      DIMENSION X(200,21),Y(200),XTX(21,21),XTXI(21,21),XTY(21),B(21),
     1          SEB(21),T(21),YC(200),Z(200)
      READ (7,1)M,N,ITYPE
    1 FORMAT (I2,I3,I1)
      DO 2 I=1,N
      X(I,1)=1.0
    2 READ (7,3)Y(I),(X(I,J),J=2,M)
    3 FORMAT (8F10.4)
C     COMPUTE XTX MATRIX
      DO 4 I=1,M
      DO 4 J=1,M
      XTX(I,J)=0
      DO 4 K=1,N
    4 XTX(I,J)=XTX(I,J)+X(K,I)*X(K,J)
C     ESTABLISH IDENTITY MATRIX
      DO 5 I=1,M
      DO 5 J=1,M
    5 XTXI(I,J)=0.
      DO 6 I=1,M
    6 XTXI(I,I)=1.
C     INVERT XTX MATRIX
      DO 9 L=1,M
      D=XTX(L,L)
      DO 7 J=1,M
      XTX(L,J)=XTX(L,J)/D
    7 XTXI(L,J)=XTXI(L,J)/D
      DO 9 I=1,M
      IF(I.EQ.L) GO TO 9
      C=XTX(I,L)
      DO 8 J=1,M
      XTX(I,J)=XTX(I,J)-C*XTX(L,J)
    8 XTXI(I,J)=XTXI(I,J)-C*XTXI(L,J)
    9 CONTINUE
C     COMPUTE REGRESSION COEFFICIENTS
      DO 10 I=1,M
      XTY(I)=0.
      DO 10 J=1,N
   10 XTY(I)=XTY(I)+X(J,I)*Y(J)
      DO 11 I=1,M
      B(I)=0.
      DO 11 J=1,M
   11 B(I)=B(I)+XTXI(I,J)*XTY(J)
C     COMPUTE DEGREES OF FREEDOM, STANDARD ERRORS, AND
C     T VALUES FOR REGRESSION COEFFICIENTS.
      NDF=N-M
      XN=N
      XM=M
      YTY=0.
      DO 12 I=1,N
   12 YTY=YTY+Y(I)**2
      BTXTY=0.
      DO 13 J=1,M
   13 BTXTY=BTXTY+B(J)*XTY(J)
```

(Continued)

Figure 4.5 Listing of FORTRAN IV Multiple Regression Analysis Program

```
      S=SQRT((YTY-BTXTY)/(XN-XM))
      DO 14 I=1,M
      SEB(I)=S*SQRT(XTXI(I,I))
   14 T(I)=B(I)/SEB(I)
C     COMPUTE COEFFICIENT OF MULTIPLE DETERMINATION.
      SUMY=0.
      DO 15 I=1,N
   15 SUMY=SUMY+Y(I)
      SUMY2=SUMY**2
      R2=(BTXTY-(SUMY2/XN))/(YTY-(SUMY2/XN))
C     COMPUTE CALCULATED Y VALUES
      DO 16 I=1,N
      YC(I)=0.
      DO 16 J=1,M
   16 YC(I)=YC(I)+B(J)*X(I,J)
C     WRITE REGRESSION COEFFICIENTS, STANDARD ERRORS, T VALUES,
C     AND DEGREES OF FREEDOM. WRITE STANDARD DEVIATION OF RESIDUALS. WRITE
C     COEFFICIENT OF MULTIPLE DETERMINATION. WRITE OBSERVED AND
C     CALCULATED Y VALUES.
      WRITE (2,17)NDF
   17 FORMAT (25X,28HMULTIPLE REGRESSION ANALYSIS//
     1          24H REGRESSION COEFFICIENTS,5X,15HSTANDARD ERRORS,5X,
     2          10H T VALUES ,I3,19H DEGREES OF FREEDOM/)
      DO 18 I=1,M
   18 WRITE (2,19)B(I),SEB(I),T(I)
   19 FORMAT (7X,F10.4,14X,F10.4,18X,F10.4)
      WRITE (2,20)S
   20 FORMAT (1H0,18X,34HSTANDARD DEVIATION OF RESIDUALS = ,F10.4)
      WRITE (2,21)R2
   21 FORMAT (1H0,15X,40HCOEFFICIENT OF MULTIPLE DETERMINATION = ,F10.4)
      WRITE (2,22)
   22 FORMAT (1H0,20X,17HOBSERVED Y VALUES,3X,19HCALCULATED Y VALUES/)
      DO 23 I=1,N
   23 WRITE (2,24)Y(I),YC(I)
   24 FORMAT (24X,F10.4,10X,F10.4)
C     TEST FOR TYPE OF DATA
      IF(ITYPE.EQ.0) GO TO 32
C     COMPUTE DURBIN-WATSON STATISTIC FOR TIME SERIES DATA
      DO 25 I=1,N
   25 Z(I)=Y(I)-YC(I)
      DWNUM=0.
      DO 26 I=2,N
   26 DWNUM=DWNUM+(Z(I)-Z(I-1))**2
      DWDEN=0.
      DO 27 I=1,N
   27 DWDEN=DWDEN+Z(I)**2
      DW=DWNUM/DWDEN
C     WRITE DURBIN-WATSON STATISTIC
      WRITE (2,28)DW
   28 FORMAT (1H0,21X,26HDURBIN-WATSON STATISTIC = ,F10.4/)
C     WRITE RESIDUALS.
      WRITE (2,29)
   29 FORMAT (33X,9HRESIDUALS/)
      DO 30 I=1,N
   30 WRITE (2,31)Z(I)
   31 FORMAT (31X,F10.4)
   32 STOP
      END
```

justified), and the number of observations are punched in columns 3–5 (right-justified). If the data is of the time-series type, then the Durbin-Watson statistic and the values of the regression residuals are usually required, and the variable ITYPE is given a value of 1 by punching this digit in column 6 of the problem definition card. For cross-sectional data the Durbin–Watson statistic is not normally wanted, and column 6 can be left blank. The computer will then read a value of 0 for ITYPE.

2. A separate data card must be commenced for each set of observations. The value of Y is punched in columns 1–10 of the card, with a decimal point in column 6. Columns 11–20 contain the value of X_2 (decimal in column 16), 21–30 the value of X_3 (decimal in column 26), and so on up to a maximum of twenty independent variables. The value of X_9, when applicable, has to be punched in columns 1–10 of a second card (decimal in column 6); similarly, the value of X_{17} appears in columns 1–10 (decimal in column 6) of a third card. The data cards must be fed into the machine in a logical order, that is, the first card (or set of cards) should contain data corresponding to the first time period's observations, the second card (or set of cards) should correspond to the second time period, and so on.

A few words of caution are required, on the use of this particular program, which was written largely for pedagogical reasons. Because it follows the computational procedures and formulae given earlier, considerable 'roundoff' errors may occur. One possible cause of this roundoff is where the numbers involved in the regression calculation are of widely differing orders. A second cause is when the matrix to be inverted, $(X'X)$ is very close to being singular, i.e., its determinant is zero. (No inverse can be calculated for such a matrix.) To alleviate the effect of roundoff, the program could be modified by asking the machine to operate in double precision mode. This means that the computer would work with numbers twice the length it normally handles. However, this is a wasteful procedure, and more sophisticated programs minimize roundoff errors through centralizing the data and use of the correlation matrix instead of the $(X'X)$ matrix.

An application

The three parameter problem given at the end of §4.5 provides a good example. The computer output from this problem is given in Fig. 4.6. From the column of regression coefficient we can write the regression equation as,

$$Y = 50{\cdot}6587 + 1{\cdot}3642\, X_1 + 0{\cdot}1139\, X_2$$

The standard errors and their corresponding T values are used to test the statistical significance of the regression coefficients. The coefficient of multiple determination, which is usually denoted by R^2, measures the proportion of variation in the dependent variable, Y, that is 'explained' by the independent variables. (For a full exposition see Johnston, J., *Econometric Methods*, New York, McGraw-Hill Book Company Inc., 1963. The numerical example above is based on one quoted in this book.)

MULTIPLE REGRESSION ANALYSIS

REGRESSION COEFFICIENTS	STANDARD ERRORS	T VALUES 6 DEGREES OF FREEDOM
50·6587	24·0608	−2·0507
1·3642	0·1432	9·5300
0·1139	0·1434	0·7943

STANDARD DEVIATION OF RESIDUALS = 3·5949

COEFFICIENT OF MULTIPLE DETERMINATION = 0·9385

OBSERVED Y VALUES	CALCULATED Y VALUES
200·0000	198·4705
206·0000	203·8136
207·0000	207·7947
220·0000	216·4380
210·0000	214·9576
216·0000	219·2757
223·0000	225·9830
233·0000	231·5539
237·0000	233·7129

DURBIN–WATSON STATISTIC = 1·6353

RESIDUALS
1·5295
2·1864
−0·7947
3·5620
−4·9576
−3·2757
−2·9830
1·4461
3·2871

Figure 4.6. Output from multiple regression analysis program

Appendix on matrix algebra

A matrix is just a way of *representing* a transformation or (as it is often called) a mapping.

Definitions. A rectangular array of real numbers enclosed in brackets and set out in the following form is called a matrix:

$$\begin{bmatrix} a_{11} & a_{12} & a_{13} & --- & a_{1n} \\ a_{21} & a_{22} & a_{23} & --- & a_{2n} \\ - & - & --- & --- & --- \\ - & - & --- & --- & --- \\ - & - & --- & --- & --- \\ a_{m1} & a_{m2} & a_{m3} & --- & a_{mn} \end{bmatrix}$$

The individual numbers a_{11} a_{12} a_{22}, etc., are called the elements. The *suffix*, i.e., the '23' if we choose a_{23} as an example, is just an easy way to identify that element (whatever it may be, e.g., 7, -32, $\frac{1}{4}$ or perhaps 0) which is in the second row, third column.

The above matrix has m rows and n columns and is said to have an order or dimension of $m \times n$. More shortly, it is called an $m \times n$ matrix.

Matrices with just one row, or just one column, are called row and column vectors respectively.

Thus $\begin{bmatrix} 3 & 1 \end{bmatrix}$ is a row vector

and $\begin{bmatrix} 1\frac{1}{2} \\ 1 \end{bmatrix}$ is a column vector

If the number of rows and columns are equal the matrix is called a square matrix or square array.

A matrix that has all its elements equal to 0 is called a zero matrix and usually denoted by the symbol O.

Thus,

$$\begin{bmatrix} 0 & 0 \\ 0 & 0 \end{bmatrix} = \mathrm{O} \quad \text{is the zero matrix of order } 2 \times 2$$

A square matrix which has all its elements on the principal diagonal (i.e., top left to bottom right) equal to 1, and all other elements equal to 0, is called an identity matrix and is usually denoted by the symbol I.

Thus,

$$\begin{bmatrix} 1 & 0 & 0 \\ 0 & 1 & 0 \\ 0 & 0 & 1 \end{bmatrix} = I \text{ is the identity matrix of order 3}$$

If two matrices have the same number of both columns and rows, and if all corresponding elements are the same, then the matrices are said to be 'equal' mathematically (though this may be felt to be stating the obvious).

Thus,

$$\begin{bmatrix} 1 & 6 & 2 \\ 4 & 3 & 7 \end{bmatrix} \text{ and } \begin{bmatrix} 1 & 6 & 2 \\ 4 & 3 & 7 \end{bmatrix} \text{ are equal matrices}$$

If we form a new matrix whose rows are the columns of the first matrix and whose columns are its rows, then the new matrix is called a transpose. The transpose of a matrix A is denoted by A^T.

Thus if

$$A = \begin{bmatrix} 3 & 2 \\ -1 & 6 \\ 7 & 4 \end{bmatrix}$$

Then its transpose

$$A^T = \begin{bmatrix} 3 & -1 & 7 \\ 2 & 6 & 4 \end{bmatrix}$$

Clearly transposing a matrix twice brings it back to its original form.

Matrix operations: Addition and subtraction are simply defined as the addition or subtraction of each element with the corresponding element in the same row and columns.

Thus,

$$\begin{bmatrix} 2 & 5 \\ 3 & 7 \end{bmatrix} + \begin{bmatrix} 2 & 9 \\ 4 & 2 \end{bmatrix} = \begin{bmatrix} 2+2 & 5+9 \\ 3+4 & 7+2 \end{bmatrix} = \begin{bmatrix} 4 & 14 \\ 7 & 9 \end{bmatrix}$$

It follows that matrices must be of the same order (i.e., same number of both rows and columns), for addition or subtraction to be defined.

Multiplication of two matrices $A \times B$ (shortened to AB) is *only* defined if B has the same number of rows as A has columns. The resulting matrix is made up of elements formed by multiplying all the elements in each row of A by all the elements in the corresponding column to B. Thus

$$\begin{bmatrix} 2 & 5 \\ 3 & 7 \end{bmatrix} \begin{bmatrix} 2 & 9 \\ 4 & 2 \end{bmatrix} = \begin{bmatrix} 2\times 2+5\times 4 & 2\times 9+5\times 2 \\ 3\times 2+7\times 4 & 3\times 9+7\times 2 \end{bmatrix} = \begin{bmatrix} 24 & 28 \\ 34 & 41 \end{bmatrix}$$

Or

$$\begin{bmatrix} 7 & 2 & 3 \\ 3 & 1 & 9 \\ 6 & 4 & 7 \end{bmatrix} \begin{bmatrix} 2 & 1 & 6 \\ 1 & 0 & 2 \\ 3 & 7 & 1 \end{bmatrix} = \begin{bmatrix} 25 & 14 & 49 \\ 34 & 60 & 29 \\ 37 & 43 & 51 \end{bmatrix}$$

To find any element in the resulting matrix (for instance the 2nd row, 3rd column in the second example) draw dotted lines through the 2nd row and 3rd column respectively, and multiply each element of the 2nd row by its corresponding element in the third column. Then add the results together.

The second row is	3	1	9	(starting on the left)
The third column is	6	2	1	(starting at the top)

The element in the resulting matrix is: $3\times 6+1\times 2+9\times 1 = 29$

By way of explanation: At the beginning of this appendix it was said that a matrix was just a way of representing a transformation. If we have a simple equation, such as $y = 4x$, then, corresponding to any value 3 (say) of x, the value of y is 12. We could say that the symbol '4' transforms 3 into 12. In matrix notation:

$$y = [4]\,x$$

This is very simple, since we have only one variable, i.e., x, to be transformed. Next suppose that there are two separate variables x_1 x_2 and their transformation into y_1 y_2 is given by

$$\begin{aligned} y_1 &= 2x_1+9x_2 \\ y_2 &= 4x_1+2x_2 \end{aligned} \qquad [I]$$

We can write this as

$$\begin{bmatrix} y_1 \\ y_2 \end{bmatrix} = \begin{bmatrix} 2 & 9 \\ 4 & 2 \end{bmatrix} \begin{bmatrix} x_1 \\ x_2 \end{bmatrix} \qquad [I(A)]$$

since the right-hand side does multiply out to be the column vector,

$$\begin{bmatrix} 2x_1+9x_2 \\ 4x_1+2x_2 \end{bmatrix}$$

and if we say that two matrices or vectors are equal then this means that each of the elements (two only in our case) are equal. These equalities are precisely the ones given by eq. [I] above.

Suppose further that y_1 y_2 are themselves the subject of a further transformation into z_1 z_2 given by (say)

$$\begin{aligned} z_1 &= 2y_1+5y_2 \\ z_2 &= 3y_1+7y_2 \end{aligned} \qquad [II]$$

or in matrix notation

$$\begin{bmatrix} z_1 \\ z_2 \end{bmatrix} = \begin{bmatrix} 2 & 5 \\ 3 & 7 \end{bmatrix} \begin{bmatrix} y_1 \\ y_2 \end{bmatrix} \qquad [II(A)]$$

x_1 x_2 have really undergone a double transformation, first into y_1 y_2 (given by eqs. [I]) and then from y_1 y_2 into z_1 z_2 (given by eqs. [II]). If we put the values for y_1 y_2 from eq. [I] into [II] we get directly the results of this double transformation (i.e., direct from x's to z's). Thus,

$$\begin{aligned} z_1 &= 2\,(2x_1+9x_2)+5\,(4x_1+2x_2) \\ z_2 &= 3\,(2x_1+9x_2)+7\,(4x_1+2x_2) \end{aligned}$$

Grouping up the terms, we have

$$\begin{aligned} z_1 &= 24x_1+28x_2 \\ z_2 &= 34x_1+41x_2 \end{aligned} \qquad [III]$$

or in the matrix notation

$$\begin{bmatrix} z_1 \\ z_2 \end{bmatrix} = \begin{bmatrix} 24 & 28 \\ 34 & 41 \end{bmatrix} \begin{bmatrix} x_1 \\ x_2 \end{bmatrix} \qquad [III(A)]$$

But putting the value of $\begin{bmatrix} y_1 \\ y_2 \end{bmatrix}$ from [I(A)] and [II(A)] gives

$$\begin{bmatrix} z_1 \\ z_2 \end{bmatrix} = \begin{bmatrix} 2 & 5 \\ 3 & 7 \end{bmatrix} \begin{bmatrix} y_1 \\ y_2 \end{bmatrix} = \begin{bmatrix} 2 & 5 \\ 3 & 7 \end{bmatrix} \begin{bmatrix} 2 & 9 \\ 4 & 2 \end{bmatrix} \begin{bmatrix} x_1 \\ x_2 \end{bmatrix}$$

The result of multiplying the two matrices above is, as we saw in the section on multiplication,

$$\begin{bmatrix} 24 & 28 \\ 34 & 41 \end{bmatrix}$$

i.e.,

$$\begin{bmatrix} z_1 \\ z_2 \end{bmatrix} = \begin{bmatrix} 28 & 28 \\ 34 & 41 \end{bmatrix} \begin{bmatrix} x_1 \\ x_2 \end{bmatrix}$$

which is the same as [III] or [III(A)].

Hence, multiplying two matrices together, according to the rules given, *does* in fact properly give the result of a double transformation. It seems that the multiplication rules are not arbitrary but have some meaning.

Comparisons: Traditional algebra and matrix algebra.

In traditional algebra $A+B = B+A$. This is easy to show by means of an example. For instance putting $A = 3$ and $B = 7$, both sides add up to ten, and so are equal.

In matrix algebra, as well, $A+B = B+A$. For example,

$$A+B = \begin{bmatrix} 2 & 6 \\ 3 & 1\frac{1}{2} \end{bmatrix} + \begin{bmatrix} 2 & 9 \\ 1 & 7 \end{bmatrix} = \begin{bmatrix} 2+2 & 6+9 \\ 3+1 & 1\frac{1}{2}+7 \end{bmatrix} \quad \begin{bmatrix} 4 & 15 \\ 4 & 8\frac{1}{2} \end{bmatrix}$$

$$B+A = \begin{bmatrix} 2 & 9 \\ 1 & 7 \end{bmatrix} + \begin{bmatrix} 2 & 6 \\ 3 & 1\frac{1}{2} \end{bmatrix} = \begin{bmatrix} 4 & 15 \\ 4 & 8\frac{1}{2} \end{bmatrix} \text{ too.}$$

Using similar simple examples the reader should show that,

'Trad' algebra	*Matrix algebra*	*Comment*
$A+B = B+A$	$A+B = B+A$	This is known as the Commutative Law of Addition.
$A+(B+C) = (A+B)+C$	$A+(B+C) = (A+B)+C$	This is known as the Associative Law of Addition.
$A(B+C) = AB+AC$	$A(B+C) = AB+AC$	
$A0 = 0$	$AO = O$	The zero matrix O acts like 0, or zero.
$A.1 = 1.A = A$	$AI = IA = A$	The identity matrix I acts like 1 or unity.
$AB = BA$	$AB \neq BA$	With the one exception immediately above.

(The sign $\neq$ means 'does not equal'. AB is short for $A \times B$.)

This last result is most important. Take the example we have been using all along, but reverse the order in which they are multiplied together:

$$\begin{bmatrix} 2 & 9 \\ 4 & 2 \end{bmatrix} \begin{bmatrix} 2 & 5 \\ 3 & 7 \end{bmatrix} = \begin{bmatrix} 2\times 2+9\times 3 & 2\times 5+9\times 7 \\ 4\times 2+2\times 3 & 4\times 5+2\times 7 \end{bmatrix} = \begin{bmatrix} 31 & 73 \\ 14 & 34 \end{bmatrix}$$

This most certainly does not equal

$$\begin{bmatrix} 24 & 28 \\ 34 & 41 \end{bmatrix}$$

since it will be remembered that for two matrices to be equal, all their corresponding elements must be equal; none of these are.

Hence, multiplying a matrix B (say) by another matrix A (say) on the left will give a matrix AB which will not be the same as the matrix BA obtained by multiplying B by A on the right. The sole exception is when A or B is I, the identity matrix.

Transformation matrices: If we multiply a square matrix A by the identity matrix I of the same order, the result, as we have seen, is A. That is

$$IA = A$$

If two of the columns of the identity matrix are interchanged, and we multiply A by this matrix on the left, the result can be shown to be the interchanging of two rows of A. On the other hand if we multiply A on the right two columns are interchanged. Thus,

$$\begin{bmatrix} 1 & 0 & 0 \\ 0 & 1 & 0 \\ 0 & 0 & 1 \end{bmatrix}\begin{bmatrix} 3 & -6 & 3 \\ 9 & -4 & \frac{1}{2} \\ 2 & 1 & 2 \end{bmatrix} = \begin{bmatrix} 3 & -6 & 3 \\ 9 & -4 & \frac{1}{2} \\ 2 & 1 & 2 \end{bmatrix} \text{— the matrix is unchanged.}$$

$$\begin{bmatrix} 0 & 1 & 0 \\ 1 & 0 & 0 \\ 0 & 0 & 1 \end{bmatrix}\begin{bmatrix} 3 & -6 & 3 \\ 9 & -4 & \frac{1}{2} \\ 2 & 1 & 2 \end{bmatrix} = \begin{bmatrix} 9 & -4 & \frac{1}{2} \\ 3 & -6 & 3 \\ 2 & 1 & 2 \end{bmatrix} \text{— the first two rows are interchanged.}$$

$$\begin{bmatrix} 3 & -6 & 3 \\ 9 & -4 & \frac{1}{2} \\ 2 & 1 & 2 \end{bmatrix}\begin{bmatrix} 0 & 1 & 0 \\ 1 & 0 & 0 \\ 0 & 0 & 1 \end{bmatrix} = \begin{bmatrix} -6 & 3 & 3 \\ -4 & 9 & \frac{1}{2} \\ 1 & 2 & 2 \end{bmatrix} \text{— the first two columns are interchanged.}$$

If we wish to multiply a whole row of a matrix A by a number then this can be done by multiplying A on the left by a matrix which is the same as the identity matrix except that the element on its principal diagonal corresponding to the row is altered to the number required. Similarly postmultiplying A (i.e., multiplying A on the right) by the same matrix will multiply the whole column of A. Thus

$$\begin{bmatrix} 1 & 0 & 0 \\ 0 & 4 & 0 \\ 0 & 0 & 1 \end{bmatrix}\begin{bmatrix} 3 & 2 & 4 \\ 5 & 6 & 1 \\ 2 & 8 & -1 \end{bmatrix} = \begin{bmatrix} 3 & 2 & 4 \\ 20 & 24 & 4 \\ 2 & 8 & -1 \end{bmatrix} \text{— the second row is multiplied by 4.}$$

$$\begin{bmatrix} 3 & 2 & 4 \\ 5 & 6 & 1 \\ 2 & 8 & -1 \end{bmatrix}\begin{bmatrix} 1 & 0 & 0 \\ 0 & 4 & 0 \\ 0 & 0 & 1 \end{bmatrix} = \begin{bmatrix} 3 & 8 & 4 \\ 5 & 24 & 1 \\ 2 & 32 & -1 \end{bmatrix} \text{— the second column is multiplied by 4.}$$

A multiple of a row can be added or subtracted to another row by multiplying on the left by a suitable transformation matrix. This matrix is arrived at by replacing the appropriate zero element in the identity matrix by the number. Postmultiplying by this transformation matrix gives a column addition or subtraction. Thus

$$\begin{bmatrix} 1 & 0 & 0 \\ 0 & 1 & 0 \\ 4 & 0 & 1 \end{bmatrix}\begin{bmatrix} 4 & 5 & 2 \\ 3 & 4 & 1 \\ 2 & 6 & -1 \end{bmatrix} = \begin{bmatrix} 4 & 5 & 2 \\ 3 & 4 & 1 \\ 18 & 26 & 7 \end{bmatrix} \text{— to the third row has been added four times the first row.}$$

$$\begin{bmatrix} 4 & 5 & 2 \\ 3 & 4 & 1 \\ 2 & 6 & -1 \end{bmatrix} \begin{bmatrix} 1 & 0 & 0 \\ 0 & 1 & 0 \\ 4 & 0 & 1 \end{bmatrix} = \begin{bmatrix} 12 & 5 & 2 \\ 7 & 4 & 1 \\ -2 & 6 & -1 \end{bmatrix}$$ — to the first column has been added four times the third column.

In all the examples so far we have restricted ourselves to multiplication by one transformation matrix only. There is no reason why this process cannot be repeated. For example if we call the successive transformation matrices $E_1\ E_2\ E_3$ and the original matrix A, then the final product will be B, given by

$$B = E_3\, E_2\, E_1\, A, \quad \text{or symbolically} \quad B = EA,$$

where E stands for the successive transformations $E_1\ E_2\ E_3$.

Clearly by the choice of suitable transformation matrices, a matrix can be transformed almost at will.

The inverse of a matrix. Inversion or division is something to which we are accustomed in traditional algebra. Thus we say $\frac{1}{6} \times 6 = 1$. Obviously it would be interesting to know if there is anything analogous to this in matrix algebra. Let us suppose that there is a matrix A^{-1} such that $A^{-1} A = I$ (where I is the appropriate identity matrix).

If $AX = B$, where A,B,X, are matrices, multiplying both sides by A^{-1} will give

$$A^{-1}AX = A^{-1}B$$

But $A^{-1}A = I$ so this gives $IX = A^{-1}B$.

But $IX = X$ (see the definitions earlier).

Hence, $X = A^{-1}\, B$.

If this matrix A^{-1} exists it is called the inverse of A.

This result is most important in the solution of linear equations. Let us take three simple linear equations, with three variables $x_1\ x_2\ x_3$:

$$\begin{aligned} a_{11}x_1 + a_{12}x_2 + a_{13}x_3 &= c_1 \\ a_{21}x_1 + a_{22}x_2 + a_{23}x_3 &= c_2 \\ a_{31}x_1 + a_{32}x_2 + a_{33}x_3 &= c_3 \end{aligned}$$

$a_{11}\ a_{12}\ c_1\ c_2$, etc., all being constants.

By the definitions of the multiplication of matrices and the identity of two matrices, this may be written as

$$\begin{bmatrix} a_{11} & a_{12} & a_{13} \\ a_{21} & a_{22} & a_{23} \\ a_{31} & a_{32} & a_{33} \end{bmatrix} \begin{bmatrix} x_1 \\ x_2 \\ x_3 \end{bmatrix} = \begin{bmatrix} c_1 \\ c_2 \\ c_3 \end{bmatrix}$$

or $\quad AX = C$ for short

giving $\quad X = A^{-1}C$ (if the inverse exists)

i.e., in full:

$$\begin{bmatrix} x_1 \\ x_2 \\ x_3 \end{bmatrix} = \begin{bmatrix} b_{11} & b_{12} & b_{13} \\ b_{21} & b_{22} & b_{23} \\ b_{31} & b_{32} & b_{33} \end{bmatrix} \begin{bmatrix} c_1 \\ c_2 \\ c_3 \end{bmatrix}$$

where $b_{11}\ b_{12}$, etc., are the elements of this inverse matrix.

Multiplying out the two matrices on the right and equalling each of the three elements of the matrix on the left with the three elements of the new matrix on the right, we have

$$\begin{aligned} x_1 &= b_{11}c_1 + b_{12}c_2 + b_{13}c_3 \\ x_2 &= b_{21}c_1 + b_{22}c_2 + b_{23}c_3 \\ x_3 &= b_{31}c_1 + b_{32}c_2 + b_{33}c_3 \end{aligned}$$

In other words, we have *solved* these linear equations for $x_1\ x_2\ x_3$ *if* we can determine the elements of the inverse matrix.

The next problem, therefore, is to try and arrive at a technique for computing the inverse.

Computation of inverse. There are many techniques for computing an inverse. For those brought up on traditional mathematics the use of determinants provides a simple though rather tedious answer. However, we have been using matrix algebra, and in particular transformation matrices so far, and these provide an interesting and rather more sophisticated solution.

Let us suppose we wish to compute the inverse of a matrix A, i.e., using our notation to find A^{-1}. Consider the matrix

$$A \mid I$$

i.e., the matrix obtained by writing the identity matrix I on the right of A (but leaving a dividing line between the two for demarcation purposes). Such a matrix is called an augmented matrix.

We now apply a series of *row* transformations to this matrix, i.e., we multiply it by a series of suitable transformation matrices $E_1\ E_2\ E_3$, etc., all of which together we write symbolically as E. These transformation matrices must be chosen so that $EA = I$, or, in other words, the A part of the augmented matrix is transformed to I, the identity matrix.

If we do this we have

$$E(A \mid I) = EA \mid EI = I \mid E$$

Since $\quad EA = I$ (as we have arranged E to do this)

and $\quad EI = E$ (since pre- or postmultiplying by an identity matrix does, by definition, leave the matrix unchanged).

But if $EA = I$, then E *is* the inverse of A by the definition of an inverse.

Hence the steps for finding an inverse are:

1. Add an identity matrix to the right of the original matrix.
2. Apply appropriate row transformations to the combined (i.e., augmented) matrix so that the original matrix is transformed into I (the identity matrix).
3. The matrix on the right will then be the inverse.

Thus, to invert
$$A = \begin{bmatrix} 2 & 1 \\ 1 & 3 \end{bmatrix}$$

Add an identity matrix to make the augmented matrix

$$A \mid I = \left[\begin{array}{cc|cc} 2 & 1 & 1 & 0 \\ 1 & 3 & 0 & 1 \end{array}\right]$$

and for simplicity let us call the top row right across of this augmented matrix R_1 and the bottom row R_2. Successive transformations of each row will be denoted by dashes (thus, first $R_1\ R_2$, then $R_1'\ R_2'$ then $R_1''\ R_2''$, etc.).

First transformation: Multiply R_1 by $\frac{1}{2}$

$$E_1[A \mid I] = \left[\begin{array}{cc|cc} 1 & \frac{1}{2} & \frac{1}{2} & 0 \\ 1 & 3 & 0 & 1 \end{array}\right] \begin{array}{l} (R_1' = \frac{1}{2}R_1) \\ (R_2 \text{ is unchanged}) \end{array}$$

Second transformation: Subtract R_1' from R_2

$$E_2\,E_1[A \mid I] = \left[\begin{array}{cc|cc} 1 & \frac{1}{2} & \frac{1}{2} & 0 \\ 0 & \frac{5}{2} & -\frac{1}{2} & 1 \end{array}\right] \begin{array}{l} (R_1' \text{ is unchanged}) \\ (R_2' = R_2 - R_1') \end{array}$$

Third transformation: Multiply R_2' by $\frac{2}{5}$

$$E_3 E_2 E_1[A \mid I] = \left[\begin{array}{cc|cc} 1 & \frac{1}{2} & \frac{1}{2} & 0 \\ 0 & 1 & -\frac{1}{5} & \frac{2}{5} \end{array}\right] \begin{array}{l} (R_1' \text{ is unchanged}) \\ (R_2'' = \frac{2}{5} R_2') \end{array}$$

Fourth transformation: Subtract $\frac{1}{2} R_2''$ from R_1'

$$E_4 E_3 E_2 E_1[A \mid I] = \left[\begin{array}{cc|cc} 1 & 0 & \frac{3}{5} & -\frac{1}{5} \\ 0 & 1 & -\frac{1}{5} & \frac{2}{5} \end{array}\right] \begin{array}{l} (R_1'' = R_1' - \frac{1}{2} R_2'') \\ (R_2'' \text{ is unchanged}) \end{array}$$

The augmented part of this is

$$\begin{bmatrix} \frac{3}{5} & -\frac{1}{5} \\ -\frac{1}{5} & \frac{2}{5} \end{bmatrix}$$

and this is the inverse of A.
A quick check shows that

$$\begin{bmatrix} 2 & 1 \\ 1 & 3 \end{bmatrix} \begin{bmatrix} \frac{3}{5} & -\frac{1}{5} \\ -\frac{1}{5} & \frac{2}{5} \end{bmatrix}$$

does equal

$$\begin{bmatrix} 1 & 0 \\ 0 & 1 \end{bmatrix}$$

5. The problem of time—I

5.1. Introduction

The problem of time can be put like this: how can we compare costs and benefits which occur at different points in time?

In view of the long time-span of many business operations this difficulty enters into a large number of corporate decisions. At one time the methods employed to cope with this problem, such as 'pay-back' for instance, were not only crude but conceptually wrong. Within the last ten years or so we have seen the widespread use of discounted cash flow and present value techniques, both of which properly take into account the time element. Both these techniques have a slightly esoteric mathematical background, and generally throughout this book—other than in chapter 4—any detailed work or mathematical formulations have been relegated to an appendix at the end of the chapter. However, the calculation of the effect of time is so basic, not only to the work in this book but to all business decision making, that it is proposed to go into it here and now.

5.2. The discount factor

Let us suppose that you are owed £100. Instead of being paid in one year's time when the debt is due, you are offered the alternative of receiving £87 now. Should you consider opting for this alternative choice?

The answer, of course, must depend on what value money has to you. If you have been in the habit of making 15 per cent per annum gross (tax is ignored at this stage) steadily in the past, you may feel justified in basing your calculations for the future on the same figure as this. If you go for the alternative choice, therefore, and have the £87 one year early, you should be able to earn 'interest' on it of $£87 \times (15/100) = £13.05$, which can be taken as £13 for practical purposes. At the end of the year, you will have the $£87 + £13$ interest $= £100$, which is precisely what you would have had if you had decided not to exercise your option. In other words £87 now is equal to £100 in one year's time. In the form of an equation:

$$£100 \text{ in one year's time} = \text{a present value of } £87.$$

To convert 100 into 87 mathematically, we have to multiply by the factor 87/100, so that we can write:

$$\underset{\text{SUM}}{\underset{\uparrow}{100}} \times \underset{\text{Discount Factor}}{\underset{\uparrow}{\frac{87}{100}}} = \underset{\text{Present Value}}{\underset{\uparrow}{87}}$$

The basic equation is therefore:

$$\text{SUM} \times \text{DF} = \text{PV}$$

using the abbreviations DF for Discount Factor, and PV for Present Value.

To arrive at the present value of a sum of money all we have to do, therefore, is to multiply this sum by a 'discount' factor. In our case, with the period of one year and a rate of interest of 15 per cent, the appropriate factor is, as we have seen, 0·87.

Generally it is tedious to have to work out this factor *ab initio*, and reference is made to tables of discount factors. Table A (page 277) does confirm that 0·87 is the correct factor to use to arrive at the present value of a sum received in one year's time at a 15 per cent rate.

PV tables apply equally whether the money is paid or received. In the example above, suppose the amount of £100 had been due in one year. If the alternative offer of £87 had not been taken up, the same interest of £13 would have been earned in the year till the debt was due, so that precisely £100 would have been available. Exactly the same identity would therefore apply.

5.2.1. Mathematical expression of discount factor

If we call the rate of interest (r), then by definition the interest on £1 after one year will be £r. If the initial sum is £2, the interest will be £$2r$, and if £P then the interest will be Pr (dropping the £ sign). The total sum (S_1), say, available at the end of one year is therefore the initial sum (P) together with this interest (Pr) earned during the year.

In symbols:

$$S_1 = P + Pr$$

or

$$S_1 = P(1+r) \tag{5.1}$$

In *compound* interest calculations, interest is given each year on the money available at the beginning of the year. The new principal available at the start of the second year is $P(1+r)$. To find the sum S_2 after two years we therefore substitute this amount for P in the formula (5.1) above, so that

$$S_2 = P(1+r)\times(1+r)$$
$$= P(1+r)^2$$

Similarly,

$$S_3 = P(1+r)^3$$

and in general, after n years

$$S_n = P(1+r)^n \tag{5.2}$$

This is the standard compound interest formula. The compound interest factor, i.e., the factor which transforms an initial sum P into a sum S_n after n years is $(1+r)^n$.

The formula (5.2) above can be rewritten as

$$P = \frac{1}{(1+r)^n}\cdot S_n$$

This is the standard present value formula. The discount factor, i.e., the factor which transforms a sum S_n into its present value now, n years earlier is

$$\frac{1}{(1+r)^n}$$

The compound interest factor and the discount factor are reciprocals. The former transforms from now to n years into the future. The latter reverses the process.

5.2.2. Examples on the use of the discount factor

Example 1. What is the present value of equal sums of £1000 received at the end of each of three consecutive years? Money spare can command 10 per cent. Using the basic equation arrived at (SUM × DF = PV) for each of the years, we have,

Year	*Sum* £	×	*Discount factor* (10%)	=	*Present value* £
1	1 000		0·909		909
2	1 000		0·826		826
3	1 000		0·751		751
					£2 486

The present value is therefore £2486. It is easy to check that these two, i.e., £1000 at the end of each year for three years, and £2486 now at 10 per cent, are the same. It is not possible to equate them directly, since they are at different levels in time, but we can make a fair comparison by finding what they are each worth after three years (columns A and B).

Alternatively, we can imagine that the £2486 is lent for the three years at 10 per cent, *and the capital is returned intact* at the end of the third year (column C). These are two ways of looking at DCF. Remembering that money spare is worth 10 per cent* the comparisons are:

	A £1 000 *for 3 years*	B £2 486 *now*	C £2 486 *lent*
Sum at start	—	2 486	
Interest for first year	—	249	249
Sum received after one year	1 000	—	—
Total at end of one year	1 000	2 735	249
Interest for second year	100	274	25
Sum received after two years	1 000	—	249
Total at end of two years	2 100	3 009	523
Interest for third year	210	301	52 } 249 }
Sum received after three years	1 000	—	2 486
Total at end of three years	£3 310	£3 310	£3 310

Example 2. A project costs £45 000 but will bring in estimated amounts of £10 000 each year at the end of each of six consecutive years. At a 6 per cent interest rate, should you invest in this project?

Year	*Sum* £	*Discount factor at (6%)*	*Present value* £
1	10 000	0·943	9 430
2	10 000	0·890	8 900
3	10 000	0·840	8 400
4	10 000	0·792	7 920
5	10 000	0·747	7 470
6	10 000	0·705	7 050
		Total PV of benefit	£49 170
		Project cost	£45 000
		Net benefit	£4 170

Since the present-day values of the returns are in total £4170 more than the amount due to be paid out now, the project, on this basis, is worthwhile.

* For further consideration of this point see 'Dual Rate Solutions' in the appendix on alternative choice decisions at the end of chapter 6.

In the example above, the sums of money which will be received or saved are the same each year. Very often this indeed is the position. For instance, the benefits obtained by building a new road will probably remain much the same for several years to come. Or when a new automated piece of machinery is installed in a factory, the benefits in terms of labour saved will be roughly the same each year. In such cases as these, when the sum received or saved is the same each year, the DCF calculation can be dramatically shortened. In our example, multiplying the yearly sum of £10 000 by 4·917 will give the total present value of £49 170. This figure (4·917) can be read off directly from the cumulative tables (Table B page 278) by looking under the 6 per cent column and along the six-year row. The work is therefore reduced to the one line calculation:

$$10\,000 \times 4{\cdot}917 = \underline{\underline{£49\,170}}$$

This cumulative discount factor, 4·917, is the total of the individual discount factors for each of the six years. Adding up the discount factors in the example above it is easy to check that they do in fact total 4·917.

Example 3. At what interest rates will it be worthwhile to invest £34 500 in a business project which is likely to bring in the following amounts of cash?

Year	*Sum*
1	6 000
2	8 000
3	10 000
4	10 000
5	10 000

Since the interest rate is not known we have to proceed by the method of trial and error. Let us start off with 6, 8, and 10 per cent.

Year	*Sum* (£)	*DF* (6%)	*Present value* (£)	*DF* (8%)	*Present value* (£)	*DF* (10%)	*Present value* (£)
1	6 000	0·943	5 658	0·926	5 556	0·909	5 454
2	8 000	0·890	7 120	0·857	6 856	0·826	6 608
3	10 000	0·840	8 400	0·794	7 940	0·751	7 510
4	10 000	0·792	7 920	0·735	7 350	0·683	6 830
5	10 000	0·747	7 470	0·681	6 810	0·621	6 210
			£36 568		£34 512		£32 612

What do these results mean?

The effect of multiplying by a discount factor is to bring the cash sum back to its present day value so that a direct comparison can be made with the investment amount (which, it is presumed, will be paid out *now*).

The comparisons are:

		At 6%	*At* 8%	*At* 10%
	Cash in (PV of all cash flows)	36 568	34 512	32 612
Less	Cash out (on investment)	34 500	34 500	34 500
	Net benefit	2 068	12	(−1 888)

If we seek only a return of 6 per cent on our money it seems that we are getting back a good deal more (2068 in fact). If we require 8 per cent, then we are, fortunately, just making it. Earlier, in example 1 we showed that when the total present value of the cash flows equals the investment amount, then this means that the discount rate is the rate of return that the cash flows are earning on the investment amount. At 8 per cent the present value of the cash flows (34 512) and the investment amount (34 500) are for all practical purposes identical. It follows therefore that the investment is making 8 per cent.

If we seek any higher rate of return than 8 per cent, then naturally the discounted benefits will not match up to the investment amount. At 10 per cent the gap is already pretty substantial; it will grow larger the higher the discount rate.

5.3. Present value and discounted cash flow

Examples 2 and 3 have been included to show the difference between Present Value (PV) and Discounted Cash Flow (DCF) analyses. In example 2 the required interest rate was given and the problem was to see if the cash flows did gain this return.

When the rate of return is given, the term *Present Value analysis* is used.

In example 3 the precise interest rate which the cash flows earned on the investment amount was calculated.

When the exact rate of return is calculated, the term *discounted cash flow*, or sometimes *internal rate of return* is used.

The main advantage of PV analysis is that only one calculation is required. In DCF analysis several calculations are usually required in order to determine the precise rate of return. The advantage of DCF analysis, on the other hand, is that, once the rate of return on a project has been established, then a quick and accurate method of comparing projects is available. If another project gives a higher rate then, *ceteris paribus*, that project will be the better one to choose. Unfortunately, other things usually are not equal. Many considerations, such as comparative risks, possible alternative projects, whether all the resources such as labour, materials, etc., can be obtained without having substantially adverse effects on other parts of the business, and the human aspects of the decision (e.g., whether the plan is politically possible and so on), are all highly relevant and important. All these factors have to be considered before any sensible decision can be made. At the moment, however, we are concentrating only on the purely mathematical factors entering into the problem. Any additional non-quantitative conditions will be temporarily ignored. Unfortunately, even on this rather restricted quantitative basis of assessment one other factor is still relevant and highly important. This can best be described by means of an example.

5.3.1. Alternative choice and opportunity loss

Let us suppose that a company has a sum of around £100 000 temporarily available and surplus to business requirements. Only two ways of investing this money are under consideration. One is to put it into a Certificate of Deposit for a period of a year. This will give a return of around 6 per cent. The other is to put it into debenture stock which not only gives a higher rate of return (around 9 per cent) but also gives this return for a longer period (three years). In both cases the exact rates are laid down in the terms of issue and there is, therefore, no need to use discount factor analyses to determine the rates of return. On our basis—indeed on any basis—there appears to be no doubt as to which is the choice to make; obviously the debenture is better than the Certificate of Deposit. A 9 per cent return is better than a 6 per cent return.

The company however customarily achieves a return on capital of around 15 per cent before tax (tax is still ignored for the moment). It is confidently expected that the £100 000 could be absorbed into the company's working capital any time after one year and earn the same rate of return as the rest of the capital. The comparisons now are:

	6% for one year: 15% for the following two years	*9% throughout*
Sum at start	100 000	100 000
Interest (6%:9%)	6 000	9 000
Total at end of year	106 000	109 000
Interest (15%:9%)	15 900	9 810
Total at end of two years	121 900	118 810
Interest (15%:9%)	18 285	10 693
Total at end of three years	140 185	129 503
	129 503 ←	
Net loss	10 682	

If the debenture choice had been taken (on the facile grounds that it appeared to offer a higher return) then the opportunity of letting the money revert to the company's funds would have been lost. This 'opportunity loss' (of 10 682) is quite substantial.

The problem of the alternative choice is this. What would the sums of money make if they were not invested in the project under consideration? In example 1 our justification for saying that £1000 for three years was equal to a 10 per cent return on £2486 *assumed* that the available money spare earned a 10 per cent rate. All alternative choice problems are faced with this same problem, i.e., what can money earn, which would be spare if the present choice were not taken up. From a decision point of view, these problems are very important and a fuller treatment of alternative choice problems is given in an appendix at the end of the next chapter.

5.4. Taxation

In a discounted cash flow or present value calculation we are comparing two sets of cash flows. First, those paid out for the investment or project (usually in one lump sum at the beginning, as indeed we have so far assumed in our examples); and second, those benefits from savings or profits (usually over many years in the future). Cash is being compared with cash. Tax will therefore need to be considered whenever it affects the cash flow. A company—provided it is making profits—has to pay Corporation Tax.* The additional profits made as a result of the proposed investment will mean that additional Corporation Tax will have to be paid, generally in the following year. In any proper DCF calculation for a business, the effects of tax must therefore be considered.

Crown departments in the U.K. are generally free from direct liability for taxes (except for the Selective Employment Tax which was not a tax on profits, but a mandatory addition to wage payments rather like NHI or Graduated Insurance Contributions). Government departments therefore do not take tax into account in their capital investment appraisal work. In order to make fair comparisons with industry, a correspondingly higher rate of return is therefore required.

Public corporations and nationalized industries are generally required by their Enabling Acts to pay taxes. However, so high is the level of investment that the corporations usually find necessary, that very large reserve of capital allowances are built up. These corporations therefore do not pay tax, and effectively their position is much the same as that of any Government department.

* In the U.K. the Corporation Tax rate at this time (1971) is 42·5 per cent. In the USA the rate is some 50 per cent. Rates around 45 per cent are fairly common throughout the world, and this 45 per cent rate will be used throughout this chapter and the next.

To all intents and purposes, therefore, tax is something which need only be considered by businesses. How then do businesses make major capital appraisal decisions such as whether to set up a new factory or buy a new machine? The cash flows from a new factory will arise from the expected increase in profits, and the cash flows from a new machine will be from labour savings. Both are cash flows 'in', in the sense that they are incremental cash flows over and above those already existing. This is the criterion that must always be applied in DCF analysis. The comparison is always between incremental cash flows 'in' (the 'benefit') and the incremental cash flows 'out' (the 'cost'). The latter usually precedes the former in time, and, as we said earlier, is often in the form of one lump sum, or at most is spread over a comparatively small number of years. It is not normally difficult to determine what the estimated cost will be, but the benefits are likely to be much more difficult to assess. Since this is particularly so in the case of investment in a new factory, it is better to concentrate on this problem, rather than on the simpler machine replacement exercise (a detailed example of which in any case is given later). Our problem therefore is to determine what the benefits will be from setting up a new factory.

Since it is pointless to make what cannot be sold, the initial approach must be through a proper evaluation of the market potential. Market research can now be regarded as a comparatively exact science, provided good use is made of sampling techniques such as Bayesian test analyses. Let us suppose that the problems of getting into the market and starting up production are estimated to take some three years. Starting at the fourth year our estimate of yearly sales is, let us say, around £1 400 000. The next step is to determine what will be the costs associated with these sales. Clearly the central management planning department will require assistance from the purchasing manager for the cost of raw materials, from the Personnel Manager for wages, and from the factory manager and the accountant *inter alia*, for overhead expenses and depreciation on the factory and plant machinery. From all these estimates a Projected Profit and Loss Account will be drawn up. One such typical Profit and Loss Account, presented in a highly abbreviated form, might be:

Profit and loss account (for the 4th year)

Sales				£1 400 000
	Less:			
		Materials	500 000	
		Direct labour	420 000	
		Overheads	310 000	
		Depreciation	80 000	1 310 000
Net profit (before tax)				£90 000

To arrive at the net cash flow from profits we have to take into account only those expenses for which cash has to be paid. The 'cash' calculation is therefore:

Sales revenue			£1 400 000
Less:	Materials	500 000	
	Direct labour	420 000	
	Overheads	310 000	1 230 000
Net cash			£170 000

In practice, these expenses will be set out in much greater detail than in the summary above, so that from the calculation point of view it is usually easier to regard the net cash figure of £170 000 as being made up of net profit (90 000) + depreciation (80 000).

By way of parenthesis it should be noted that depreciation is technically a non-cash expense. The cash spent on the purchase of a fixed asset is paid out at the time of its acquisition, and the depreciation expense is just the accountant's way of spreading this purchase figure over a given number of years in the accounts. Net profit of course is the residual figure when all expenses are taken away from sales. Broadly speaking it would therefore represent cash but for the fact that one expense—depreciation—is a non-cash expense and should not have been subtracted. Since depreciation has in fact been deducted in arriving at the net profit figure, it must be added back to get at the cash figure. Additionally, one major assumption of an entirely different nature is also made in these calculations, and this is that the book value of sales, for example, is equal to the cash received from sales. Provided that there is not much change in the debtors from one year to another, and not too many bad debts, this will be a fair assumption. Since all these figures are estimates of the future, and the precise debtor position at any time can hardly be foreseen, it seems to be the only possible assumption to make. Similar remarks apply to the payments for materials and all expenses. There is also the implied assumption that stocks are not being irregularly built up, i.e., that purchases line up with the cost of materials sold.

From the Estimated Profit and Loss Account we therefore deduce that the net benefit in this year will be:

Net cash flow from profits = £170 000.

Because of the increase in profits there will be additional Corporation Tax to pay. In arriving at taxable profits, the Inland Revenue do not allow the companies' assessment of depreciation to stand. They insist that their own calculation of depreciation, i.e., capital allowances, is deducted instead. If we suppose that these capital allowances are £100 000, then the tax computation will be:

Net profit	90 000	
Add book depreciation	80 000	
Net cash flow from profits	170 000	(Received during the year 4)
Less Capital allowances	100 000	
Taxable profit	70 000	

Corporation tax at, say, 45 per cent is due on this £70 000. Because the basic figures are £170 000 and £100 000, it is easier to regard this as 45 per cent of (£170,000 – £100 000).

The cash flow arising from the increased tax payable is therefore equal to:

Tax on cash flow from profits:	45 per cent of £170 000 =	£76 500
Less Tax saved by capital allowances:	45 per cent of £100 000 =	£45 000
	Net =	£31 500

and this in general is payable in the following year, i.e., the fifth year from the start.

Summing up the cash flows in the conventional form with each year on a horizontal line (but only putting in the figures we have been dealing with) we have:

Year	(a) *Cash flow from profits*	(b) *Tax on this profit*	(c) *Capital allowances*	(d) *Tax saved by capital allowances*	(e) *Net cash flow*
1	—	—	—	—	
2	—	—	—	—	
3	—	—	—	—	
4	170 000	—	100 000		
5		76 500		45 000	
6					

The net cash flow for any year under column (e) will be made up of the cash from profits, column (a), less the tax on these profits, column (b), plus the tax saved by capital allowances, column (d), so that:

$$(e) = (a) - (b) + (d)$$

5.4.1. Monthly discount tables

The net cash flow from profits, i.e., the difference between cash from revenue and the cash paid out for expenses, will probably be spread throughout the year. It is unlikely, to say the least, that it will all occur on the last day of the year. Yet that is the assumption on which the discount tables (Table A and Table B, pages 277 and 278) have been constructed.

A more realistic assumption is that the benefit is spread equally over the 12 months of the year. Discount tables constructed on this assumption (Tables C and D, pages 279 and 280) generally give slightly truer assessments of the DCF rate. Which set of tables (A and B, or C and D) should be used for any particular problem will depend on the facts of the case.

5.4.2. A basic example

The purchase and installation of some new automatically controlled lathes will cost an estimated £24 000, but only two men instead of eight will be needed to operate them. It is estimated that the savings in wages, etc., will amount to around £6000 per year for six years. At the end of the six years it is estimated that the net scrap value, after allowing for the costs of removal, will only amount to some £200. The new lathes will qualify for a cash (investment) grant of 20 per cent and also for annual allowances at the rate of 20 per cent on the reducing balance.* Assess the financial viability of this investment, assuming that your company uses a 10 per cent criterion rate for investment appraisal. The Corporation Tax rate is 45 per cent.

The calculation of the capital allowances is:

Year				*Cash grant*	*Capital allowances*
		Cost	24 000		
	Less	Investment (cash) grant 20%	4 800	4 800	
		Net cost for annual allowances (AA)	19 200		
1		Annual allowance (20%)	3 840		3 840
			15 360		
2		” ”	3 072		3 072
			12 288		
3		” ”	2 457		2 457
			9 831		
4		” ”	1 966		1 966
			7 865		
5		” ”	1 573		1 573
			6 292		
6		” ”	1 258		1 258
			5 034		
		Sold for (estimated)	200		
7		Balancing allowance	4 834		4 834

Since the main savings are in wages, and these will occur steadily month by month throughout the year, it seems reasonable to use Tables C and D

* See Table E page 281 for the recent U.K. investment allowances.

for the discount factors. It is true that tax will be paid in one lump sum, but this is likely to be nearer the middle than the end of the following year, so C and D should be more accurate for the tax element, too.

The *after tax calculation* of the total present value of the cash flows for the benefits from savings is:

Year	(a) *Savings*	(b) *Tax on savings*	(c) *Capital allowances*	(d) *Tax saved by capital allowances*	(e) *Net cash flow*	*Discount factor (10%)*	*Present value*
1	6 000 ↑		3 840		4 800 } 6 000 }	0·950	10 260
2	│	2 700	3 072	1 728	5 028	0·864	4 344
3	│	↑	2 457	1 382	4 682	0·785	3 675
4	│	│	1 966	1 106	4 406	0·714	3 146
5	↓	│	1 573	884	4 184	0·649	2 715
6	6 000	↓	1 258	708	4 008	0·590	2 365
7		2 700	4 834	566	200 } (−2 134) }	0·536	(−1 037)
8				2 175	2 175	0·488	1 061
			Total present value of investment benefits				26 529

Present value of net benefits (26 529 − 24 000) = 2529.

Investment clearly is worth while since the present value of the investment benefits (26 529) exceeds the present value of the investment costs (£24 000) by £2529. Basically, what we are doing here is bringing back the cash values of both the costs and the benefits to their equivalent value today and then comparing them. This is what present value analysis sets out to do. Obviously we shall be happy to pay out £24 000 now, if we are immediately handed back £26 529.

Had we used Table A instead of Table C for the discount factors, the figure for the present value of the investment benefits would have worked out at 25 391. The difference of (26 529 − 25 391) 1138 between the figures is material. Choosing the right set of discount tables is important if we wish to establish the correct rate of return. If we are solely concerned with comparisons between projects, then, for practical purposes, any set of tables can be used, provided the same set is used throughout.

In the above calculation we put the £4800 for the cash received from the investment grant, and the £200 for the cash received for scrap, directly into the net cash flow column. An alternative treatment is to deduct these from the initial outlay on the investment, so that net investment cost is:

	Initial outlay		24 000
Less	Cash grant (assumed received after one year)		
		$4800 \times 0{\cdot}950 = 4560$	
	Plus scrap value (assumed received at end of year 7)		
		$200 \times 0{\cdot}536 = 107$	4 667
	Net investment cost		£19 333

If this is done the present value of the investment benefits will also be reduced by an equivalent amount (£4667), since the cash grant and scrap figures will not then be included in the cash flow column. The relative difference between the two sides will of course remain unchanged. Probably the first method of presentation is a little better since it does keep separate the costs and the benefits. Moreover, there is one other substantial advantage from this separation. If we wish to determine the precise rate of return (i.e., the DCF or internal rate of return) then it is simpler to have to consider alterations in only one side (the benefit side), when trying to match up the two sides. In this case we leave the investment cost at £24 000, so that we can take the net cash flow straight from column (e) in the example above. Trying rates of 15 per cent and 16 per cent gives:

Year	*Net cash flow*	*Discount factor* (15%)	*Present value*	*Discount factor* (16%)	*Present value*
1	10 800	0·928	10 022	0·924	9 979
2	5 028	0·807	4 058	0·796	4 002
3	4 682	0·702	3 287	0·686	3 213
4	4 406	0·610	2 688	0·592	2 608
5	4 184	0·531	2 222	0·510	2 134
6	4 008	0·461	1 848	0·440	1 764
7	(−1 934)	0·401	(−776)	0·379	(−733)
8	2 175	0·349	759	0·327	711
			£24 108		£23 678

Interpolation gives the rate as

$$\left(15 + 1 \times \frac{108}{430}\right) = 15{\cdot}25 \text{ (to two decimal places)}$$

Hence, the *after tax* rate of return on the investment is 15·25 per cent.

The *before tax calculation* of the total present value of the cash flow for the benefits from savings, set out for comparison purposes, is:

Year	*Sum*	*Discount factor* (10%)	*Present value*	
1/6	6 000	4·551	27 306	(using Table D)
1	4 800	0·950	4 560	(using Table C)
7	200	0·536	107	(using Table C)
	Total present value of investment benefits		£31 973	

Present value of net benefits (31 973 − 24 000) = £7973.

To determine the precise rate of return we again have to use the method of trial and error. Trying 24 per cent and 25 per cent we have

Year	*Sum*	*Discount factor* (24%)	*Present value*	*Discount factor* (25%)	*Present value*
1/6	6 000	3·340	20 040	3·276	19 656
1	4 800	0·892	4 282	0·888	4 262
7	200	0·245	49	0·233	47
			24 371		23 965

Interpolation gives the rate as

$$\left(24 + 1 \times \frac{371}{406}\right) = 24{\cdot}91 \text{ (to two decimal places)}$$

Hence, the *before tax* rate of return on the investment is 24·91 per cent.

It is evident that the before tax calculation is much easier to make. Unfortunately, however, it does give a widely distorted figure for the rate of return, since it is a fact of life that Corporation Tax must be paid. Because it does not give a true rate of return, it follows that investment projects assessed on this basis and compared with an agreed cut-off rate may be incorrectly passed or failed. Raising the cut-off rate will not put this right, since the effect of tax is not consistent; indeed it varies with many factors such as the annual allowance rate, whether any investment grant is given or not (and at what rate), and so on.

5.5. The after wage inflation calculation

If wage rates in the past have been subject to an annual inflation of say 4 per cent, then it may well be realistic to assume that this rate is likely to continue into the future. As the illustration below shows, savings will increase with inflation and so will the present value of the benefits. The investment cost, on the other hand, since it is paid out now, will in general remain unaffected. The effect of taking inflation into account is to increase the true money rate of return. The incidence of inflation is therefore an argument in favour of investment. This is true whether the investment is in new machinery (as above), or in a new factory (when the benefits in terms of net revenue will be subject to price inflation at the prevailing rate).

In the preceding example introducing the effects of inflation would mean that the wage savings instead of staying at £6000 per annum would increase by, say, 4 per cent each year. After one year the savings would be £6240, after two years £6490, and the amount would increase each year.

The *after tax, after wage inflation calculation* of the total present value of the cash flow from savings is therefore:

Year	*Savings*	*Tax on savings*	*Capital allowances*	*Tax saved by capital allowances*	*Net cash flow*	*Discount factor* (10%)	*Present value*
1	6 000	—	3 840	—	4 800 6 000	0·950	10 260
2	6 240	2 700	3 072	1 728	5 268	0·864	4 552
3	6 490	2 808	2 457	1 382	5 064	0·785	3 975
4	6 750	2 921	1 966	1 106	4 935	0·714	3 524
5	7 020	3 038	1 573	884	4 866	0·649	3 158
6	7 301	3 159	1 258	708	4 850	0·590	2 862
7		3 285	4 834	566	200 (−2 719)	0·536	(−1 350)
8				2 175	2 175	0·488	1 061
				Total value of the investment benefits			£28 042

Present value of net benefits (28 042 − 24 000) = £4042. To determine the rate of return let us try 18 per cent and 20 per cent.

Year	*Net cash flow*	*Discount factor* (18%)	*Present value*	*Discount factor* (20%)	*Present value*
1	10 000	0·915	9 882	0·907	9 796
2	5 268	0·776	4 088	0·756	3 983
3	5 064	0·657	3 327	0·630	3 190
4	4 935	0·557	2 749	0·525	2 591
5	4 866	0·472	2 297	0·438	2 131
6	4 850	0·400	1 940	0·365	1 770
7	(−2 519)	0·339	(−854)	0·304	(−776)
8	2 175	0·287	624	0·253	550
			24 053		23 235

Interpolation gives the rate as

$$\left(18+2\times\frac{53}{818}\right) = 18{\cdot}13 \text{ per cent.}$$

5.6. The profitability index and comparisons

When comparing projects which have the same, or roughly the same, investment cost, the figure for the present value of the cash flows from the benefits fairly reflects the value of the investment. When, however, the investment bases are widely different, ranking according to the present value of the benefits is conceptually incorrect. For if double the amount is invested, then obviously we require double the return. However, the *ratio* of the present value to the investment amount, does give a good guide as to what return is being obtained on the investment base. This ratio is called the Profitability Index and is defined as

$$\frac{\text{Present value of the benefits}}{\text{Investment}}$$

To recapitulate, in the example of the proposed investment in automatically controlled lathes we have used two techniques:

1. Present value analysis (with a 10 per cent cut-off rate).

and 2. DCF analysis.

In order to preserve generality of approach we should list the third technique, i.e., the use of:

3. The Profitability Index (though this may well be regarded as a logical extension of present value analysis rather than as a separate technique of its own).

We have also used three degrees of rigour:

1. BTBI (before tax and before inflation), i.e., ignoring the effects of both tax and inflation.
2. ATBI (after tax and before inflation), i.e., taking into account the effects of tax, but ignoring inflation.
3. ATAI (after tax and after inflation), i.e., taking into account the effects of both tax and inflation.

The comparisons, set out again for convenience, are:

Present Value (*at* 10 *per cent*)

BTBI 31 973 − 24 000 = 7973

ATBI	26 529 − 24 000	= 2529
ATAI	28 042 − 24 000	= 4042

DCF

BTBI	24·91%
ATBI	15·25%
ATAI	18·13%

Profitability index (at a 10% rate)

BTBI $\frac{31\,973}{24\,000} = 1{\cdot}332$

ATBI $\frac{26\,529}{24\,000} = 1{\cdot}105$

ATAI $\frac{28\,042}{24\,000} = 1{\cdot}168$

When comparing capital investment appraisal methods, the following points should be noted:

Present value analysis is a quick and easy technique for determining whether a particular project measures up to an agreed criterion rate of return. It gives a clear GO or NO GO answer, but that is all.

Both the DCF rate and the Profitability Index (PI) have the additional advantage that they enable projects to be ranked, so that comparison between alternative projects is possible. There are, it is true, slight variations in the PI figures if different PV cut off rates are used in its calculation, but these are so small that they are immaterial for practical purposes. The PI calculation is usually easier than the DCF calculation, but on the other hand the DCF calculation gives directly the figure for the rate of return on the project. To sum up, either DCF or PI can be used for ranking and comparison purposes. As we shall see later PI is generally more satisfactory when comparing projects with differing lives.

If we examine the DCF figures for our investment project it is obvious that calculations made ignoring tax are wildly over optimistic and incorrect. Even calculations made taking into account tax, but ignoring inflation, are pretty far from the truth. The argument that in any country inflation applies 'equally' to all investment projects, and can therefore be ignored, is as fallacious as the comparable argument for ignoring tax. Inflation rates are not all equal. Wages, consumer goods, services, and capital goods all show slightly different but material changes in inflation rates. The incidence of inflation, like the incidence of taxation, varies with the project. It, too should not be ignored when comparing alternative investments.

5.7. Currency debasement and inflation—private sector calculation

In the original example (§5.4.2) the savings—which were entirely from a reduction in wages—were £6000 per annum for six years. Using a 10 per cent cut-off rate and allowing for tax, the total present value of the benefits from investment was £26 529. When we took wage inflation into account the effect (§5.5) was to increase this figure to £28 042.

What we have not taken into account so far is the effect of currency debasement or *money* inflation, that is the fact that £100 received in ten years time is worth a lot less than £100 received now, not because of the additional interest that could be earned if the money were received now (this, of course, has already been *specifically* allowed for by the use of the discount factor), but because currency debasement means that it will purchase considerably less, i.e., its value, in real terms, has decreased considerably. When we arrive at the total present value we add up all the yearly figures for the present value in the last column. Adding them up seems only meaningful if equal sums have the same real value whatever year they may be received in.

To deal with money inflation we therefore have to reduce the Present Values of the later years by the annual amount of the currency debasement. If we take this to be 4 per cent (i.e., the money inflation rate equals wage inflation rate), we have to multiply the present values by the discount factors for 4 per cent. The full calculation taking into account both wage inflation and money inflation is:

Savings	Tax on savings	Capital allowances	Tax saved by capital allowances	Net cash flow	Discount factor (10%)	Present value (money terms)	Discount factor (4%)	Present value (real terms)
				4 800	0·950	10 260	0·979	10 045
6 000	—	3 840	—	6 000				
6 240	2 700	3 072	1 728	5 268	0·864	4 552	0·941	4 284
6 490	2 808	2 457	1 382	5 064	0·785	3 975	0·905	3 596
6 750	2 921	1 966	1 106	4 935	0·714	3 524	0·870	3 066
7 020	3 038	1 573	884	4 866	0·649	3 158	0·837	2 643
7 301	3 159	1 258	708	4 850	0·590	2 862	0·805	2 304
	3 285	4 834	566	200	0·536	(−1 350)	0·774	(−1 045)
				(−2 719)				
			2 175	2 175	0·488	1 061	0·744	789
Total present value of the investment benefits						£28 042		£25 682

The figure £25 682 refers to total present value of the benefits in real terms taking into account wage inflation and currency debasement. The obvious figure to compare this with is the total present value before any form of inflation is considered, i.e., £26 529.

It may seem surprising that these two figures differ at all. On the face of it, we have added 4 per cent on, in the savings column, and then knocked it off, in the penultimate column. Some part of the difference will vary with the precise discount factor used in the penultimate column, that is, whether it is from Table A or Table C and whether we start it at year one or year two. But whatever factor is used, there will always be some difference due to the fact that the 'tax saved by capital allowances' is subject to money inflation, but is unaffected by wages inflation. Additionally, if the money inflation rate varies from the wage inflation rate there will necessarily be another source of variation between the present value figures.

In practice, the difference is not usually very large and if a high degree of accuracy is not required a satisfactory figure for comparison purposes might seem to be obtained by ignoring all the effects of inflation. Unfortunately, this is not correct. What we have still to take into account is the effect of currency debasement on the investment, as opposed to the benefit, side.

Typically, we will borrow the money for the investment by way of a debenture.* This gives a fixed money rate of interest. Currency debasement, however, will affect these interest payments in just the same way as it affects the benefits. Clearly, we cannot take currency debasement into account on one side and ignore it on the other. The choice is therefore, to take account of the effects of currency debasement on both sides, or to ignore it for both sides. The latter is obviously simpler and easier. This point is further taken up in §6.4.1.

We arrive, therefore, at this conclusion: In investment analysis the effects of currency debasement can generally be ignored, but strictly the effects of wage or price inflation on the benefit side should be taken into account.

This rule is most important. It means that the ATAI (After Tax After Inflation) figure is conceptually *the correct one to use in DCF analysis work.* It must be noted that the ATBI (After Tax Before Inflation) figure is the *one generally used* and this gives good results, particularly for project ranking purposes. The inflation figure has an additional hidden hedge against rising costs, etc.

* If we borrow by way of a bank loan the rate may vary but will still not be directly affected by inflation.

5.7.1. Currency debasement and inflation—public sector

Earlier on we said that government departments by right, and nationalized industries and public corporations in practice, can and do ignore tax. For these non-business cases, therefore, we have to consider the effect of wage or price inflation on the before tax rate of return. Using our terminology we need to consider the relation between the BTBI and the BTAI figures. So far BTAI has not been considered at all.

Fortunately, to compare the rate of return (R_{AW} say), (i.e., the return after taking into account wage or price inflation at an estimated rate r_w), with the normal rate of return (R) ignoring tax, is not too difficult. We need to remember that the present value P_n of a sum S_n after n years is given by the formula

$$P_n = S_n \frac{1}{(1+R)}^n$$

If I is the investment cost and R is the DCF or internal rate of return then

$$I = \frac{1}{(1+R)} S_1 + \frac{1}{(1+R)^2} S_2 + \text{-----} + \frac{1}{(1+R)} n\, S_n \qquad (5.3)$$

After wage or price inflation the sums (S) will be increased by the compound interest factor $(1+r_w)$ and we shall have a new R_{AW} determined by the equation

$$I = \frac{1}{(1+R_{AW})}(1+r_w)\, S_1 + \frac{1}{(1+R_{AW})^2}(1+r_w)^2\, S_2 + \text{etc.} \qquad (5.4)$$

With a rate of money inflation or currency debasement r_m, the real value of a sum of money S_1, after 1 year is

$$S_1 \frac{1}{1+r_m}$$

and a sum of money S_2 after 2 years is

$$S_2 \frac{1}{(1+r_m)^2} \ldots, \text{etc.}$$

Hence we have:

$$I = \frac{1}{(1+R_{AA})} \frac{(1+r_w)}{(1+r_m)} S_1 + \frac{1}{(1+R_{AA})} \frac{(1+r_w)}{(1+r_m)} S_2 + \ldots, \text{etc.}$$

(Where R_{AA} is the true rate of return after price or money inflation and currency debasement.) Comparing eq. (5.3) with the equation immediately above we see that

$$\frac{1}{1+R} = \frac{1}{(1+R_{AA})} \frac{(1+r_w)}{(1+r_m)}$$

Cross-multiplying and working this out,

$$R_{AA} = \frac{R + r_w - r_m + Rr_w}{(1 + r_m)}$$

This is the full formula for the effect of both wage or price inflation (r_w) and money inflation or currency debasement (r_m).

If we put $r_w = r_m$ (i.e., wage inflation equals money inflation), then

$$R_{AA} = \frac{R + Rr_w}{1 + r_m} = R$$

and we see that the effect of one is to cancel the other out.

Ignoring currency debasement, on the grounds that it applies to *both* the investment and the benefit side we have,

$$R_{AW} = R + r_w + Rr_w$$

This formula is only applicable to those cases where tax can be ignored, i.e., in general to all non-business or public sector calculations. In this formula it must be remembered, too, that the inflation rate and the rates of return before and after inflation are all expressed as percentages. For instance, if the before inflation return is 15 per cent $\{= (15/100)\}$ and the rate of inflation is 4 per cent $\{= (4/100)\}$, then the true after inflation rate of return is

$$R_{AI} = \frac{15}{100} + \frac{4}{100} + \frac{15}{100} \times \frac{4}{100} = \frac{19{\cdot}6}{100} = 19{\cdot}6\%$$

In countries where the wage or price inflation rate is very high (e.g., in Brazil, where it has been around 20 per cent), the effect of inflation is so substantial that it completely distorts and makes meaningless any DCF rate of return which is calculated ignoring inflation. Even in a country with an inflation rate of only around 4 per cent, comparisons of projects made ignoring inflation can produce figures that are all awry. For instance, let us consider two alternative social investment projects, *X* and *Y* whose rates of return, ignoring inflation, are estimated to be 2 per cent and 10 per cent respectively. The true rates of return are:

For *X*, $$2 + 4 + \frac{2 \times 4}{100} = 6{\cdot}08\%$$

For *Y*, $$10 + 4 + \frac{10 \times 4}{100} = 14{\cdot}4\%$$

Comparing 2 per cent with 10 per cent is a very different matter to comparing 6·08 per cent with 14·4 per cent.

6. The problem of time—II

6.1. Sensitivity analysis

Throughout the analysis so far certain figures for the investment costs, savings, rates of inflation, length of effective life of the new asset, scrap value, Corporation Tax rate and capital allowance rates have been assumed. All these figures are just our best estimates of what is expected to happen in the future. Some are based on figures which have remained fairly stable for many years, e.g., capital allowances. Even here there are some grounds for expecting possible changes or alterations,* if not in the annual allowance rates, certainly in the U.K. in the investment grant rate. However, it is unlikely that they will vary very much in their overall effect. In the past they have been reasonably stable, and we may expect them to remain so in the future. One figure—the scrap value—is so small that any variations in it are not likely to be material. One figure—that for the investment cost—can probably be estimated pretty accurately; any variation here between actual and estimate should be fairly small. Savings per year, length of life and inflation, even Corporation Tax, are all at the other end of the spectrum. All are comparatively uncertain, but all affect the DCF rate of return on the investment (or the present value of the benefits, if present value analysis is being used). But to what *extent* will they affect these investment appraisal calculations? How sensitive will the PV or DCF rate be to a drop in the actual savings below those estimated? How sensitive to a decrease in the life of the investment? How sensitive to a small increase in the investment cost? How sensitive to a drop in the inflation rate, or to an increase in Corporation Tax rate?

It is mathematically satisfying, but unfortunately not very realistic, to calculate the effect of an increase or decrease of each of these variables by a fixed percentage figure. Not realistic because, of course, in making such a comparison there is the implied assumption that all these changes are *equally* likely. Clearly this is not so. An increase of as much as 10 per cent in investment cost is fairly unlikely. On the other hand our estimates for savings are based on much more shadowy figures, and a

* See Table E page 281 for the recent U.K. investment allowances.

10 per cent error is quite possible. What we really need to decide on is what are the equally likely but possible errors in making these estimates. Such a list might well be:

1. An investment cost increase of 5 per cent.
2. A decrease in annual savings of 10 per cent.
3. A decrease in the effective life of the project from six to five years.
4. A Government freeze on prices and incomes and hence a drop in the inflation rate to nil.
5. A Corporation Tax increase to $47\frac{1}{2}$ per cent for the first three years, followed by an increase to 50 per cent for the last three years.

The problem is to determine what effect these figures will have on the present value, the PI and the DCF rate. Once again, we use the basic example given in §5.4.2. and §5.5.

1. An investment cost increase of 5 per cent. The calculation of the new investment base is:

	Old investment	24 000
Add	$\frac{5}{100} \times 24\,000$	1200
	New investment cost	£25 200

The present value of the investment benefits will be unchanged at 28 041, if we ignore the slight effect that the 5 per cent rise will have on the annual allowances.

The profitability index is therefore:

$$\frac{28\,042}{25\,200} = 1{\cdot}113$$

To determine the DCF rate, let us try 15 per cent and 16 per cent:

	Net cash flow	*DF* (15%)	*PV*	*DF* (16%)	*PV*
1.	10 800	0·928	10 022	0·924	9 979
2.	5 268	0·807	4 251	0·796	4 193
3.	5 064	0·702	3 555	0·686	3 474
4.	4 935	0·610	3 010	0·592	2 921
5.	4 866	0·531	2 574	0·510	2 482
6.	4 850	0·461	2 236	0·440	2 134
7.	(−2 519)	0·401	(−1 010)	0·379	(−955)
8.	2 172	0·349	759	0·327	711
			25 397		24 939

Interpolation gives the rate as

$$\left(15+1\times\frac{197}{458}\right) = 15{\cdot}43\%$$

2. A decrease in annual savings of 10 per cent i.e., a decrease in basic savings from 6000 to 5400 per annum, adjusted for the expected 4 per cent rise in inflation.

The calculation is:

	Savings	*Tax on savings*	*Capital allowances*	*Tax saved on capital allowances*	*NCF*	*DF* (10%)	*PV*
1.	5 400		3 840		4 800 / 5 400	0·950	9 690
2.	5 616	2 430	3 072	1 728	4 914	0·864	4 246
3.	5 841	2 527	2 457	1 382	4 696	0·785	3 686
4.	6 075	2 628	1 966	1 106	4 553	0·714	3 251
5.	6 318	2 734	1 573	884	4 468	0·649	2 900
6.	6 571	2 843	1 258	708	4 436	0·590	2 617
7.		2 957	4 834	566	200 / (−2 391	0·536	(−1 174)
8.				2 175	2 175	0·488	1 061
							£26 277

The present value of the benefits is 26 277.
The profitability index is therefore:

$$\frac{26\,277}{24\,000} = 1{\cdot}095$$

The calculation of the DCF rate is along similar lines to that made for the investment cost increase. The rates to try are 14 per cent and 15 per cent and the rate works out at 14·56 per cent.

3. A decrease in the effective life of the project from six to five years. This requires a material adjustment in the capital allowances calculation, since it is now proposed to sell the new machinery after five years. The last part of this calculation will read:

Year 5		Tax written down value (as before)	6292
	Less	Sold for (estimated)	200
Year 6		Balancing allowance	6092

The calculation of the new present value for the benefits follows along similar lines to that in (2) above. The figure is 25 606.

To find the DCF rate, try 12 per cent and 14 per cent. The exact rate is 13·78 per cent.

4. A drop in the wage inflation rate to nil. No further calculations are required here, since what we have arrived at, in effect, is the normal after tax but before inflation figure. Restated, for comparison purposes, the figures are:

Present value of the investment benefits:	£26 529
Profitability index:	1·105
DCF rate:	15·25 per cent

5. An increase in Corporation Tax to 47½ per cent (for the first three years) and to 50 per cent (for the last three years). The only alterations will be to the tax on savings, and the tax saved by capital allowances.

The present value of the benefits works out at	£27 501
The profitability index at	1·146
The DCF rate at	17·17 per cent

Summary. If we list all these possible errors and compare the results with the original figures, we have:

	DCF Rate	*Net PV (at 10%)*	*PI*
1. Basic figures	18·13%	4 042	1·168
2. Investment cost increase of 5 per cent	15·43%	2 842	1·113
3. Decrease in savings of 10 per cent	14·56%	2 277	1·095
4. Decrease in life to 5 years	13·78%	1 606	1·067
5. No wage inflation	15·25%	2 529	1·105
6. Corporation Tax increase	17·17%	3 501	1·146

It is evident that a Corporation Tax increase will have little effect. On the other hand, a decrease in life to five years, or a decrease of around 10 per cent in the yearly savings, will markedly reduce the rate of return. It is these figures therefore, if any, whose accuracy and reliability needs to be checked and investigated. Provided it is felt that the likelihood that any one of these errors will occur is sufficiently small, and provided that 13 per cent is regarded as a satisfactory figure, then no further action is required. If, however, there seems to be a reasonable chance that one or more of these errors in estimating may occur in combination, then the analysis must be taken a step further. Consider the effect of a decrease in life to five years *and* an increase in investment cost of 5 per cent. The net cash flow can be taken from §5.5 (for the first five years) and then as adjusted for the calculation in (3) above. If we try 10 and 12 per cent rates, we have,

	NCF	*DF* (10%)	*PV*	*DF* (12%)	*PV*
1.	10 800	0·950	10 260	0·941	10 163
2.	5 268	0·864	4 548	0·840	4 425
3.	5 064	0·785	3 975	0·750	3 798
4.	4 935	0·714	3 524	0·670	3 306
5.	4 866	0·649	3 158	0·598	2 910
6.	(−2 251)	0·590	(−1 328)	0·534	(−1 202)
7.	2 741	0·536	1 469	0·477	1 307
			£25 606		£24 707

The present value of the benefits is £25 606

Profitability index is $\frac{25\,606}{25\,200} =$ 1·016

DCF rate is $\left(10 + 2 \times \frac{406}{899}\right) =$ 10·90 per cent

The DCF rate represents a drop of (18·13 − 10·90 =) 7·23 per cent from the basic figures. This compares with decreases of (18·13 − 13·78 =) 4·35 per cent and (18·13 − 15·43 =) 2·70 per cent in the individual component figures.

Since 4·35 + 2·70 is slightly less than 7·23, it seems that the cumulative effect of two errors is a little greater than the sum of the individual errors. (Taking the extremely unlikely case when ALL the errors are put together it is easy to show that the net effect would be to cause the rate of return to fall to below zero.) Figure 6.1 shows all the results of the sensitivity analysis, in graphical form.

6.2. Uneven lives

One conclusion to be drawn from the above analysis is that the project is very sensitive to a shortening in its expected life. Very often this is the case. Unfortunately, estimating the precise life of a project is a very difficult thing to do in practice. Really there are two different, though related, problems here. The first is how to deal with cash flows or other benefits which continue as far as can be seen into the future. A typical example of this problem would be investment in a new factory producing standard or staple goods, the need for which is likely to continue almost indefinitely. The second is how to compare projects which have shorter

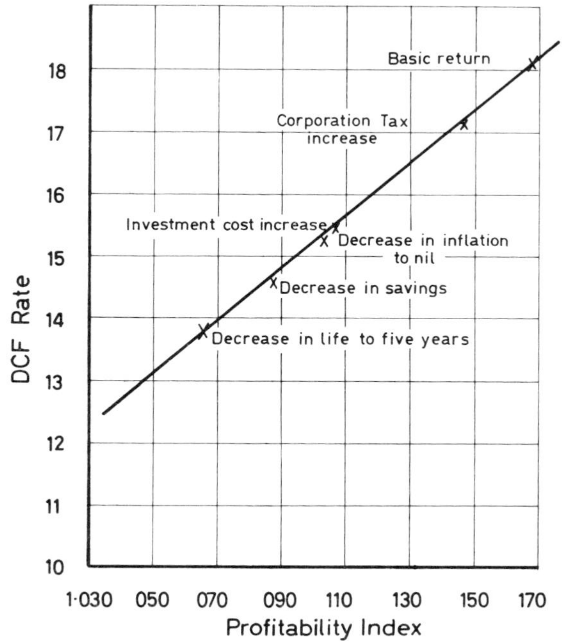

Figure 6.1. *Sensitivity analysis*

but *differing* life-spans. This problem links up with the more general problem of alternative projects, and the rate of interest that surplus funds can earn, since if one project should finish before another there will be spare money available for a while. We have already seen in an earlier example (§5.3.1) that because a project has a higher rate of return it does not necessarily follow that it is better. In that example a return of 6 per cent for one year was preferable to 9 per cent for three years because the spare money could earn 15 per cent. Let us try the effect of using the profitability index as a criterion for assessing the two alternative projects compared there. With the *cut-off rate of 15 per cent* for determining the present value, and using Tables A and B for the discount factors (since monies are received at year ends), we have

Project A (i.e., £6000 for one year AND the £100 000 returned at the end of that year—since 6 per cent *on* a base of £100 000 implies that the base is still available):

$$\text{PV} \quad 106\,000 \times 0{\cdot}870 = £92\,220$$

$$\text{PI} \quad \frac{92\,220}{100\,000} = 0{\cdot}922$$

Project B (i.e., £9000 for three years and the £100 000 returned at the end of the third year):

PV	9000 × 2·283	=	20 547
	100 000 × 0·658	=	65 800
			£86 347
PI	$\frac{86\,347}{100\,000}$	=	0·864

The profitability index therefore correctly gives project A as better than project B. This result is most important. The conclusion to be drawn from it is that in real-life circumstances where money spare does of course have a value—so that effectively there really is a background cut-off rate against which the returns on projects can be compared—then the profitability index does seem to be a better measure for capital investment appraisal work than the DCF rate of return. This may shock traditional British users of the DCF or internal rate of return method. For them the DCF rate is the *true* indication of the rate of return on a project and so rating a project by DCF must be best. As we have seen this just is not true. One project can have a substantially higher DCF rate than another; yet to prefer it on these grounds is wrong, and can lead to an incorrect decision.

At a 15 per cent rate project A is better than project B. At rates higher than 15 per cent the gain that project A has over project B must increase, since A will have the additional benefit of the extra rate for the two years. If we work out the profitability indexes for the two projects for various present value cut-off rates we have

	Profitability index	
PV rates (as a percentage)	*Project A*	*Project B*
0	1·060	1·270
6	0·999	1·081
10	0·964	0·975
12	0·947	0·928
15	0·922	0·863
20	0·883	0·769
25	0·843	0·688

At a criterion rate of approximately $10\frac{1}{2}$ per cent, the profitability index ranks projects A and B as equal. This means, in effect, that the loss that project A (at 6 per cent) makes in the first year in comparison with B (at 9 per cent) is made up in the later two years by the increased gain that A enjoys over B which is still earning at the same rate. At rates higher than $10\frac{1}{2}$ per cent for spare funds, A will gain more, and accordingly will

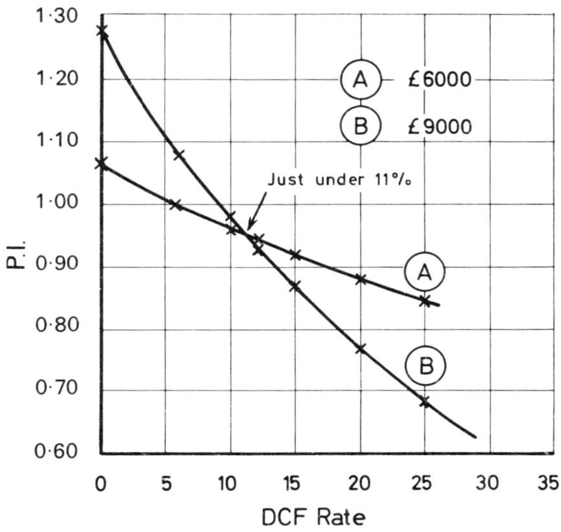

Figure 6.2.

be a better proposition than B. At lower rates B will be better than A. Figure 6.2, shows the position.

Many British firms are geared to the use of DCF rather than PV or PI analysis. If for this or any other reason the use of DCF is still felt to be expedient or desirable, the only approach which is at all conceptually satisfactory in comparing projects with differing life-spans is to proceed as follows:

> Estimate the value that the project with the longer life will have at the time when the shorter project reaches the end of its life. This value, of course, will be higher than its own residual balance at the end of its life because of the remaining years of working life still available. Put this figure into the DCF calculation as a terminal cash flow, and then make the comparison between the two projects which now have the same life-span.*

This approach, fortunately, will also deal with the former of the two problems posed at the beginning of this section, i.e., how to deal with benefits which continue as far as can be seen into the future. Here the best solution is arbitrarily to end the cash flows at some fairly distant date—fifteen, twenty, or twenty-five years are the horizons often chosen—and put in the value of the business as an ongoing concern at that date as a terminal cash flow. It may be argued that estimating the value of a business so far into the future is a task which is almost impossibly difficult. Fortunately, so powerful is the reducing effect of the discount factor at this

* This technique does not deal with the background rate of return problem: it does however provide a simple and effective method for most practical purposes.

period in time that any inaccuracies would have to be large to be appreciable. For instance an error of £100000 in twenty-five years time at a rate of 15 per cent is equivalent to a difference of only (100000 × 0·030) £3000 now.

6.3. Follow-up of discounted cash flow

How good are decisions made with the aid of DCF or PV analysis? Unfortunately, the conclusion that must be drawn from the results of recent surveys carried out in the U.S.A. is not very good! One large corporation that had only passed projects which satisfied a criterion rate of 11 per cent, had actually achieved in practice an overall 7 per cent. Other figures lend support to the view that the actual rates achieved have been substantially less than the estimated DCF rates, sometimes indeed they are as low as half the original figures.

Why have there been these differences between the estimated and the actual figures? DCF and PV techniques do properly take into account the value of time. On analysis, it has become evident that the errors have been in those basic figures which make up the costs and benefits. These figures have often been wildly optimistic. It seems that involvement in a project tends to blunt one's critical judgement of these factors.

The only way to deal with this sort of wild guesswork is to have, as routine, a standard follow-up procedure for capital investment appraisals. Most of the primary data entering into the calculations will have been supplied by non-financial staff, such as managers in the production, personnel, marketing, and research and development departments. All these estimated figures must subsequently be compared with the actual results. The benefits from doing so will be twofold. First, it will soon become apparent where the errors in estimating have been occurring. Second, the very fact that it is known that the original figures will subsequently be audited must make those people who supply the estimates much more careful and responsible in their work. Most, though not perhaps quite all, projects will warrant a post audit on these lines. In some cases, when the project is closely integrated with other work, the cost of separating the expenses and the benefits properly to be attributed to the project may be excessive: indeed it may sometimes be unrealistic if much apportioning of overheads is necessary. Having said this it nevertheless remains true that the benefits from having a standard follow-up procedure carried out by staff, not themselves involved in the preparation of the original figures, cannot be overestimated.

Reverting to the original estimate (§5.4) for the profit and loss account for the fifth year of the business, let us suppose that when the actual figures become available and are set out against these estimates, the position is:

		EST		*ACT*
Sales		1 400 000		1 200 000
Purchases		500 000		420 000
Direct labour		420 000		408 000
Overheads:				
Variable	180 600		158 400	
Fixed	129 400		146 600	
		310 000		305 000
Cash flow from profits		170 000		67 000
Tax on previous year's profit (at 45%)		76 500		30 150
Tax saved by CA's		45 000		45 000
Net cash flow		138 500		81 850

Let us assume that the original investment amount was estimated to be £1 000 000, that the expected life was twenty years, and that the anticipated scrap value at the end is nil. Let us further assume, just for the purpose of this example, that there was no build-up in the initial years, in other words, production and selling at the full rate started in the first year. We can then calculate the expected DCF rate quite simply, since

$$\frac{\text{investment}}{\text{yearly cash flow}} = \frac{1\,000\,000}{138\,500} = 7{\cdot}22$$

and Table B gives the rate as something over 12 per cent.

If these actual results in year 5 are regarded as typical, then we can use them as a good guide to all future cash flows. The actual cost of the investment will also be available by this time. It may be that this figure differs in total from the original estimate of £100 000. Payments, too, may not all have been in one lump sum, but more likely in the pattern shown below. To arrive at the true DCF rate with the revised figures, let us first try 6 per cent.

Year		*Sum*	*DF (at 6%)*	*PV*
−1	Land	10 000	1·060	10 600
0	Buildings and plant	73 600	1·000	73 600
1	Working capital	7 000	0·943	6 601
				£90 801

The cash flow from profits gives a present value at 6 per cent of

$$81\,850 \times 11{\cdot}470 = £90\,420$$

It follows that the actual DCF rate of return is a little under 6 per cent.

Table 6.1

				Figures supplied by:					
	EST	*ACT*	*VAR*	*Marketing sales*	*Personnel*	*Purchases*	*Production*	*Accountant*	*Other*
Sales	1 400 000	1 200 000	−200 000	x					
Purchases	35·7%	35·0%	+0·7%			x			
Direct labour	30·0%	34·0%	−4·0%		x		x		
Variable overhead	12·9%	13·2%	−0·3%				x	x	
Fixed overhead	129 400	146 400	−17 000				x	x	x
Corporation Tax	45%	45%	—					x	
Capital allowances	100 000	100 000	—				x	x	x

To find out what has caused this drop from an estimated 12 per cent to approximately half that rate, we need to compare the actual with the estimated basic figures and then to analyse the differences. Since purchases, direct labour, and variable overheads are all likely to be directly variable with sales, these items must first be expressed as a percentage of sales.

Table 6.1., shows the layout:

In the appendix at the end of chapter 8, on the measurement of management, the analysis of the variances into controllable (i.e., 'performance' variances), and uncontrollable ('non-performance' variances) is carried on a stage further, beyond that shown above.

6.4. The rate of interest

So far the problem of the availability of money for an investment, or the cost of providing it, if it is not there, has not been considered. Always, until now, the supposition has been that the money is available; the only decision needing to be made is how to spend it; for example, whether on project A or project B. The ground covered to date has consisted entirely of an analysis of the best techniques for comparing and evaluating alternative projects.

6.4.1. Corporations

What is the cost of capital for a corporation? On the face of it, the cost of borrowing money, net of tax, would appear to be an adequate answer. To proceed from this to the criterion cut-off rate we need, presumably, to add some extra percentage to cover the risk which must be inherent in any project, since the benefits lie in the future and can therefore only be estimated. The current market rate of interest (10 per cent) for irredeemable or long-term debentures in the U.K. is not typical. Nevertheless, if we take this rate and adjust for Corporation Tax at 45 per cent, the after-tax cost of long-term money will work out at $(10-4\frac{1}{2}) = 5\frac{1}{2}$ per cent. (The tax deduction is justified, since debenture interest is a charge against profits though this assumes, it is true, that taxable profits are being made). Taking this to be the case, the criterion rate should be,

	After-tax cost of long-term money	$5\frac{1}{2}$ per cent
Add	Risk cover, depending on the degree of risk inherent in the project but say	$2\frac{1}{2}$ to $5\frac{1}{2}$ per cent
	Cut-off rate (after tax)	8 to 11 per cent

and broadly these figures agree with the cut-off rates used by the capital investment appraisal departments of the larger corporations.

These figures need, however, to be treated with considerable caution for a number of reasons. As we saw in the section on the follow-up of

DCF, projects which have been passed because they exceeded an agreed cut-off rate, when subjected to a post audit, have generally fallen considerably short of that agreed rate. Typically, if a 10 per cent cut-off rate has been used the average rate actually achieved has been only 7 per cent, so that the shortfall has been around 30 per cent of the original rate. If, therefore, it is required that an average of 9 per cent really be achieved, and it is felt likely that the percentage drop from estimate to actual may well continue at the same (30 per cent) figure, then the cut-off rate should be set as high as 13 per cent! Hopefully, the very fact that post audits have discovered such high discrepancies in the past will mean that measures will be taken to close the gap. In that case the cut-off rate should still be revised up from the 9 per cent, but not to so high a figure as 13 per cent. Nevertheless, just to leave the rate at 9 per cent must mean that the facts are not being faced up to properly.

The simple approach to the cost of capital calculation outlined above is, however, conceptually incorrect since it is wrong to base the cost of capital for any investment project solely on the cost of borrowing money to cover that project. Partly this is because there is a limit to the amount of borrowing that a company can undertake, but mainly because each project must not be looked at in isolation but rather as part of the overall corporate planning policy.

The factors that limit the borrowing of a company are extremely varied and complex. Table A—the model set of articles given in an appendix to the Companies Act 1948, and frequently used in whole or in part by U.K. companies—says that borrowing '(apart from temporary loans obtained from the company's banks in the ordinary course of business) shall not at any time, without the previous sanction of the company in general meeting, exceed the nominal amount of the share capital of the company for the time being issued'. Usually this legal limit far exceeds the actual amount of borrowing that a company wishes to undertake. A much more important practical limitation is the amount of 'gearing' (here used as the ratio of long-term debt to total invested capital, i.e., debt to total issued shares, reserves and long-term debt) regarded as safe. This ratio varies considerably between industries and trades, but the upper limit is generally around 33 per cent. It is true that British companies tend to be undergeared, i.e., they do not recognize, and use to the full, the benefits from cheap debenture money. No doubt this is a legacy of the belief that to be able to pay one's own way is the right approach, and that to borrow is wrong. Nowadays, there is an increasing acceptance that this view is not only outdated, but unfair to the shareholders and to the company, both of whom are being deprived of the advantages that accrue from a sensible planning policy which sees control of debt as part of its total financial strategy.

As we have said, the limit on the amount of debt that a company can have is generally set by the gearing ratio. Now it may be that the particular project we are considering can have its funds provided by way of a debenture loan because the gearing ratio is not up to the maximum permissible. This means that for the next project there will be no available leeway for a further debenture issue, and hence it will have to be financed from retained earnings, or by a further issue of equity capital (itself a major proposition which can only be undertaken occasionally and when market conditions are right). The cost of these types of capital may be different from the cost of loan money. Clearly it would be wrong to pass the first project on the grounds that it was being financed cheaply, if this meant that, later, a more worthwhile project would have to be rejected. The company must look at the overall position and pass those projects which, it is anticipated, will give the highest return. It follows that a uniform criterion rate should be applied to all projects, and that this rate should be arrived at by considering the cost of all forms of financing which go to make up the total supply of available funds within the planning period.

What then are the costs of these various forms of capital, and what will be the proportion of each type in the mix of total funds available? Conventional approaches to this problem tend to concentrate on the mix of funds making up the capital already employed. For example:

		Cost (%)	*Weight* (*in fraction of total capital*)	*Weighted rate*
Equity:	Ordinary shares	10	$\frac{3}{4}$	7·500
	Debentures	$5\frac{1}{2}$	$\frac{1}{4}$	1·375
				8·875

In the above calculation the cost of debentures interest is shown after tax since, as we have noted, debenture interest can be deducted in arriving at taxable profits. To determine the cost of equity capital *per se* is not easy. Fortunately, however, we are not interested in the cost of *any* capital already invested in the business since this is a sunk cost. For decision-making purposes we only need to know the cost of those additional funds which, over a period of time, will be available for new investment projects. Such money will come in the main from:

(*a*) debentures

and (*b*) retained earnings

and (rarely) from

(*c*) new issues of ordinary shares.

The precise proportion of the total amount that each of these sources of funds provides will be different for each company. It will depend mainly on the 'slack' available in the long-term debt capacity, and the after-tax after-dividend volume of retained earnings. Each of these, in turn, will depend on a number of factors, some special to the industry or trade in which the company is trading, some special to the company at that period in time, and some extraneous to both. For example, the 'legal' limit on dividend distribution in the U.K. some while ago inevitably affected the amount of retained earnings.

Having estimated the proportion of each of these sources of funds in the total mix, the next step is to determine the cost of each constituent. We have already arrived at the figure of $5\frac{1}{2}$ per cent for the after-tax cost of a 10 per cent debenture. The relationship between after-tax earnings and the market price of shares is given by the price/earnings (P/E) ratio. Unfortunately, for our purposes, the market price reflects future expectation of growth. It does not give the cost of shares which are earning profits at the current rate. A better guide is the P/E ratios of those companies with an expectation of stable future profits. This means, in practice, taking companies whose earnings over the past few years have been unexceptional and steady. The P/E ratio of such companies is of course well below the national average (at present under 20 in the U.K.). It is difficult to be precise but the figure is probably between 10 and 12 to 1. Inverting this ratio, and multiplying by 100 we have around 9 per cent as the 'cost' of this form of capital. If, for the sake of argument, we assume that retained earnings and debenture money go equally into the provision of marginal capital—the precise proportion being special to the company concerned—this gives as the cost of that capital:

	Cost (%)	*Weight*	*Weighted cost*
Retained earnings	9	$\frac{1}{2}$	4·50
Debentures	$5\frac{1}{2}$	$\frac{1}{2}$	2·75
		Cost of capital	7·25

and this rate ($7\frac{1}{4}$ per cent) is also more or less in line with generally accepted ideas of the cost of capital, and is probably a little more useful as a basis for the assessment of the appropriate cut-off rate, than the earlier calculations.

It is only fair to add that some analysts argue that the historical total, rather than the marginal, approach to the cost of capital is the correct one. Sometimes their calculation of this cost is based on an attempt to find out the true amount of funds currently tied up in the business, and then to compare this base either with the profit level that is being made, or perhaps with the level of profits that management regards as acceptable. As a first step this means constructing a balance sheet with assets and liabilities at their true as opposed to their book value. The average before-tax profit on invested capital (i.e., net assets) for British industry has been a little over 13 per cent. If we take the book value of assets as a very rough guide to their real value, this gives an after-tax cost of capital of approximately $7\frac{1}{2}$ per cent.

All these approaches are highly theoretical. They give figures which range widely round a mean of some 7 per cent or so. Before this or some similar figure can be used for determining the cut-off rate two factors must be considered. A tentative suggestion for one of them—risk—was included in the original calculation for the cut-off rate at the beginning of this section.

Risk is a complex matter. The basic work on the lead up figures has already been covered in §6.1, the section on sensitivity analysis. How possible alterations in these figures can affect a corporation faced with making a decision on a project is given in an appendix on *risk* at the end of this chapter. This analysis has been relegated to an appendix for two reasons. First, the problem of weighing risk against value is not restricted to time alone. Second, the approach is fairly sophisticated, and its application is likely to be confined to those larger corporations, conglomerates, and transnationals who are involved in weighing projects of many types and sizes.

In practice, industry in the U.K. does not put in a specific allowance for risk in quantitative terms. Instead, a cut-off rate which implicitly includes some allowance for risk is used. This after-tax cut-off rate generally lies between 8 per cent and 11 per cent.

The other factor is inflation and this has already been discussed when we estimated the rate of return on savings or profits accruing from the investment. There it was argued that if the effect on the benefit side has been taken into account, it would clearly be wrong to exclude it from the cost side. The business problem, therefore, is this. What effect, if any, will inflation have on the cost of capital? The elements that go into the provision of the total capital fund are retained earnings and debentures (i.e., borrowed money). Retained earnings are cash flows from profits, and throughout the life of the project they will be affected by inflation. Since the cost of a debenture is fixed at the time of issue, it will not be affected, in money terms, by inflation. If we suppose that debentures make up the bulk of the capital required, then we can easily make a fair comparison between money costs and money benefits. In this case, it will be remembered, the correct figuring for the benefit side in our basic example is the *after* wages inflation calculation.

If we make the comparison in real terms we have to take account of currency debasement on the cost side. We therefore have to reduce the debenture interest payments over the years by the appropriate discount factor for money inflation. The precise effect will depend on the proportion of debenture money in the total mix. There will, theoretically, always be some reduction in the cost in real terms unless the company policy is to finance all new expenditures entirely from internal sources. We can confirm, therefore, the original proposition when we said that 'the existence of inflation is in general an argument in favour of investment'.

6.4.2. Private

The above analysis was concerned solely with decisions that businesses should make when comparing investments made now with benefits received later in time.

It is not only companies, however, who have to decide on the value that time has for them. People have to do so all the time. In one sense practically all human decisions come into this 'jam today or jam tomorrow' category. Presumably, if we just wish to get as much satisfaction today as possible, we shall spend all that we want to, up to the limit of our cash resources. But this will almost certainly mean going short sometime in the future, and the distant future, at any rate is comparatively uncertain. As against this we may wish to save money, not to spend tomorrow, but just because we like the feeling of security that money available in the bank gives. It might seem that we are defining the value that money has to us fairly precisely when we take out an endowment insurance policy, since here we are paying out sums of money currently, to get back a larger sum at a later date. But this is not necessarily so. Endowment policies reflect business interest rates, since firms engaged in this form of insurance need to earn a commercial rate of return just like any other company which wishes to stay in business. All that taking out an endowment policy means is that we are making a marginal utility decision, i.e., we are deciding what sum we are prepared to invest at that predetermined interest rate which the insurance market offers. This rate may be affected a little by the demand but not much. It is never worth while for an insurance company to continue issuing endowment policies if it can put the available funds to better use elsewhere.

It is not easy to determine our personal time preference rate. So many of the factors concerned are imponderable, unquantifiable, and above all impossible to isolate. In a sense, all decisions relating to time are marginal decisions, but this is particularly so for personal expenditure decisions. We must have the bare necessities of life to keep going, even if the reward for giving up benefits now in favour of benefits that could be received in the future is very great. Many personal decisions do take account of time. Investment in a house is a good example. Since the money is usually borrowed from a bank, or by way of a mortgage, the comparison with a business considering investment in a project, and taking into account the cost of capital required to do so, seems pretty close. But possession of a house of some sort is a basic requirement for normal civilized existence. Only in the marginal sense of expenditure on a house over and above that basic requirement does such a decision show a true preference rate. Moreover, many people put money into houses, not because they rate future benefits from home ownership so highly, as because they feel that property is a stable form of investment that will appreciate in value over the years. All that they are saying is that investment in property is a better financial proposition than other forms of investment, such as shares. The future benefits they are concerned with are not from just dwelling in a house.

6.4.3. Social

Private persons and companies have to make decisions in which they weigh up the value of money paid out now for benefits which will be received in years to come. The central government, local government and public corporations and bodies also have to make these decisions. Land use (e.g., motorway planning), defence and education are obvious examples. Some classical economists argue that the collective (Government) decision on these matters merely reflects, via the democratic process, the summation of individual time preference rates. On this argument it is the mean of all personal time preferences, and local and central government institutions just provide the machinery by which this is put into practice.

It is hard to believe that this is true in any real sense. If it is so, correlation is certainly an irrational and chancy affair, since the average person (whose decision goes to make up this choice) has not the faintest idea what the present social time preference rate is, even if he knows what the term means. In any case, society is built on the need for governments to take decisions which do not just mirror our personal preferences. Decisions must be made by the elected representatives of the people; decisions in which community is put above self. It is this that Burke told the electors of Bristol many years ago and the message is more relevant today. Defence is one classic example of this: education is another. Are we really able to decide personally whether money should be spent on us or on the education of our children?

The first point, made right at the beginning of this book, was this: If expenditure on a new machine or factory can give a return of x per cent, then the only way to justify spending the money available on research and development or management or advertising, etc., was to show that the return on these alternatives would exceed x per cent. Further, the return must also exceed the cost of capital by some substantial margin. Much the same argument applies to expenditure by the Government or by nationalized industries. Let us concentrate, for the moment, on the latter.

Early in the 'sixties, targets were set for the return on net assets for the nationalized industries in the U.K. Electricity was the highest at 12·4 per cent (before depreciation), British European Airways was 6 per cent; the railways were supposed to break even, and so on. However, cost-minded economists argued on these lines: 'All the funds come from the same source—the Exchequer—and all are spent on the public. So why should different rates of return be required?'

The Post Office rate was the first to be set at the new 8* per cent target figure. For many reasons this seems to be an appropriate overall rate. It ties up pretty well with the average after-tax figure achieved by private industry, and since the nationalized industries do not normally have to pay tax, the comparison is fair.

The next step is to argue that all public expenditure whether directly via civil service departments or local governments, or indirectly through nationalized industries or public corporations, should earn around this rate. Otherwise, how can the expenditure be justified? This does not mean that the manifest financial return on the capital employed should be equal, since the customary financial revenue is only a small part of total benefits. But if *all* benefits are expressed in money terms then this is so.

When public money is being employed, the rate the Government has to pay for long-term (undated) debt would appear to provide a good basis for setting the cost of this form of capital. It seems obvious that expenditure should at least earn a rate of return higher than this rock bottom, cost of government capital, rate. But there are two further steps before we are finished. First, why should the Government (social) rate differ from the private and the company rate? Put another way, if all benefits are being included why should available funds earn more in one sector than in another?

Finally, and prophetically, why should this same rate not apply throughout the E.E.C. and, in the final analysis, throughout the world, or wherever man may be? The forces acting towards economic unity are very strong, as of now. Only the political world is divided. And nowadays the flag follows trade.

6.4.4. Conclusion

The very fact that standardization on some quasi-magical figure such as 8 per cent seems sensible now, itself poses one simple question. Why 8 per cent? Why should man's overall time preference rate be 8 per cent, and not 6 per cent or 10 per cent or 20 per cent?

To answer this we have to look at both of the two sides involved, that is at the supply of money for future investment, and also the demand for it. Supply seems to depend on a variety of factors, some acting in one direction, some in another. Man's expectation of life must be a potent influence. If—to take one extreme case—we all expect to live only for a year or so,

* Now (1971) 10% for *optimal* expenditure.

then to invest now for the future is practically pointless. Since man's expectation of life is in fact steadily increasing all the time, then, on this argument, interest rates should decrease. But whatever they should do, the long-term trend is for them to increase. A more important factor would therefore appear to be the level of savings. This is determined by the excess of earnings over the amount required for consumption. In poor countries the population must spend all its earnings on the purchase of day to day necessities. Nothing is left over for saving. However, in comparatively rich countries 'expenditure rises to meet income' according to Parkinson's law! On this basis, for there to be any increase in savings, the rise in real earnings must exceed or equal our capacity to adjust our expenditure habits to meet it. The key word here is probably 'habits'; most people tend to have a savings/expenditure pattern which is determined very much by the norm of the civilization in which they live.

On the other side of the penny we have the use that companies (or government bodies) can make of the money that is invested voluntarily or otherwise with them. In a free enterprise economy, the growth of technological expertise and knowledge determines the use that can be made of available money by a business, and this probably provides the pattern for the use of all money. Elsewhere we argue that technological growth is almost certain to follow a Sigmoid Curve pattern, and that, at this moment in time, we are well into the upturn, or the early exponential part, of this curve. The rate of technological progress, and with it the real business time preference rate, are therefore likely to increase for quite a while, then slowly flatten out, and finally die away.

Appendix on risk

In this appendix a stochastic as opposed to a deterministic approach is used. Chapter 7 is devoted to stochastic problems, and this section could have been included there. However, this application has been put in here as it is self-contained and relates entirely to time.

Earlier (in §6.1), on sensitivity analysis, we argued that it must be very difficult to arrive at firm figures for the expected costs and benefits. These figures themselves depend on arriving at good estimates for key factors such as sales, selling costs, manufacturing costs, and wages.

The conventional way to deal with this sort of problem is to construct an 'uncertainty profile' for each of the key factors. In an article, 'Investment Policies that Pay Off', in *Harvard Business Review* (January-February 1968) David B. Hertz (formerly with Arthur Andersen & Co, now a director of McKinsey & Co) suggested that, for example,

> Estimates of revenues from a proposed new plant, might indicate that there is a two-thirds chance of their falling within \$40 000 of an 'expected'—or average over the long run—\$250 000 a year, that there is only one chance in ten of their falling below \$180 000, but that there is also one chance in ten that they will exceed \$350 000.

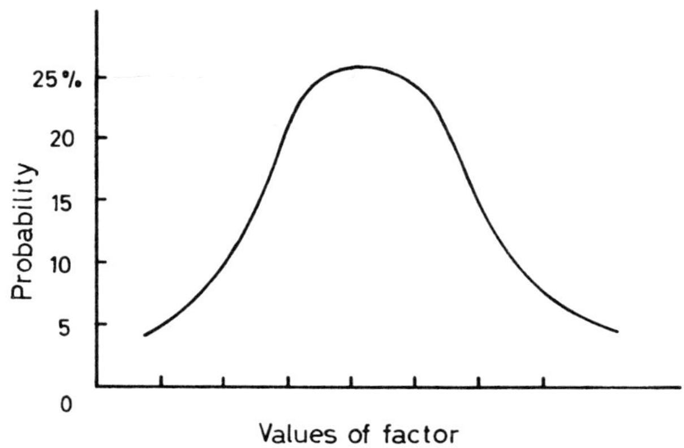

Figure 6.3. Uncertainty profile

From this and similar information the uncertainty profile can be drawn up. Only a few points need to be entered. The curve is then drawn through these points on the assumption that the spread follows a normal probability distribution pattern (see Fig. 6.3).

Once an uncertainty profile has been established for each key factor, the technique is to sample, repeatedly, at random from the distributions of all of these variables. Each combination will give a different DCF rate of return on investment. Each calculation will be long and tedious. Fortunately, computer programs exist to cope with this situation (e.g., PROP or PROSPER, by ICL).

Some 1000 or so different combinations will usually suffice, and from the results a probability distribution, called a 'risk profile', is built up. Figure 6.4 shows the

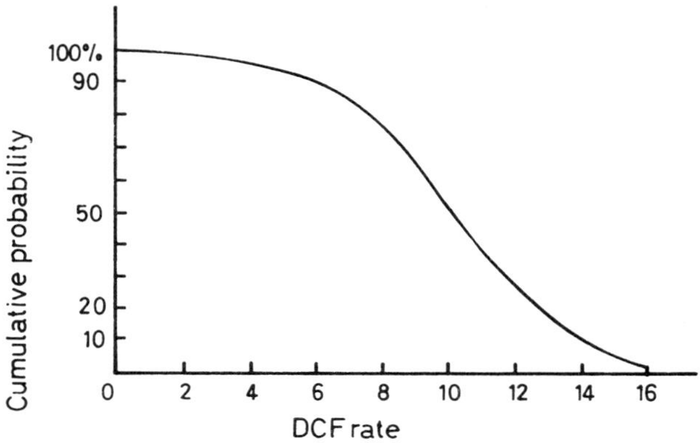

Figure 6.4. *Risk profile*

results of a typical simulation. It is easy to read off from this figure the probability that any required rate of return will be achieved. In this case there is a 90 per cent probability that at least a 6 per cent return will be obtained.

It is now possible to compare accurately two or more investment alternatives. If the risk profiles for two possible investments are drawn, they may either not overlap, as in Fig. 6.5, or they may cross, as in Fig. 6.6.

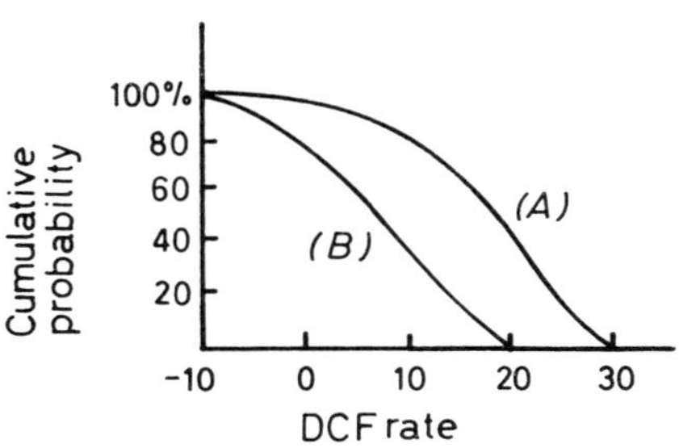

Figure 6.5.

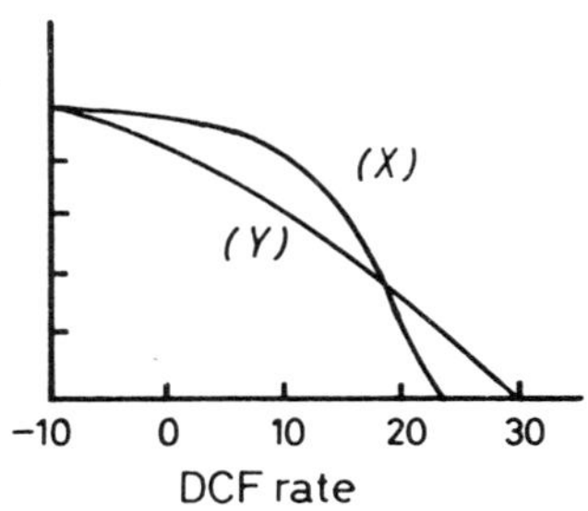

Figure 6.6.

If the risk profiles are as in Fig. 6.5, then clearly (*A*) is absolutely better than (*B*), since it offers a greater probability of achieving each and every given rate of return. As between (*X*) and (*Y*) the position is not so clear. It depends, in the last analysis, on the relative importance that management attaches to a reasonable chance of a high rate of return (Y), or being fairly sure that the rate will not fall to a very low figure (X).

The problem, then, is one of balancing return against risk; or, put more precisely, to weigh the relative advantages of a high rate of return against a high variability. Fortunately, it is possible to quantify this latter concept. The measure of the spread of a distribution that statisticians generally use, as was noted in §4.5, is the 'standard deviation'. The approach, therefore, is to plot a graph of the DCF rate of return against the standard deviation (expressed as a percentage).

Each point on the graph will represent an individual investment project. Its x co-ordinate will be the estimated average rate of return for that project, and its y co-ordinate the percentage standard deviation, i.e., the measure of its uncertainty or variation from that average rate; Fig. 6.7 shows a typical set of results.

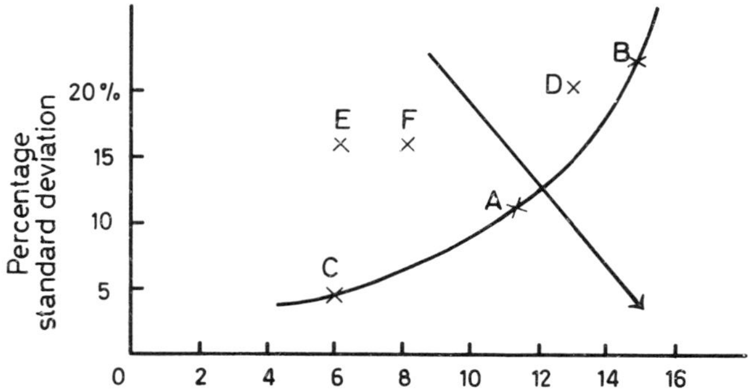

Figure 6.7.

Clearly, project C is better than E, and F than E. What is required is a combination of a small standard deviation and a high rate of return so the results should be in the general direction indicated by the arrow. The points A, B, C (each representing an investment project) lie on the 'efficiency frontier'. Once the efficiency frontier for a company has been determined, the objective must be to improve on this position, that is, to take on projects beyond this frontier.

Obviously, the efficiency frontier provides a good guide for ranking projects when it is required to take *both* risk and return into account.

Appendix on alternative choice decisions

The basic problem that we have to consider here arises from the fact that money tied up in a particular project means money not available for other projects. One project may seem better than another—because it gives a higher DCF rate. If, however, it ties up funds for an inconvenient length of time, this may mean that from an overall point of view it was a bad choice. Before giving the general approach to alternative choice problems in capital investment appraisal, two rather specialized, but in practice quite important, problems are considered. The first is dual rate DCF, i.e., where the alternative choice is restricted to the investment of funds temporarily surplus to the requirement of one particular project; the second is double solutions.

Dual rate DCF.* How does a company go about borrowing money for a capital investment project? One way is to issue debenture stock. The market rate for debentures in the U.K. is currently around 10 per cent, which means that the after-tax cost to a profit earning company is around $5\frac{1}{2}$ per cent. Alternatively, an approach to the bank manager can be made. The precise rate at which such a loan will be made will vary with the credit rating and financial stability of the borrower. There is, however, a substantial difference between these two methods of borrowing. The cost of a debenture issue in money terms will not vary; the cost of a bank loan will vary with the Bank Rate. In periods of depression, when trade is likely to be bad, profit figures low, and cash in short supply, Bank Rate will probably be high. The burden will be heaviest just when it will be most hard to bear.

Both the DCF and present value approaches assume that the same interest rate will be applied throughout the period. This may not be the case for two reasons. The first we have already seen—the possible change in the paying rate due to Bank Rate alterations if the investment money is borrowed from the joint stock banks. The second is not quite so obvious. Some projects will have surplus funds arising temporarily during the course of the project. It is not likely that the earning rate on such funds will be the same as the paying rate on the investment amount. The before-tax rate which surplus money in the bank would earn is around 4 per cent or 5 per cent, so that the gap between the earning rate and the paying rate would be pretty substantial.

Surplus cash flows will not necessarily arise in every project: much depends on the method of financing. They may only occur during temporary periods or when a sinking fund is being built up to meet later substantial negative cash flows. Some projects will have a small terminal negative cash flow for tax reasons, such as a balancing charge after the sale of assets.

* Taken from Dewhurst, R. F. J., *Mathematics for Accountants and Managers*, Heinemann, pp. 100/103.

Let us revert to the first example (§5.2.2, example 1). The calculation there showed that cash flows of £1000 p.a. at the end of each of three years were equal to a return of 10 per cent on a capital of £2486. If we now suppose that the money is borrowed by means of a debenture, issued at 10 per cent and repayable at the end of the period of three years, it follows that there will be spare cash available during the life of the project. If the earning rate for this spare cash is 4 per cent, then ignoring tax throughout, we have:

Year 0	Debenture £2486 issued and money used for project.		
			Surplus cash
Year 1	Received from project	1000	
	Paid debenture interest	248	752
			752
Year 2	Received from project	1000	
	Paid debenture interest	248	752
	Add interest on £752 for 1 year at 4 per cent		30
			1534
Year 3	Received from project	1000	
	Paid debenture interest	248	752
	Add interest on £1534 for 1 year at 4 per cent		61
			2347
	Less repayment of debenture		2486
	Difference		139

The fact that the earning rate (4 per cent) is not as great as the paying rate (10 per cent) means that the investment amount is not now repaid over the 3 years. In the conventional meaning of the phrase, the project cannot be said to be earning 10 per cent.

There can be little doubt that dual rate analysis is more realistic than single rate. Inevitably, any funds that will be available in practice for short periods will not earn as much as the long-term rate that has to be paid for borrowed capital.

Dual rate calculations can be made using the present value method (when both rates must be nominated) or the DCF method (when one rate, usually the earning rate, is nominated) and the paying rate is then found. PROP or PROSPER by ICL also cover dual rate analysis of capital investment projects.

Double solutions. There is one other problem which is of especial interest, since the standard DCF approach apparently gives two contradictory answers. This problem occurs when there is a large negative terminal cash flow, e.g., a balancing charge or a balloon payment on a debenture at the end of the project's life. Let us consider a very simple example.

Project A has an investment cost of £100 and the benefits are £300 at the end of year 1, and (−£210) at the end of year 2. That is, in the usual layout:

Year	*Cost*	*Benefits*
0	100	
1		300
2		−210

To arrive at the exact DCF rate we always have to use the method of trial and error. If we start with 40 per cent, the net present value of the benefits (107·1) exceeds the investment cost. On the face of it the investment is therefore making more than 40 per cent. This is confirmed by taking the rate at 100 per cent. The present value of the benefits (97·5) then is less than the investment cost. Interpolation gives the rate as between 88 per cent and 89 per cent. However, if we try a 10 per cent rate, i.e., a rate substantially lower than 40 per cent, instead of the present value of the benefits having increased, we find that it has fallen (to 99·3). Interpolation gives another rate at which investment cost equals benefits, between 11 per cent and 12 per cent. It seems therefore that the project can be said to have two rates of return, one around 11 per cent, the other just under 89 per cent. Which is the 'right' one?

The problem is easily solved if we remember that a return of 11 per cent implies that spare cash available during the life of the project is earning 11 per cent, and a rate of 89 per cent, that spare cash is earning 89 per cent. We only require, therefore, to know what rate money spare will earn. If we refer to the investment of this spare money as project B, the critical factor is the rate of return that project B gives. Figure 6.8 shows the curve of equal return as between the DCF rate for spare cash for project A measured along the horizontal axis, and the rate of return available on project B measured along the vertical axis.

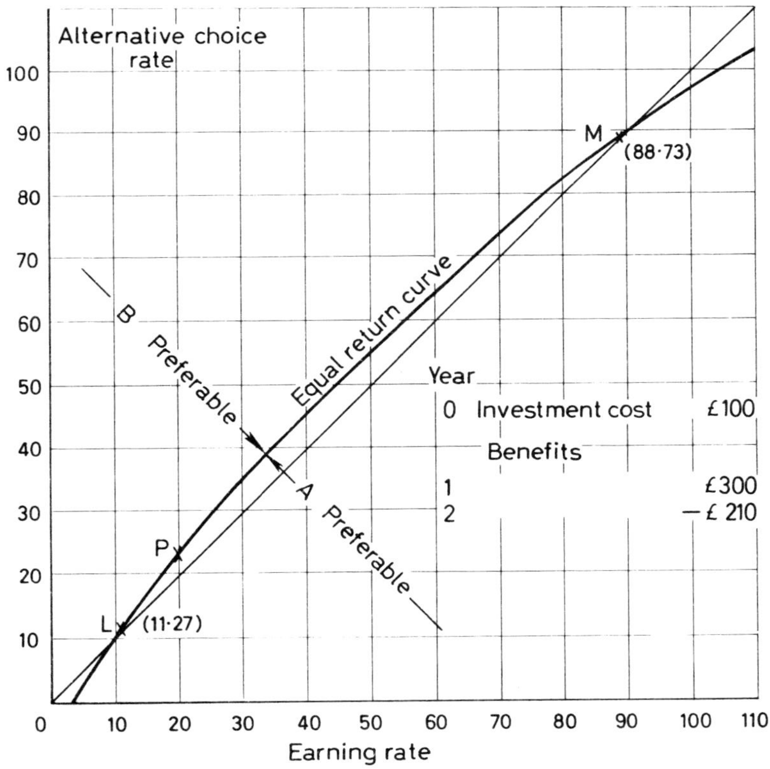

Figure 6.8.

If we suppose that the earning rate on spare cash is (say) 20 per cent, the corresponding point on the curve of equal return is P. If the rate of return on project B is above P, i.e., exceeds 23 per cent (approximately), then B is preferable to A. Conversely, A is preferable to B if the return on B is below P.

Between the points L and M the equal return curve lies above the line OLM, so that for a given earning rate on A the rate for the alternative choice B must be greater than this to make B the right choice. Looked at the other way round, when a fixed rate of, say, 40 per cent is available for B, the right choice will still be A if it has only a slightly lower rate of return.

If we assume that the alternative choice rate equals the earnings rate then the decision rule is simple. For rates between 11 per cent and 89 per cent choose A. For rates less than 11 or over 89, choose the alternative project B.

Alternative choices. We have argued throughout that the alternative use to which funds can be put is always a critical factor. Since we have a problem which must take into account the availability of cash at any moment in time, and any other restraints there may be, a linear programming type of solution seems to be indicated. The mathematical expression is as follows:

Let b_j be the net present value of project j and x_j the fraction of project j accepted (so that $0 \leqslant x_j \leqslant 1$ for all j from 1 to n, where n is the number of alternative projects under consideration).

We require to maximize the objective function:

$$\sum_{j=1}^{j=n} b_j x_j$$

This objective function will be subject to various cash constraints.

Let the amount of the cash outlay required in the t'th period on the j'th project be c_{tj}, and let C_t be the maximum possible expenditure in that period, then

$$\sum_{j=1}^{j=n} c_{tj} x_j \leqslant C_t \quad \text{for all } t \text{ from 1 to } T$$

where T is the time horizon.

Additionally, there are almost certain to be other restraints. These can be either:

1. physical shortages of the goods and services needed for production, e.g., shortages of skilled personnel, special raw materials, etc.

The objective function, which we wish to maximize, will remain unchanged, but the constraints will now be extended as follows:

If project j requires the use of d_{rs} of a certain constraint r, whose maximum availability is D_r, then

$$\sum_{j=1}^{j=n} d_{rj} x_j \leqslant D_r \quad \text{for all } r \text{ from 1 to } R$$

where R is the number of these constraints.

2. imposed constraints, i.e., constraints imposed by, or accepted by, management. Management, for instance, may be concerned with the effect that project allocation will have on the figures shown in the published Balance Sheet and Profit and Loss Account. Lending banks, shareholders and, to a lesser extent, creditors and trade unions, all have their own techniques for assessing and analysing these reported results. Banks may be concerned with the current ratio and the liquidity ratio, institutional investors with the gearing, and so on. Setting out these ratios in abbreviated form, and putting in typical figures for the acceptable limits, we have a further series of constraints in linear programming form. Thus,

$$\frac{\text{Current assets}}{\text{Current liabilities}} \leqslant 2$$

$$\frac{\text{Quick assets}}{\text{Current liabilities}} \leqslant 1$$

$$\frac{\text{Long-term debt}}{\text{Invested capital}} \leqslant \frac{1}{3}$$

and these constraints must be met for all periods of time from now to T, the time horizon.

The above analysis of the optional use of funds, whilst apparently comprehensive, gives rise to a number of problems. The time horizon needs careful consideration. Too short a time, and the solution is not necessarily the same as the one that would be obtained by taking a longer and more complete time coverage. (Inevitably, too, whatever the time period may be, there will always be some projects which will be unfinished. The best way to deal with these projects is to give them a terminal scrap value along the lines mentioned in §6.2, on uneven lives.) Too long a time horizon on the other hand, and the figures at that time in the future become so uncertain as to be almost meaningless. This problem of uncertainty is indeed one of the main grounds for criticizing the use of a linear programming approach to these problems. For periods well into the future it will be almost impossible to determine what the constraints—cash or otherwise—are likely to be.

Some time, not too far away, the over-all planning of a business will be determined on these lines. Until then, linear programming techniques are likely to be confined to problems of a more sub-optimal nature.

7. Stochastic decisions

7.1. Introduction

Weighing the consequences of one decision against another would be comparatively easy if the various consequences could all be foretold with complete certainty. Unfortunately, this is never the case. Any statement as to what may happen in the future can only be an estimate. The best that can be said is that one estimate is more likely to be correct than another or, more likely, that there is perhaps a fifty-fifty chance that the estimate will be substantially correct. How can we deal with these vague figures? How can we deal with chance? Clearly we need, as a first step, to discuss the basic tenets of the mathematical theory of probability.

7.2. Basic rules of probability

Suppose we toss a penny in the air, what is the probability that it will come down 'heads'? If it is an evenly-balanced coin, and we toss it in a random way, common sense tells us that there is a half-chance that it will be 'tails', and a half-chance that it will be 'heads'. The probability that it will come down 'heads' is, therefore, 1/2. Of course, if it is a double-tailed penny there is no chance that it will come down 'heads', so the probability is 0. If it is a double-headed coin, then it is certain that it will come down 'heads', so that the probability is 1. The range of probabilities varies, as we see, from 0 upwards to 1—the latter being the measure of cast-iron certainty. Every probability must lie somewhere between 0 and 1. This is the first rule of probability.

In the original situation, with the normal penny, the coin can come down with either a head or tail on top (ignoring the very faint chance that it might come down to rest standing on its side). The sum of the two probabilities is

$$\frac{1}{2}+\frac{1}{2} = 1.$$

This demonstrates the second rule of probability, that is:
the probability of the various, mutually exclusive, and exhaustive states, must add up to one.

7.2.1. Independent events

The probability rules relating to independent* events can best be demonstrated by considering the example of a six-sided dice. With a normal, fairly-loaded dice, all sides have an equal chance of coming up on top. The chance, p (say) that any particular side will come up is 1/6th. This follows directly from the second basic rule which says that all possible, mutually exclusive, probabilities must add up to one. Since $6p = 1$, then p must be 1/6.

If we toss the dice 120 times, a given side should occur on average around $(1/6 \times 120) = 20$ times. Suppose that each of the times the dice was thrown we also tossed a normal double-sided penny in the air. How often would the combination of the given side of the dice, and a head (say) of the coin occur? Since the side will occur twenty times on average, the combination of the given side and the head of the penny will be ten times on average, i.e., as a fraction, $10/120 = 1/12$. Since the probability of the side turning up is 1/6th, and of the head of the penny turning up is 1/2—the joint probability (which we have seen to be 1/12) is the product of the side probability (1/6) and the head (1/2). As an equation:

Joint probability of side and head		*Probability of side*		*Probability of head*
1/12	=	1/6	×	1/2

In probability terminology, we write:

the probability of event A as	$P(\text{A})$	for short
" " " " B as	$P(\text{B})$	for short
the joint probability of events A and B together as	$P(\text{AB})$	for short
and then the rule is:	$P(\text{AB}) = P(\text{A}) \times P(\text{B})$	

Just to make our rules fairly complete we also note that $P(\text{AB}) = P(\text{BA})$. This is a statement of what is, perhaps, fairly obvious. The probability of a head and a side is the same as that of a side and a head.

7.2.2. Conditional probability

In life, the probability estimates often vary with (that is they depend on) the occurrence, or otherwise, of various factors. In a business the proba-

* By independent events we mean *statistically* independent events—that is the occurrence of one event will not effect the probability of the occurrence of the other event. (See the next section on conditional probability.)

bility that next year's sales will be around £1 million might, for instance, be conditional on whether or not our usual yearly contract with the British Railways is renewed or not. The symbol $P(\mathrm{B}\,|\,\mathrm{A})$ means the probability of event B (e.g., achieving sales of £ million) occurring, given that event A (e.g., getting the British Railways contract) occurs. The dividing line is vertical. This is important, as otherwise the symbol could be misconstrued as meaning the probability of 'B divided by A'.

With independent events $P(\mathrm{B}\,|\,\mathrm{A}) = P(\mathrm{B})$, since if B and A are not related then the probability of B is not altered by whether A has occurred or not. This equation is, in fact, the mathematical *definition* of the interdependence of two events A and B.

For dependent events the relationship is:

$$P(\mathrm{B}\,|\,\mathrm{A}) = \frac{P(\mathrm{AB})}{P(\mathrm{A})}$$

and

$$P(\mathrm{A}\,|\,\mathrm{B}) = \frac{P(\mathrm{AB})}{P(\mathrm{B})}$$

Cross multiplying, these become:

$$P(\mathrm{AB}) = P(\mathrm{A}) \cdot P(\mathrm{B}\,|\,\mathrm{A}) \qquad (7.1)$$

and

$$P(\mathrm{AB}) = P(\mathrm{B}) \cdot P(\mathrm{A}\,|\,\mathrm{B}) \qquad (7.2)$$

It is easy to verify that these are true. Let us revert to the dice and coin problem. Suppose that in the event that a two, four, or six is thrown, a normal coin is also tossed, but if a one, three, or five is thrown, a coin which has both sides 'heads' is tossed.

There are twelve possible, equally likely, combinations. They are represented by the lines joining the dice and the coin:

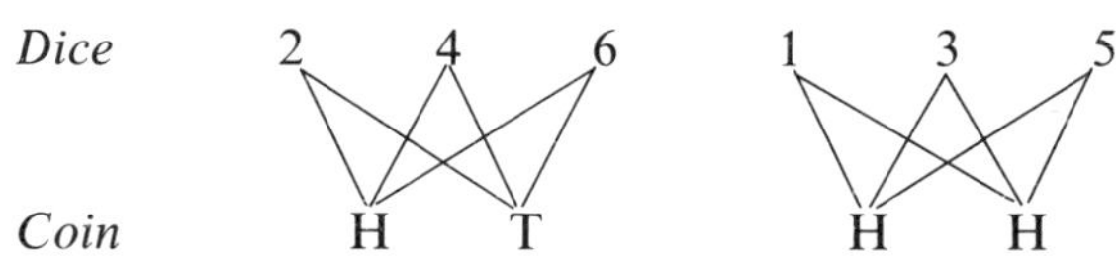

Suppose the two specific events we are concerned with are

the number two coming up on the dice — call this event A
the tail of the coin coming up — call this event B

Then,

$P(\mathrm{A}) = 1/6$ (since all sides of the dice are equally likely to be on top)
$P(\mathrm{B}) = 1/4$ (this is only one out of the four equal possibilities)
$P(\mathrm{B}\,|\,\mathrm{A}) = 1/2$ (since if a two is thrown, the coin tossed is a fair one)
$P(\mathrm{AB}) = 1/12$ (since only one line joins the two and a 'tails')

We can verify eq. (7.1), that is:

$$P(\text{AB}) = P(\text{A}) \cdot P(\text{B} \mid \text{A})$$

because $$1/12 = 1/6 \times 1/2$$

Equation (7.2) gives a value for $P(\text{A} \mid \text{B})$ of $\dfrac{P(\text{AB})}{P(\text{B})}$

$$= \frac{1/12}{1/4} = \frac{4}{12} = \frac{1}{3}$$

which implies that the probability of a two on the dice throw, given that a 'tail' has occurred on the coin toss, is 1/3. This reverse result effect is important and will be of use in the later sections of this chapter.

By taking any other combinations of the sides of the dice and the coin as events A and B, it can be shown that the above equations apply in every case.

7.2.3. Conditional and classical probability theory

In classical probability theory the procedure is always to work from known probabilities and hence to arrive at the answer. This approach is eminently suitable for almost all scientific calculations. It has many business uses too. For instance, it enables the maker of mass-produced watches to predict the chance that any of his retailers will return more than a certain number of defective watches in a given period; or it will enable the supplier of household central heating oil to calculate when his tanker should call to top up each domestic tank under the recorded weather conditions. (The object here is to cut down the number of calls per year to the minimum consistent with keeping the tank from running out.)

For business or social decisions at a high level, however, the probabilities are not usually known in advance. Maybe they can be guessed at; usually such guesses are not very accurate. However, further information can perhaps be obtained. Probably the best example is provided by the problem of whether to launch a new sales product or not. 'First guess' probabilities in this sort of situation are notoriously subjective and inaccurate. However, a test marketing result, although not itself in any way conclusive, will provide enough information to enable a recalculation of the probabilities to be made. The modified probabilities may well be adequate for decision making purposes. At any rate, they should be better. In probability terminology the original probabilities will be called prior probabilities, and the revised probabilities, posterior probabilities.

7.2.4. A Bayesian example

By way of example let us suppose we are considering whether to market a new technical book. What bothers us most of all is whether or not a rival firm is likely to produce a similar book at the same time. Our own rough assessment of the probability that it will market is 0·2. It follows that the probability that it will not market is 0·8. Let us call these $P(M)$ and $P(N)$ respectively for short. The prior probabilities, written down for reference, are therefore,

$$P(M) = 0{\cdot}2$$
$$P(N) = 0{\cdot}8$$

In the past we have often been able to get information as to whether the rival firm will market or not from a friend of ours who works in an associated company. He is not, however, exactly a top level man, his information is secondhand, and has not always been very accurate. How good it has been can best be judged by looking at the record of the number of times that our friend's predictions have been right. Table 7.1 gives these results.

Table 7.1

		Rival firm markets similar book	*Rival firm does not market similar book*
		(M)	(N)
Z_1	Friend said it would market	9	6
Z_2	Friend said it would not market	1	4

This record has been constructed by taking the ten times in the past when the rival firm has marketed a similar book, and noting that nine times our friend had predicted this, and once only was he wrong. On the other hand when we consider the ten times when the rival firm had not marketed, he still said they would in six cases. Clearly he has a slight predilection towards believing that the rival firm will market, and this emotional attitude is not unusual. Had the figures under N, and opposite Z_1 and Z_2, been two and eight respectively, then obviously we could say that his information was on the whole pretty accurate. Test marketing results based on a comprehensive market research analysis can be of this order of accuracy.

Since we had exactly ten examples in the past for each of the two situations M and N, the table is easily converted into a statement of probabilities by putting a decimal point in front of each of the figures. In conditional probability terms we have

$$P(Z_1|M) = 0{\cdot}9 \qquad P(Z_1|N) = 0{\cdot}6$$
$$P(Z_2|M) = 0{\cdot}1 \qquad P(Z_2|N) = 0{\cdot}4$$

What we are concerned to find is the new probabilities that the rival firm will or will not market, given that our friend says either that they will, or will not. In conditional probability terms we need to find

$P(M \mid Z_1)$, $P(N \mid Z_1)$—i.e., the probabilities if our friend says they will market.

$P(M \mid Z_2)$, $P(N \mid Z_2)$—i.e., the probabilities if our friend says they will not market.

First we calculate the joint probabilities:

$$P(Z_1 M) = P(Z_1 \mid M)\, P(M) = 0{\cdot}9 \times 0{\cdot}2 = 0{\cdot}18$$

and $$P(Z_1 N) = P(Z_1 \mid N)\; P(N) = 0{\cdot}6 \times 0{\cdot}8 = \underline{0{\cdot}48}$$

giving $$P(Z_1) = P(Z_1 M) + P(Z_1 N) \qquad = \underline{0{\cdot}66}$$

(since M and N are the only states Z_1 can be associated with).

Using our reverse result effect,

$$P(M \mid Z_1) = \frac{P(MZ_1)}{P(Z_1)} = \frac{0{\cdot}18}{0{\cdot}66} = 0{\cdot}27 \text{ approximately}$$

and $$P(N \mid Z_1) = \frac{P(NZ_1)}{P(Z_1)} = \frac{0{\cdot}48}{0{\cdot}66} = 0{\cdot}73 \text{ approximately}$$

These calculations are repeated on the same lines with Z_2 replacing Z_1. Putting the two together we have:

	Joint probabilities		*Marginal probability*	*Posterior probabilities*	
Friend gives answer	$P(Z \mid M)P(M) = P(ZM)$	$P(Z \mid N)P(N) = P(ZN)$	$P(ZM)+P(ZN) = P(Z)$	$P(M \mid Z) = \frac{P(MZ)}{P(Z)}$	$P(N \mid Z) = \frac{P(NZ)}{P(Z)}$
Z_1	0·18	0·48	0·66	$\frac{0{\cdot}18}{0{\cdot}66}$	$\frac{0{\cdot}48}{0{\cdot}66}$
Z_2	0·02	0·32	0·34	$\frac{0{\cdot}02}{0{\cdot}34}$	$\frac{0{\cdot}32}{0{\cdot}34}$
	$P(M) = 0{\cdot}20$	$P(N) = 0{\cdot}80$	1·00		

The posterior probabilities are therefore:

$$P(M \mid Z_1) = 0{\cdot}27 \qquad P(N \mid Z_1) = 0{\cdot}73$$
$$P(M \mid Z_2) = 0{\cdot}06 \qquad P(N \mid Z_2) = 0{\cdot}94$$

It is interesting to note how these probabilities have changed from the prior probabilities. If we suppose that our friend tells us that the rival firm will not publish (Z_2), then the new revised probabilities are 0·06 that they will publish, and 0·94 that they will not. These results are hardly surprising. All they are doing is expressing in quantitative form the fact that if we start off thinking it unlikely that they will market (0·2), and our friend confirms this (Z_2), then this reinforcement of our views leads us to a revised probability (0·06) which even more strongly expresses our belief that they will not market. The opposite effect occurs, of course, if our friend says that they will market (Z_1).

7.2.5. Sensitivity

How sensitive are these posterior probabilities to errors in:

(*a*) our prior probabilities

(*b*) the accuracy of our friend's predictions?

First, we assume our friend's predictions remain unchanged throughout at:

	M	N
Z_1	0·9	0·6
Z_2	0·1	0·4

but the prior probabilities of marketing $P(M)$ are allowed to vary from 0·0 through to 1·00. The new posterior probabilities that the rival firm will market have been worked out in the same way as before. They are shown in Table 7.2:

Table 7.2

	$P(M)$					
	0·00	0·20	0·40	0·60	0·80	1·00
$P(M \mid Z_1)$	0·00	0·27	0·50	0·69	0·86	1·00
$P(M \mid Z_2)$	0·00	0·06	0·14	0·27	0·50	1·00

The probabilities that the rival firm will not market, whether prior $P(N)$, or posterior $P(N \mid Z_1)$ or $P(N \mid Z_2)$, hardly require to be shown separately, since in every case they, together with the corresponding probability that the rival firm will market, add up to 1. For example, when $P(M)$ was taken to be 0·2, $P(N)$ had to be 0·8, since M or N are the only two possible mutually exclusive possibilities.

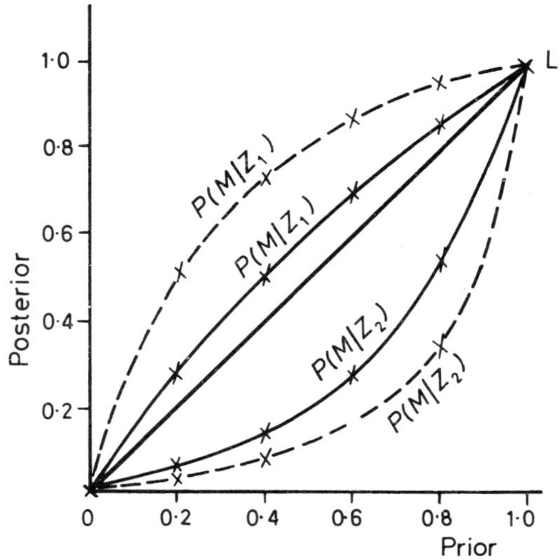

Figure 7.1.

Figure 7.1 shows the curves of the posterior probabilities $P(M|Z_1)$ and $P(M|Z_2)$ plotted against the values of $P(M)$ using the figures from Table 7.2. These curves are the unbroken lines.

The line joining the points OL is the line of no change between the prior and posterior probabilities. The greater the distance of the curves from this line, the greater the change. The effect of the inside information is fairly substantial when it indicates that the rival firms will not market, and relatively slight when it indicates that marketing is likely. It follows that, in the former case, the posterior probabilities are sensitive to any error in the prior probabilities.

We next turn to the effect that changes in the reliability of the information given to us by our friend will have on the posterior probabilities. Let us now assume that his record in the past has been better, in fact in line with good test marketing results, say,

	M	N
Z_1	0·9	0·2
Z_2	0·1	0·8

This means that in the past when the rival firm has not marketed a similar book our friend has still predicted the correct result 0·8 of the times.

The new posterior probabilities are shown in Table 7.3:

Table 7.3

	$P(M)$					
	0·00	0·20	0·40	0·60	0·80	1·00
$P(M \mid Z_1)$	0·00	0·53	0·75	0·87	0·95	1·00
$P(M \mid Z_2)$	0·00	0·03	0·08	0·16	0·33	1·00

The curves of the posterior probabilities are shown in Figure 7.1 as dotted lines. The curve for $P(M \mid Z_1)$ now has a completely different shape. Within the range 0·4 to 1·0 for the prior probabilities, it is fairly close to the horizontal. The posterior probabilities range from 0·75 to 1·0. Within this range the results are relatively insensitive to any error in the prior probabilities. Of course all this is only reflecting on graphical form the almost obvious fact that the predictions are pretty accurate.

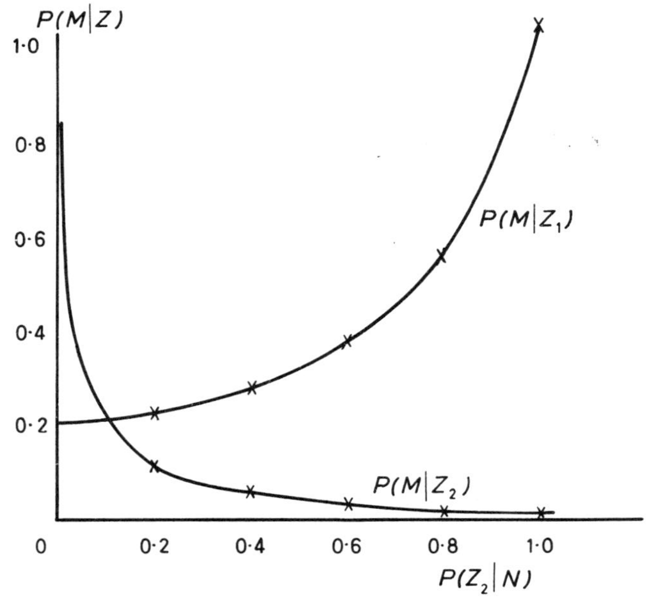

Figure 7.2.

Let us analyse the effect of changes in the accuracy of these 'test market' predictions. Figure 7.2 shows the resulting posterior probabilities corresponding to changes in the predictions. The prior probabilities have been kept constant throughout with $P(M) = 0{\cdot}2$ and $P(N) = 0{\cdot}8$. The test marketing results, given that the rival firm did market, have also been kept constant with $P(Z_1|M) = 0{\cdot}9$ and $P(Z_2|M) = 0{\cdot}1$. However, the test market predictions, given that the rival firm did not market, i.e., $P(Z|N)$, have been allowed to vary from 0 to 1. The horizontal axis shows the values of $P(Z_2|N)$. The value of $P(Z_1|N)$ can be derived from the identity $P(Z_1|N)+P(Z_2|N) = 1$. The vertical axis shows the changes in the required posterior probabilities that marketing will occur, i.e., $P(M|Z)$. The two curves for $P(M|Z_1)$ and $P(M|Z_2)$ show these probabilities given that the prediction is that the firm will, or will not, market respectively. The further along the horizontal axis away from the origin, the greater the accuracy of the prediction. Near to the origin, when the predictions have proved to be widely inaccurate, the effect on the posterior probabilities is dramatic. A slight change in the predictions gives a large swing in the resulting probabilities.

7.3. Expected value

Reverting to the original situation, outlined in §7.2 when we had a normal penny which has a head on one side and a tail on the other, suppose we are told this:

If the coin comes down 'heads' we receive 60p, but if it comes down 'tails', nothing. What are we prepared to pay for this? What is its value to us?

Presumably the simple answer is (on average) just 30p. We could express this expected value by an equation such as

Probability × *Sum*	=	*Expected value* (*EV*)
1/2 × 60p	=	30p

Had the terms included, as well, a payment of 40p in the event that the coin came down 'tails', the total value to us would be arrived at in a similar way. Thus,

Probability × *Sum*	=	*EV*
1/2 × 60p	=	30p
1/2 × 40p	=	20p
Total expected value	=	50p

Hence, to arrive at the total expected value of any particular decision choice we multiply the money value of each choice by the probability of its occurrence, and add up all these products.

7.3.1. Bayes' decision rule

This rule says that where there are several possible courses of action available, the decision maker should make that choice which has the highest total expected value. For instance, my two possible choices might be either to throw a dice or toss a coin. Suppose that if I get a one or a two on the dice, then 90p, is paid; if I get a three, four or five, then 150p is paid, and if I get a six, then 600p is paid. Is this preferable to a straight choice with a coin of 500p if I get 'heads', and nothing if it is 'tails'? The calculations of the total expected values of the two possible decision choices are:

Dice	*Probability × Sum*		*EV*
	2/6 × 90p	=	30p
	3/6 × 150p	=	75p
	1/6 × 600p	=	100p
	Total expected value	=	205p
Coin	1/2 × 500p	=	250p
	1/2 × 0p	=	0p
	Total expected value		250p

Bayes' decision rule, therefore, gives the coin as the best choice.

It is relevant to note that this is not the only possible criterion on which decisions can be based. It would be possible, for instance, to argue that the dice choice should be made because this gives the possibility of the highest return of all (i.e., 600p). When the precise probabilities are a matter for guess or conjecture, that is, when a high degree of uncertainty is present, such a decision rule may well be used. This decision rule is called maximax. Alternatively, maximin can be used; this too will give the dice. The argument there is that, if luck is not on our side, we shall at least receive 90p, from the throw of the dice, as against nothing if we throw tails. This choice implies that we feel that things may go badly and that in such circumstances we want to be as well-off as possible. We wish to be protected.

7.4. Decision trees

Let us, however, assume for the moment that the probabilities are reasonably firm and that we intend to use Bayes' decision rule. A helpful method of presentation is by the use of a decision tree. The dice/coin alternative choice would then appear as shown in Fig. 7.3.

To arrive at the total expected value at A, we multiply all the possible sums by their respective probabilities. This gives a total expected value of 205p (as against 250p, for B). Proceeding leftwards, the correct decision choice as between the two is to take B, as this has a higher expected value. Decision tree analysis proceeds by this method of moving from right to left, which is referred to as 'rollback'. Usually the framework is much

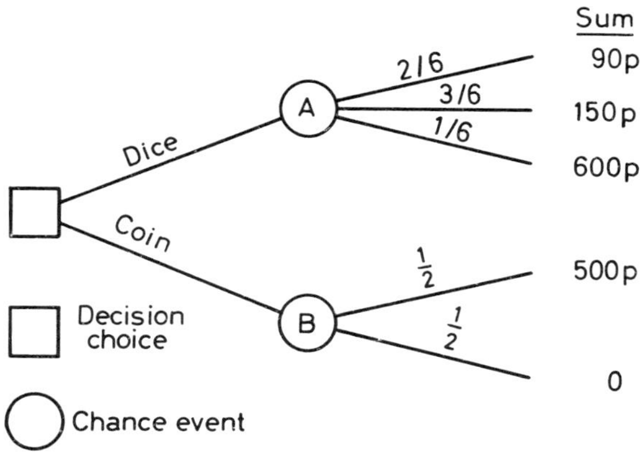

Figure 7.3.

larger than in this simple case, but the same approach applies. The method can be summed up as follows:

1. Proceed from right to left.
2. At every chance event find the total expected value.
3. At every decision point choose that course of action with the highest expected value.

7.4.1. Calculations involving expected value

Among the decisions which are the most difficult to make in business are those involving substantial sums of money, sums which will bring in good profits if things go as hoped for, but a large loss if expectations are not achieved. For instance, in a guided weapons factory, when setting up an assembly line which is initially designed solely to produce for one large Government order, one problem will be whether or not to produce an extra number of these missiles for stock. After all, it can be argued that there may be repeat orders from the U.K. Government, or foreign governments may become interested. It is all a matter of politics, and politics are notoriously a chancy thing. If no orders are received, then all the extra cost of production is a total loss. If orders are received to cover the full amount produced for stock, then a very substantial saving will be made. But perhaps the order will be for just a few more than the stock we have in hand. In that case, the production line will have to be set up again in any case. Deciding on the right thing to do in such circumstances is very difficult. It is further complicated by the fact that to keep the production line going means paying out money now, and any savings that may occur will be sometime in the future, when the sale is made.

It is not only at high price levels that problems like these occur. A grocer or greengrocer will be faced with the question as to how much of a perishable food (e.g., milk, fruit, vegetables) to stock. Any seasonal business will be faced with this problem in one form or another. Weed-killing, for instance, has its main season in early spring. Weed-killing equipment such as spray tanks, will be manufactured throughout the year. Much of the manufacture of this year's models will, therefore, be programmed during the otherwise quiet winter months. How much shall be produced? Outside catering is another and much more chancy trade. How many fancy cream cakes or how many ice-cream dishes shall be prepared for a holiday weekend or for a village fete?

7.4.2. A basic example

This fresh cream cake problem is a suitable example to follow up. Such cream cakes are purchased, we assume, only in whole trays, and past experience has shown us that it is most unlikely that less than three trays or more than five trays will be sold. Each tray costs £6 to purchase and has a selling price of £10. We shall, presumably, purchase either three or four or five trays since the demand, we know, is almost certain to be one of these three. Table 7.4 shows the profits for all those combinations laid out in matrix form.

Table 7.4

	Purchase (choice)		
Demand (event)	3	4	5
3	12	6	0
4	12	16	10
5	12	16	20

To arrive at the profit for a purchase of four trays and a demand of five we deduct the cost of $4 \times 6 =$ £24, from the sales of $4 \times 10 =$ £40. (Since we cannot sell what we have not got, the sales must only consist of the four trays that we have purchased.) The difference, i.e., £40 − £24 = £16, is the conditional profit for a purchase of four trays, given that a certain event (a demand for five trays) has taken place. Table 7.4., can therefore, in a loose sense, be regarded as a table of conditional values or profits.

How can we decide what are the probabilities that the demands will be for three or four or five trays? Presumably we can either rely entirely on past data, or we can use these in conjunction with some suitable method of forecasting. If we have to make our decision some days in advance of the event, it may be sensible to rely solely on past figures and regard them as providing the best available guide. Analysis of the figures for the same period over the last few years gave these results:

Demand	*No. of trays*	*Probability*
3	15	0·3
4	25	0·5
5	10	0·2
	50	1·0

(The probability in the last column has been worked out from the number of trays demanded in the past, i.e., from the second column.)

The three possible courses of action are to purchase either three, four, or five trays. If we purchase three, then the profits corresponding to demands for three, four or five trays are £12, £12, and £12, and the associated probabilities are 0·3, 0·5, and 0·2. The total expected value (EV) of this decision to purchase three trays is therefore:

$$\begin{aligned} & & & \text{£} \\ & \text{EV (purchase 3)} &= 0{\cdot}3\times 12+0{\cdot}5\times 12+0{\cdot}2\times 12 =& \ 12 \\ \text{Similarly,}\ & \text{EV (purchase 4)} &= 0{\cdot}3\times 6+0{\cdot}5\times 16+0{\cdot}2\times 16 =& \ 13 \\ \text{and,}\ & \text{EV (purchase 5)} &= 0{\cdot}3\times 0+0{\cdot}5\times 10+0{\cdot}2\times 20 =& \ 9 \end{aligned}$$

The choice which gives the highest expected value is the purchase of four trays. Therefore, if we follow Bayes' decision rule, this will be the number we will order.

7.4.3. Perfect information

If the decision as to the number of fancy cream cake trays that we require is left until the event is near, it is likely that we shall be able to predict the demand very accurately. Almost certainly we shall know the state of the weather and—if we leave it right to the very last moment—we shall in theory have a very good idea of the number of people attending. Using our experience, these factors, taken together, should enable us to predict the demand almost precisely. But leaving the decision until the last moment, brings with it certain drawbacks. It means sending transport to collect the fancy cream cakes, and this means extra wages and transport expenses. The net cost may be, in fact, fairly small. But is the extra information worth the cost? What is the real value of this 'perfect' information to us, at this moment in time, when we are considering whether to go ahead and purchase now or to wait until the day? There are three possibilities. Perfect information may indicate that the demand will be for either three, or four, or five trays. If it is three, then what benefit will this be to us? Undoubtedly, if we are told that it will be three, the correct course for us is clear—we will order three. This way we maximize our profit. Now the probability, as of now, that we shall be given this information (that is, the demand will be for three trays) is 0·3. Under conditions of certainty the expected value or profit of this possibility is, therefore,

$$0{\cdot}3 \times 12 = £4.$$

For the other possibilities, that is for demands of four or five trays, the profits we shall be able to get will be £16 and £20 respectively, and the probabilities that these will occur will be 0·5 and 0·2. The total expected profit under certainty is therefore:

$$0{\cdot}3 \times 12 + 0{\cdot}5 \times 16 + 0{\cdot}2 \times 20 = £15{\cdot}6.$$

This is the expected profit if we wait. If we do not wait, then the expected value of our profits (presumably taking the choice of purchasing four trays, which Bayes' decision rule told us to do) is £13. The additional benefit from waiting is

$$£15{\cdot}6 - £13 = £2{\cdot}6.$$

If the estimated addition in cost, due to the extra wages and transport expenses is greater than this, then the sensible decision is to go ahead and order the four trays now rather than to hold on for perfect information.

7.4.4. Opportunity loss

There is another way of looking at this fancy cream cake problem; one in which we concentrate on the loss in the event that a wrong decision is made rather than looking at the positive gain from making a correct decision. Let us run through the possibilities again. If the demand is for three trays, then an order of three will be the best choice. Orders of four, or five trays will produce losses of $1 \times 6 = £6$ and $2 \times 6 = £12$ respectively when compared with the best choice. For a sale of four, the best choice is to order four. Purchases of three and five will involve losses of £4 and £6

Table 7.5

	Possible purchase (choice)		
Demand (event)	3	4	5
3	0	6	12
4	4	0	6
5	8	4	0

compared with this. For a sale of five, the best choice is to order five. Purchases of three and four will involve losses of £8 and £4. These figures are shown in Table 7.5. A table of losses, such as this, is usually referred to as an Opportunity Loss Table.

Now the chances that each of these possible losses will occur is known, since the probabilities that the demand will be for three, four or five trays are respectively 0·3, 0·5 and 0·2. We can, therefore, produce an Expected Opportunity Loss (EOL) for each decision. The calculation is precisely similar to the calculation of expected value:

$$
\begin{aligned}
& & & \text{£} \\
\text{EOL (order 3)} &= 0{\cdot}3 \times 0 + 0{\cdot}5 \times 4 + 0{\cdot}2 \times 8 &=& \ 3{\cdot}6 \\
\text{EOL (order 4)} &= 0{\cdot}3 \times 6 + 0{\cdot}5 \times 0 + 0{\cdot}2 \times 4 &=& \ 2{\cdot}6 \\
\text{EOL (order 5)} &= 0{\cdot}3 \times 12 + 0{\cdot}5 \times 6 + 0{\cdot}2 \times 0 &=& \ 6{\cdot}6
\end{aligned}
$$

The obvious choice is to purchase four; since this way expected loss is minimized. This, of course, gives the same choice as the expected value calculation. In the opportunity loss approach we wish to minimize our loss as seen 'downwards' from the level of the best decision we could have taken, given perfect information. In the expected value approach, we wish to maximize our gain 'upwards'. Together, therefore, expected value and expected opportunity loss must equal the expected profit under certainty for every choice. Using the figures above:

$$
\begin{aligned}
& & & & \text{£} \\
\textit{Order } 3 \quad & \text{EV(3)} + \text{EOL(3)} &=& \ 12 + 3{\cdot}6 &=& \ 15{\cdot}6 \\
\textit{Order } 4 \quad & \text{EV(4)} + \text{EOL(4)} &=& \ 13 + 2{\cdot}6 &=& \ 15{\cdot}6 \\
\textit{Order } 5 \quad & \text{EV(5)} + \text{EOL(5)} &=& \ 9 + 6{\cdot}6 &=& \ 15{\cdot}6
\end{aligned}
$$

7.4.5. A complete decision tree

We are now in a position to consider a complete decision choice: one taking account of all possibilities; these include not only obtaining perfect information but also imperfect information. With all these possibilities the mathematics can quickly become heavy, and a simpler example seems more suitable. We therefore restrict the alternative choices and the events to two each.

Suppose that we are considering whether to purchase four, or to purchase five, of a particular item. It does not really matter what these items are. Perhaps we are a boutique owner, and we are trying to decide whether to buy four or five dresses of a new 'way out' design (with obviously a short sales life and little or no scrap value if not sold) from a travelling salesman. The dresses will sell at around £15 each and their cost is £6, so the profit on each dress sold is £9. Past experience leads us to believe that we can usually rely on selling four or five of such boutique dresses and we assess the probability of selling four at 0·8, and of five at 0·2. If this seems a trivial problem—and it is unlikely that the boutique owner would agree on this point—then all we have to do is regard the figures as being in thousands of pounds and as applying to guided missile installations.

The pay-off table is:

		Purchase (choice)	
		4	5
Demand (event)	4	36	30
	5	36	45

The calculations follow along the same lines as in the preceding 'three choice' problem. Dropping the £ signs, they are:

$$\begin{aligned} \text{EV (purchase 4)} &= 0{\cdot}8 \times 36 + 0{\cdot}2 \times 36 &&= 36 \\ \text{EV (purchase 5)} &= 0{\cdot}8 \times 30 + 0{\cdot}2 \times 45 &&= 33 \\ \text{EV (perfect information)} &= 0{\cdot}8 \times 36 + 0{\cdot}2 \times 45 &&= 37{\cdot}8 \end{aligned}$$

Obviously our choice is to purchase four, or else to go for Perfect Information, and we shall do the latter only if, and only if, it costs us less than $(37{\cdot}8 - 36 =)$ 1·8.

Perfect Information is, however, rather an abstract theoretical consideration. It is unlikely, in real life, that even *ex cathedra* advice will be so reliable. What can be done is to turn to other people for their professional advice. In the case of the boutique shop this will probably mean asking a friend in the trade. In the case of the guided missile project it may mean a complicated market research by a firm of specialized marketing consultants. Whatever way is really irrelevant to our purpose. Suppose that we know of a test market firm that has been turning out results of a reasonable order of accuracy. When their analysis has been restricted to the consideration of two choices only, their past record has shown this pattern:

	A	*B*
A	0·9	0·1
B	0·1	0·9

Across the board it seems that they have been correct 90 per cent of the time.

Given this information it is easy to calculate what the posterior probabilities will be. The calculation is:

Joint probabilities		*Marginal*	*Posterior probabilities*	
$0{\cdot}9 \times 0{\cdot}8 = 0{\cdot}72$	$0{\cdot}1 \times 0{\cdot}2 = 0{\cdot}02$	0·74	$\frac{0{\cdot}72}{0{\cdot}74}$	$\frac{0{\cdot}02}{0{\cdot}74}$
$0{\cdot}1 \times 0{\cdot}8 = 0{\cdot}08$	$0{\cdot}9 \times 0{\cdot}2 = 0{\cdot}18$	0·26	$\frac{0{\cdot}08}{0{\cdot}26}$	$\frac{0{\cdot}18}{0{\cdot}26}$
0·80	0·20	1·00		

With the usual notation for posterior probabilities:

$$P(4 \mid 4) = 0{\cdot}97 \qquad P(5 \mid 4) = 0{\cdot}03$$
$$P(4 \mid 5) = 0{\cdot}31 \qquad P(5 \mid 5) = 0{\cdot}69$$

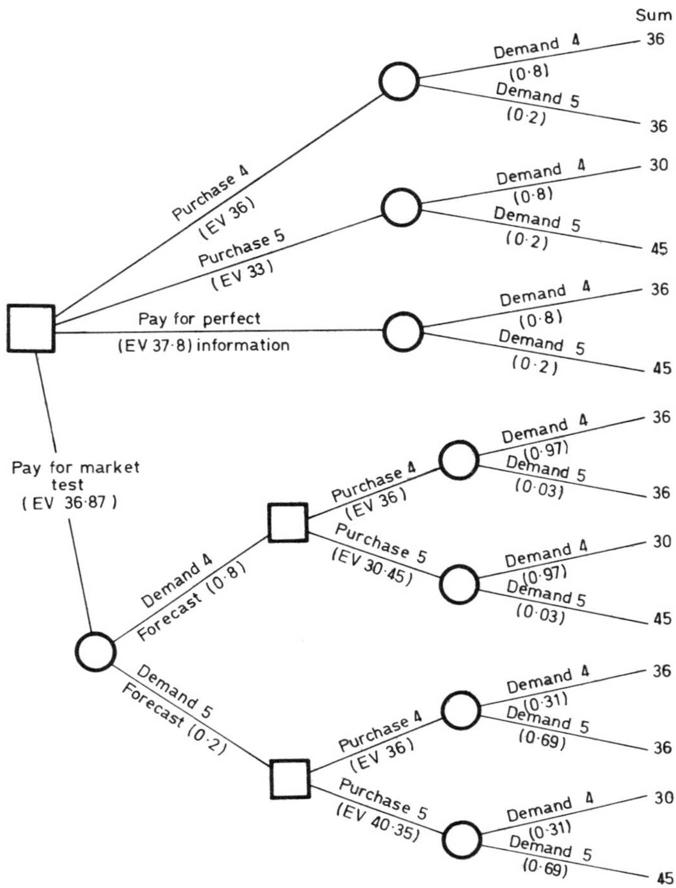

Figure 7.4. Decision tree

It is important to remember that, at this stage, we do not know what the test results will give and so we do not know which of the rows above to use for our posterior probabilities. There are two possibilities, and these are that the test may indicate four, when the top row will be relevant, or it may indicate five, when the lower row will be appropriate. As of now we can only say with our present information our expectation of the first result is 0·8, and of the second, 0·2.

Figure 7.4 shows the decision tree for all the possible courses of action. The top and middle sections follow along the same lines as the earlier example. If we go for the test market, there are two possible indications. For each indication we have two possible choices, i.e., to purchase four, or to purchase five. The expected value of the first is 36, and of the second is 30·45. Bayes' decision rule tells us to choose the first between these two. This rule also makes us choose the latter (with an EV of 40·35) as between the bottom two. The total expected value of the test market choice is therefore:

$$0{\cdot}8 \times 36 + 0{\cdot}2 \times 40{\cdot}35 = 36{\cdot}87$$

As between going for the test market or a straight purchase of four or five we shall clearly go for the test market provided the cost of this information is less than (36·87 − 36 =) 0·87.

Finally, it is interesting to see the effect of variations in the accuracy of the test market information on the expected value of this choice, and hence on the amount we shall be prepared to pay for this information. Table 7.6, shows the expected value against the assessed accuracy of the test market.

Table 7.6

Percentage accuracy	*Expected value (EV)*	*Benefit from test*
50	36	—
60	36	—
70	36	—
75	36·09	0·09
80	36·30	0·30
90	36·87	0·87
100	37·80	1·80

No benefit should ever arise when the test is only 50 per cent accurate, since a 50 per cent accuracy is achieved by random choice. In our case, no benefit is derived from the test unless it is nearly 75 per cent accurate. The benefit rises steeply as we approach 100 per cent accuracy, i.e., perfect information. Perfect information is a special case of imperfect information. Figure 7.5 shows the results for all the percentages from 50 to 100.

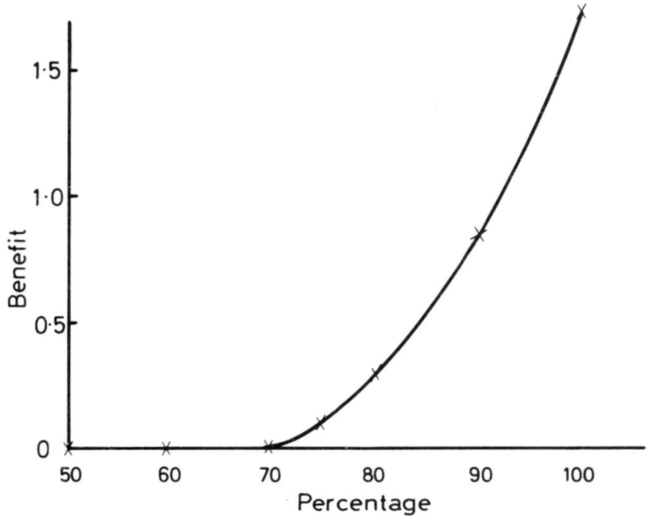

Figure 7.5.

7.5. Problems and limitations of decision tree analysis

This completes the basic framework for stochastic decision making. A number of substantial problems still remain. For instance:

7.5.1. Complexity

The possible choices in real life are often not restricted to numbers as small as two or three. In such cases decision tree analysis by hand is tedious and complicated. Computer programmes are available for this work and the use of computers is particularly suitable when the effect of variations in the figures is being investigated. Sensitivity analysis on these lines should indeed be regarded as the norm, rather than as an additional refinement, when dealing with decision problems, since all figures relating to the future are inherently uncertain. The effect that inaccuracies in the basic figures will have on the final decision should always be determined.

There is a further reason for using a computer in decision tree analysis. If the decision tree is at all complex and extends for some distance in time the effect of the various choices on the resources available to the business as a whole must be considered. Typically decisions will involve time (see §7.5.2) and the availability of a scarce resource such as cash will be affected by the decisions made. The interaction of these decisions with the requirements of other sections of the business would generally be too complicated to work out manually.

7.5.2. Time

The problem of time in decision tree analysis has so far been ignored. Reverting to the dice/coin decision choice shown in the first decision tree, suppose that the 500p would not be received until a year from now. The present value of this sum of money to us now—assuming that money spare can earn 10 per cent—is $500 \times 0{\cdot}909 = 454{\cdot}5$p. Since we have to multiply this sum by the probability (1/2), the total expected value now, of this choice, is $1/2 \times 454{\cdot}5\text{p} = 227{\cdot}25$p. To take account of time the third rule, therefore, needs to be modified. It should read:

At every decision point, choose that course of action which has the highest expected *present* value.

The precise rate of interest to be used for the discount factor, and all the other considerations relating to time, have been covered in the preceding two chapters. Incorporation of these results in decision tree analysis by this modification of the third rule is comparatively simple and straightforward.

7.5.3. Utility

Until now it has always been assumed that the true worth of the expected value can be accurately arrived at by multiplying the probability by the sum of money involved. But is this really so? Is a businessman for example always prepared to gamble on a project which presents a half chance of a superlative profit, but a half chance of an enforced liquidation, just because the mathematical expression of the expected value of this 'risky' choice is a little higher than that of some other steady 'safe' choice. People do not operate like this. The subjective value, the real value to us, as opposed to the mathematical expected value, is referred to as utility. These values of course will vary from person to person and corporation to corporation. How can we go about determining them?

Suppose I go in for one of the top commercial T.V. games in which, at any stage, I can either continue or stop, and the cash prizes get higher and higher. Let us say that I have arrived at the position where I can either take the money I have already won, or go on for the jackpot of (say) £100 000 which is available in one of the two boxes facing me. If I choose the wrong box I get nothing. The odds of getting the jackpot are obviously 50–50 (i.e., $\frac{1}{2}$ as a fraction). On a strict mathematical basis I should take the chance if the money I have already won is £50 000 or less. But in real life a sum of, perhaps, £20 000 certain is probably thought of as being as valuable as a half chance of £100 000. On a graph with money values plotted against preference this will be indicated by the point A (see Fig. 7.6).

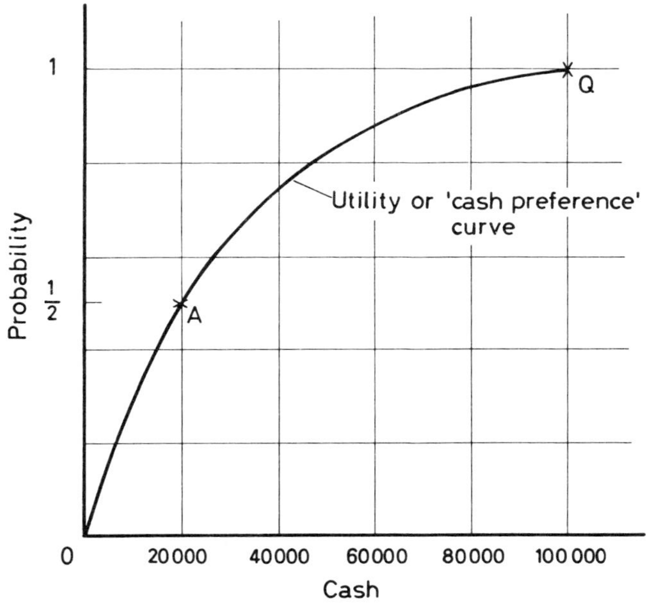

Figure 7.6.

Two other points must lie on the preference curve. The origin O must certainly do so, since the value of no chance at all of £100 000 is obviously nil. Similarly the value of £100 000 absolutely certain is precisely £100 000 so the point Q must be on it too. The preference curve has been drawn freehand through the points OAQ. Theoretically other preference points should also be put in. In practice these three will usually give a good indication of the curve.

The strict mathematical preference 'curve' is obviously the straight line OQ (it is this line which effectively has been used in all the decision tree analyses so far). But the conservative preference curve OAQ more truly reflects real life preferences, and it is this one which should be used in decision tree analysis. When dealing with a business or corporation, the use of a 'personal' preference curve, such as this one, as a substitute for the entrepreneurial preference curve of the business is not correct, unless it is a one man firm. The preference curve for each decision making body needs to be established by techniques such as the one we have outlined. Moreover, such curves need to be updated regularly, since feelings change with the passing of time.

7.5.4. Stochastic decision trees

In the decision tree, shown in Fig. 7.4, there were only two possibilities that we considered, if the decision made was to purchase four. These corresponded to a demand for four, or a demand for five. The associated probabilities were 0·8 and 0·2. If we enlarge the scale of the example and imagine that the decision under discussion was whether to purchase forty, rather than four, it is almost certain that the possibilities would be greater in number than two. They might well range from say thirty-seven to forty-three. The associated probabilities (as perhaps in Table 7.7, for example) would be much more difficult to work out.

Table 7.7

Demand	*Probability*
43	0·05
42	0·10
41	0·20
40	0·30
39	0·20
38	0·10
37	0·05

If the scale of the example is increased still further, so that the decision is whether to purchase 400 or not, the range of the possibilities will be likely to be much greater still. The practical problem is not that of dealing with this increased number. Computerized decision tree analysis is now, as we have said, a very quick and effective tool. The real problem is that no decision maker would find it easy to assign even the simple probabilities as in Table 7.7 above, let alone for the more complex case when the scale was further increased. All that he would probably be prepared to estimate is what the most likely value would be, and what the extreme values are, that is those values outside of which the probabilities are so slight that they can be ignored. If we make the assumption that the distribution round the most likely value is normal, then it is possible to replace the large number of discrete possibilities by a continuous distribution curve. This curve will be the normal curve whose mean is the most likely value and whose base extends 3σ, i.e., three standard deviations, either side of this mean to the two extreme values.

This stochastic tree approach is basically a simulation technique.* At each chance event the branches are replaced by continuous probability distributions. At the chance event a random selection is made by the computer on each iteration. This decision tree approach produces results which themselves are in the form of probability distributions for each of the possible decisions. They can then be compared by taking into account both the expected value and the shape of each probability distribu-

* Compare with the example given in the appendix on risk at the end of chapter 6.

tion. One decision may show a curve with a high mean expected value, but with a long 'tail' extending so far as to include the possibility of a substantial loss. Another branch may show a curve with a slightly lower mean expected value, but with a probability distribution clustered tightly around this mean. The decision maker can then weigh the benefits of a high expected value choice, but one which has a high variation, against another less rewarding though more stable choice.

Some computer programmes for decision tree analysis proceed on the basis of evaluating all possible paths. Others eliminate branches of the tree on some specified basis such as that of possessing both a lower expected value and a higher variance than an alternative branch. All sophisticated programmes allow for the introduction of sensitivity analysis and the effects of the difference between utility and cash value.

7.6. Business use of decision tree analysis (D.T.A.)

In the *Harvard Business Review* of May/June, 1970, Mr Brown, an Associate Professor of Business Administration at the University of Michigan, reported on the use made by U.S. companies of decision tree analysis. The survey was conducted in 1969 and some twenty American companies were investigated. It must be noted that the mix of companies in the survey was based on their known use or interest in decision tree analysis. Even on this artificial selection basis the results were striking enough.

The experience of the Du Pont organization which pioneered the application of D.T.A.—much as it pioneered network analysis some ten years earlier in time—is a good point at which to start. Du Pont first used D.T.A. as a serious management technique around 1960. According to the Manager of the Management Services Division, D.T.A. has still not reached the point where it has a major impact on high level decisions. This failure, he argues, has been mainly due to the absence of educational effort aimed at the senior decision makers. At a slightly lower level he finds that D.T.A. is being commonly applied in association with conventional analysis. Frequently, it has been used as a scientific tool to support the main argument.

At General Electric—another company that has been active in employing D.T.A. for several years—decision theory has been found to be a useful tool in the area of plant applications. More than five-hundred instances of the application of computerized D.T.A. have been recorded there in the past four years.

Not all companies that have tried D.T.A. have been so marginally impressed as Du Pont and General Electric. The Ford Motor Company has passed some 200 senior executives through a brief D.T.A. course in the last few years yet, except for some middle management applications, little use has been made of decision theory by the organization as a whole. In support of D.T.A. it is argued there that this is probably due in part to the natural reluctance of very senior managers to adjust to such unconventional techniques.

From the whole spectrum of the twenty companies in the survey one or two clear findings emerged. The first and perhaps the most important was that the success or otherwise of D.T.A. in an organization depended on the way it was applied. Most successful was the direct approach in which the decision theory analyst worked directly with the senior executive, was responsible to him and reported the results straight to him. The least successful was the 'arms length' approach in which the analyst was employed and controlled from a central services department. In such cases, the executive seemed to regard the analyst as a rival whose aim was to disrupt the decisions that he, the executive, had arrived at by less sophisticated techniques, but which he intuitively felt to be right.

The extreme example of the 'arms length' analyst is the outside consultant and the survey suggested that consulting firms did relatively little D.T.A. work for their clients. McKinsey's were the one significant exception to this rule. In parenthesis, it may be remarked that the reverse situation seems to apply in the U.K. Here, very little use is yet made of D.T.A. even by the big corporations. However, some consultants do use D.T.A. to support their conclusions.

This dichotomy between the intimate and the arms length approach highlights one other important feature of D.T.A., which emerged from the survey. It seems that senior executives were understandably reluctant to put down figures when the information available was relatively uncertain, but, much more importantly, disliked disclosing some of the true reasons that entered into their private decision making. Sometimes these reasons were simply that the information was secret or confidential. Sometimes, however, they were much more intangible. The survey included one instance of an elaborate analysis of possible locations for a European subsidiary. The logical manifest reasons were, in reality, dominated by the subjective factor that the personnel wanted to be near the International School in Geneva.

At first sight the existence of such irrational factors might seem to be an argument against decision theory. The reverse, however, is really the case. Decision tree analysis, because of its logical form and layout, draws attention to and brings out into the open these apparently illogical but emotionally significant factors which play a part in decision making. In a sense, the whole purpose of this book is to concentrate on these factors, to try and bring them to the surface, and finally to attempt to put money values on them, either directly or by inference.

8. The measurement of management

8.1. Introduction

The phrase 'measurement or evaluation of management', in the specific sense of measuring in quantifiable units, has been much used recently. Generally its usage has been confined to the problem of finding the value that senior employees have to a company. In this sense, employees, or 'management', are regarded as an asset to the corporation. Sometimes they are compared with fixed assets, such as machinery and plant; more often with intangible assets such as goodwill or copyright. If they are an asset, then, so the argument runs, they should be included in the Balance Sheet along with all the other assets that go to make up a profit making corporation. The importance of this new view of the Balance Sheet and Profit and Loss Account is unquestionable, and it is tempting to follow it up here.* But, although such statements of account attempt to record the situation in much more meaningful terms than current presentations, they are still statements of what the position is at the present, or, more accurately, of what it has been in the immediate past. From a decision point of view any evaluations which record the past are irrelevant (other than as providing a guide to the future). All we are concerned with is the effect that any change in management will have, and how to evaluate such changes. Since we are concerned with the effect on the business, we need to consider the manager and his department as our basic unit.

Theoretically there seem to be three possible approaches to measuring any change in the efficiency of a department by its manager. These are:

1. A direct test made on the individual manager of his knowledge, and an assessment of the academic correctness of his approach to the man/machine management problems in his department. Many such tests exist. The National Foundation for Education Research in England and Wales lists around 300 tests. No doubt these tests do measure

* A brief outline of this new approach is given in an appendix to this chapter.

accurately certain things such as specialized knowledge, I.Q., and so on. The only problem is whether there is necessarily any real correlation at all between these tests of knowledge and aptitude, and that effective skill in management which we wish to quantify. Tests really measure ability in tests. Even skill in management is not an absolute factor. The skill required for one job may be very different from that required by another.

2. A direct check of the manager's output *at his job*. Sometimes it is possible to measure directly an increase in the working capacity of the individual manager. This approach can be quite effective at operator, or even supervisor level, but top level managerial efficiency, with its emphasis on high ranging intangible decisions, is, obviously, very difficult to quantify this way.
3. A direct check made, on the business, of the benefit to the *business*, measured in terms of the increased profits or decreased costs provided by the department.

Unquestionably, the last of these choices is the one that it is best to follow up. We are, after all, trying to measure the benefit that increased managerial efficiency brings to the company, not to the individual. Since we are really trying to evaluate this change in a manager's performance, presumably some scheme, which gives standards of performance for the managers will be of some help? Management By Objectives (MBO) sets out to provide just this sort of plan. Within this framework we need of course, as well, techniques which will enable us to measure variations in managerial efficiency from this preset standard. First, however, let us discuss the basic structure.

8.2. Management By Objectives (MBO)

Suppose that our business is a medium/large engineering company and (just for the sake of exposition) assume that we are only concerned with the next twelve months. The over-all aim of management for this next year will normally be to increase profits to a certain figure, subject as we have seen, to various provisos as to size and security. This exact figure will be determined by a number of factors, such as the previous year's profit figure of the company, by some measure of what the company *should* be earning (e.g., that of a similar sized company in the same industry),* by certain factors special to the company in the coming year (for instance, the effect of heavy promotional advertising in the previous year), and finally and most importantly, by the share of the market that it is

* The rate of return (before tax) in the engineering industry in the U.K. has been around 14 per cent—that is just above the national average of 13 per cent.

estimated that the company can achieve in the coming year. All these factors taken together will give the planned net profit figure for the coming year. This is the objective for the company as a whole. For the very top level of management, this is the preset standard. But net profit consists of sales less expenses, so, at the second level, we must have standards for sales and costs.

Sales. The overall sales figure itself will be made up of export sales and the various home area sales. Each area—to pursue this particular 'branch' further—is made up of the total of the sales of the various representatives in that area. We are now down to each individual salesman's objective. A salesman's key objective in terms of sales will only be achieved if he is

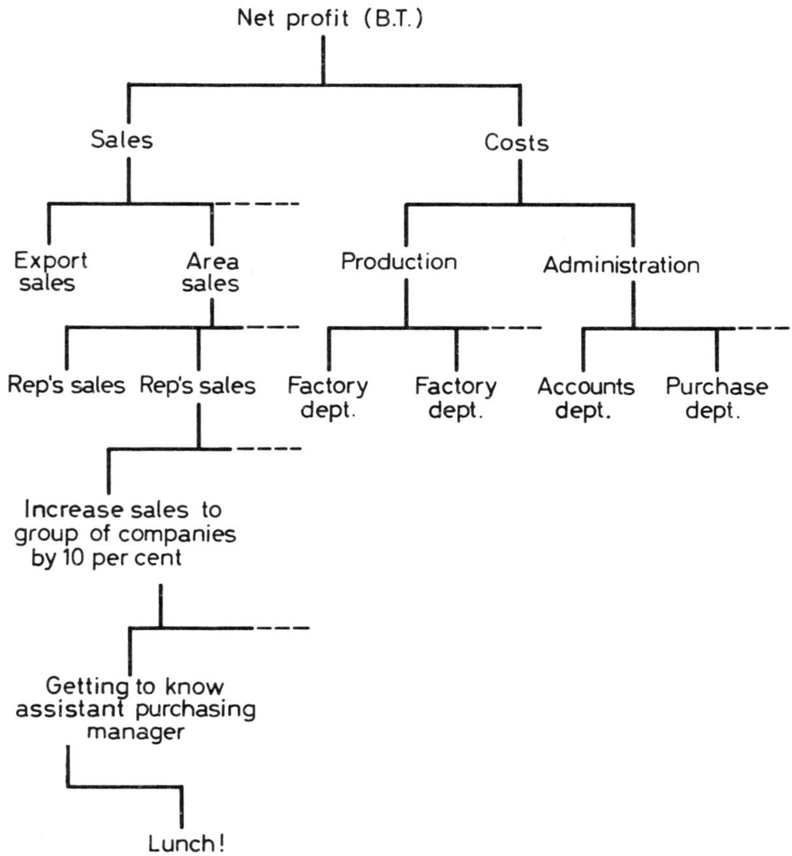

Figure 8.1.

successful in his subsidiary objectives. One of these might be to increase his sales to an important group of companies by 10 per cent. This, in turn, may mean getting to know an assistant purchasing manager at the head office of this group of companies, and getting some valuable orders from him. Getting to know the assistant purchase manager may depend initially on his agreeing to a lunch meeting arranged, perhaps, through a mutual acquaintance. This will be the key objective at this level. This is the way business works! Figure 8.1 shows the position set out in the form of a tree chart.

Can we now determine the benefits from increased sales? To what extent will any increase enable an Area Sales Manager to reach his sales target, and what effect will this have on overall profitability? Fortunately, this connection is easy to make, since any increase in sales brings a cash benefit to the company equal to 'sales *less* variable costs'. This direct or marginal costing method has been used throughout this book. Nevertheless, a simple example is included here to show how the approach would work out.

Let us suppose that one of the products made is a small hovercraft, designed for leisure use, and that the standard selling price of the hovercraft is £245. Present production is around forty per month. Sales' revenue is, therefore, £9800. Of the total monthly costs of £9350, fixed costs account for some £6550 and variable costs £2800. Variable costs per hovercraft are, therefore, $\frac{2800}{40} = £70$. For each additional unit sold the marginal income will be the sales value (£245) less the variable costs (£70), i.e., £175. (Fixed costs, by definition, do not alter and so do not come into the calculation.) It follows that, if sales can be increased by just over ten hovercraft, the cash benefit to the company is £1750.

Production. Can we use the same approach for the other branches of the tree, i.e., the production and administration departments? Let us consider these seriatim. If M.B.O. is used, each factory manager will know what his objective is in terms of the number of units he must produce at standard cost or better. Most likely his production is determined for him by the sales side of the business in any case. What he can do is to reduce costs by efficient production. Provided that he has been given an objective based on a standard cost of each of the types of units produced and provided his actual costs are assessed, then the variance gives a precise indication of how well he is doing. However, this is subject to two important provisos.

First, such information can only be obtained if his department is a cost centre and an accurate system for calculating standard costs is in operation. Second, many costs in a department are outside the control of the manager (e.g., allocations of general overheads, materials price as opposed to materials usage variance, etc.). All costs must, therefore, be split into controllable and uncontrollable costs. The manager can only be assessed on the former.

It is important to realize that an individual split up of costs must be made for each manager whose performance is being rated. Any division of the variances between controllable and uncontrollable, is only likely to be appropriate for one manager. Taking our example, the materials price variance is not a controllable variance for the factory manager although it may be for the purchasing manager.

Assessing which costs are controllable and how they should be calculated for each manager is crucial to the assessment of the value of a manager's performance and the benefit he gives to the firm. It is also rather technical and specialized. All this work has therefore been relegated to an appendix at the end of this chapter.

Reverting to the first problem of the provision of accurate standard costs, traditional standard costing techniques are generally adequate when the volume of production remains sensibly constant, so that figures based on past historical data can be used with only comparatively minor adjustments, such as for increase in prices of raw materials, labour rates, etc.

When the volume of production varies substantially, a more accurate assessment of the division between variable and fixed costs than that provided by conventional accounting methods is required.

By way of an example, suppose we are concerned with one department only and that this department has two outputs M1 and M2. The direct costs of M1 M2 (i.e., direct labour, direct materials and direct expenses) are, we suppose, some a_1 a_2 per unit. In marginal costing terminology, we would say that these are the marginal costs per unit of M1 M2. If x_1 x_2 units are produced the total marginal cost is $a_1 x_1 + a_2 x_2$. To arrive at total cost we have to add the fixed costs C (say). If we split C up into c_1 and c_2, as between M1 M2, in some arbitrary manner, then $C = c_1 + c_2$ and total cost Y (say) is given by:

$$Y = a_1 x_1 + a_2 x_2 + C$$

Assuming we have a series of values for Y, x_1 and x_2 going back over a number of months, we shall be able to use the technique of regression analysis to determine the true values for a_1, a_2 and C. It must be remembered that if the results cover a substantial period of time, and the incidence of inflation is likely to be material, then all costs should be reduced to a common base in time. The only remaining problem is how to ensure that the fixed overhead costs are fairly split up between the products.

From the point of view with which we are concerned, that is the *alterations* in standard costs due to changes in throughput (which in general will be externally generated), the allocation of fixed costs between products is *irrelevant*. However, in order not to leave the problem utterly unresolved the following points are made for the record.

In a simple case, such as that outlined, with only two products, it is probable that the figure for C, the total fixed costs, as thrown up by the analysis, will be fairly substantial. If it is necessary to arrive at a total cost for each product, the split of C into c_1 and c_2 will be important. Since we have arrived at an accurate figure for the direct costs for each product, it may seem realistic to split C into c_1 and c_2, in the ratio of these direct costs. Of course, it must be emphasized that any allocation of overheads is by nature arbitrary, but a split along these lines does make use of the available information.

When the number of different products or throughputs is substantial, as will generally be the case, both the absolute value of C, the fixed costs, and its value in relation to total costs is likely to decline. Consequently, the split up of the fixed costs to each of the products is likely to be better and product standard costs prepared on this basis should be much more realistic.

Administration. Finally, let us consider the various services and control departments in the head office. Each department may require some special additional analysis, but the technique outlined below, is of fairly general application. The accounts department is central to the financial analysis of the whole business organization; moreover the actual performance of the accounts department is very difficult to assess. It provides, therefore, a good basic example to pursue in some depth.

The main problem arises because the output of the accounts department, like all service departments, is not exogenous;* almost all the work is for other departments in the organization. Moreover, the demand (e.g., for cost figures, monthly profit and loss accounts, estimates for contracts, budgets, etc.) probably varies from month to month, certainly from year to year. How can we assign 'costs' to the preparation of these figures? In theory it might seem possible to find the man-hours spent by the various members of the staff on each of the types of accounts and management figures. Primitive records, analogous to these, are kept by clerks in professional accountants' offices with a view to charging out the work done subsequently to clients. Such records are never kept in the accounts department of an ongoing business organization. Not only would it take up far too much of the clerks' time, but even to try to do so is to attempt the impossible. When the machine operator invoices sales, should this go down as sales day-book analysis, or as monthly or yearly profit and loss account work, or as preparation of customers' accounts, or as providing the basic figures for analysing sales price variances and volume variances

* Here used in the sense of 'outside the business'.

for standard costing? It is, of course, all of these and more. Clearly, some different form of analysis is required. As a first step let us consider what the *outputs* of the accounts department are. A typical list, presented under main headings, for convenience, might be:

1. *Monthly work:* Monthly profit and loss accounts for the business as a whole. Departmental profit and loss accounts. Lists of debtors outstanding (ageing schedules). Preparation of private salaries. Preparation and updating of short-term flexible expense budgets for the departments. Cash budgets for the business as a whole.
2. *Standard cost figures* of products, by batches, and/or by departments or processes. Variance analysis.
3. *Estimates:* Compilation of estimates for contracts, proposed new products, etc.
4. *Capital investment appraisal:* DCF calculations for new factories, plant, machinery, lease or buy choices, etc.
5. *Yearly profit and loss accounts and balance sheet* (and the associated work with auditors), work for the A.G.M., etc.
6. *Sundry work*—e.g., share transfer work, analysis of competition, trade associates, possible merger or take-over companies, etc. Balance sheets and other special work. Break-even charts, etc.

The amount of work involved in some of these (e.g., the monthly profit and loss accounts and the ageing schedules) may well remain sensibly constant; others, such as the compilation of costing estimates and capital investment calculations, are likely to vary considerably. Figures will certainly be available for the volume of work undertaken for each of the individual items either, month by month or quarter by quarter. Past cost figures for the accounts department, taken as a whole, should be equally readily available. The only qualification as to the suitability of these figures for our purpose is that they must all have been prepared on the same basis (e.g., as to overhead allocation).

In order to determine the total benefit provided by the services of the accounts department, we must first find the cost associated with each item in the above list.

If we call the cost of the individual items

$$b_1 b_2 b_3 --- b_n$$

and, if we suppose that the number of units of output of the various items are

$$x_1\ x_2\ x_3\ ---\ x_n$$

then the total cost T (say) of the accounts department will be given by the equation,

$$T = b_0 + b_1 x_1 + b_2 x_2 + b_3 x_3 + \text{---} + b_n x_n$$

Since we assume that we know what the past outputs have been, we shall have available a series of figures going back in time for x_1 x_2, etc.

For the most recent time period (period 1, say)

$$T_1 = b_0 + b_1 x_{11} + b_2 x_{12} + b_3 x_{13} + \text{---} + b_n x_{1n}$$

and for the period before this,

$$T_2 = b_0 + b_1 x_{21} + b_2 x_{22} + b_3 x_{23} + \text{---} + b_n x_{2n}$$

and so on.

The standard statistical technique for multiple correlation analysis can be applied to these data and will give the best values for b_0 b_1 b_2 b_3---b_n on a least squares basis. Sometimes, it is possible, although impossibly tedious, to work out a graphical 'solution' of these linear equations by trial and error. With any suitable programme, however, the computer will provide the answer in a matter of seconds. All this has been covered in §4.5, the section on regression analysis.

The analysis should not go back much in time. The effect of inflation on the total cost figures can be taken into account by uprating the early values for T by a suitable index to the equivalent values today, or, more conventionally, by using the earliest period as a base, and adjusting all the later figures to this base. The end result of this analysis will be a series of figures for the costs of unit outputs of the various items of the accounting department. Consequently, at any time we can lay down what the relationship should be between cost and the associated total output. Hence we can set an objective—a standard might be a better word— in the sense that for any output there is a corresponding cost. Therefore, the work of the accountancy office can be measured against a known standard. It is easy to see that this approach—*mutatis mutandis*—can be applied to *all* service departments. Although it is virtually impossible to quantify such department's production by the more conventional methods (since no profit directly accrues from their work) regression analysis can put money figures on their various outputs.

Many criticisms can be levelled against this approach. For instance, how can it cope with:

(*a*) Changes in staff.

(*b*) Changes in office layout (e.g., the introduction of new business machines —even a computer!).

(*c*) Taking account of the *quality* of the work done.

Briefly:

Changes in staff will iron out if the company we are dealing with is fairly large. It is, in any case, the responsibility of the department manager to see that he has good staff. This is part of his job. He is being rated on this, and it is precisely this which we are taking into account.

If he inherits a poor subordinate who has a responsible job, it may be some time before this situation can be satisfactorily dealt with. (This can be seen as an example of the intractible general problem of allocating long-term liabilities to the short term for assessment purposes.) If the subordinate has been there a while, his work will have been included in the standard costs which have, after all, only been arrived at by analysis based on historical data.

If it is still regarded as necessary to take account of the effect of one or more subordinates in the analysis, the best approach is to use dummy variables. In parenthesis, one beneficial by-product of such a method is that the parameter associated with the dummy variable gives a value for the subordinate. This way, even the work of assistant managers and other subordinates can be quantified.

Better business machines will improve output. If the improvement arises from the choice of better and more appropriate machines, then this, too, is to the credit of the manager, and will improve the department's output. But if the improvement arises from a technological break-through —the benefit from which is generally available—then this might seem to defeat the analysis. One defence is that we are dealing with short-term solutions, and such break-throughs may not arise within this period. Again, however, if we introduce a dummy variable into the regression analysis (see §4.5.2) we can still bring in figures from both before and after the introduction of the new machine.

Finally, the matter of quality. To some extent this is something with which the analysis cannot cope. But this is only the case in respect of the quality of work done, or advice given at very high levels. At most levels (e.g., in the preparation of costs, budgets, or private payroll figures) if quality of output suffers, what usually happens is that the work is returned to the accounts department. More time must, therefore, be spent in putting it right. And this, of course, is covered by the analysis.

8.3. Recapitulation of techniques

What we have shown so far is that techniques do exist which can first measure, and then translate into money terms, the output from all the parts of a business. Since we can measure the output in money terms, we can evaluate the benefit from more efficient manager control. We can list the techniques as:

1. *The marginal revenue approach:* This is mainly applicable to sales, but the approach can also be used for low levels in the production process. For instance a machine operator who increases his production will benefit the company by the marginal revenue (that is

sales less variable costs). When the operator is working at a machine which is part of a long production line, the net benefit is not so easy to isolate. We need to assess the contribution that the operator makes to the production line. To arrive at this benefit, the revenue in the above calculation must be replaced by a transfer price for his finished product. The simplest calculation of the transfer price will be one based on the standard cost of his work. If the operator receives units which have already been through various processes, the net benefit from his work is:

Transfer price of unit after his operation *less* transfer price before his operation and raw materials used in this operation.

2. *Standard costing:* This is applicable, in theory, to any department which is a cost centre. In practice, its most appropriate use is found in a factory department in which measurable units are produced. The most important step in this analysis is to split the variances into those which are genuinely controllable, from the point of view of the manager in charge, and those which are not. The detailed work is given in the appendix.

3. *Regression analysis:* This is most suitable for service departments or, indeed, any department whose output is non-exogenous. Some substantial problems occur when applying these techniques, and many of these difficulties have already been briefly considered.

   In operator costing, the calculation of the transfer price depends on the appropriateness and accuracy of standard costing. In the factory department, the corresponding analysis depends on the correct money assessment of the units produced. This will be simple if there is just one department and its product is sold, i.e., goes to final demand. If we have a series of departments, then the problem of assessing the transfer price arises. This problem is entirely analogous to the transfer price on a production line. Fortunately, its solution by input output analysis is comparatively easy.

4. *Input output analysis.* In §4.7, the section on this type of analysis, a simple technique for measuring the output of a department in money terms, was arrived at. This technique was applicable when the output of the department was not in direct sales to the public, but was in the form of partly finished goods to another department. As we have said, this approach can also be applied, *mutatis mutandis*, to the operator costing problem. It seems, therefore, that input-output analysis needs to be included as the final basic technique.

8.3.1. Integration of techniques

At first sight all these may seem to be separate techniques for dealing with different problems. In reality they are all aspects of the same problem. The problem is that of first assessing what the costs should be corresponding to varying levels of production or throughput of services or goods, and then splitting up these costs into those that are controllable and those that are not.

Our treatment of these has been a little superficial, but at least it is evident that some attempt can be made to shed the cold light of quantitative analysis on these dark areas.

Appendix on controllable variances

It is not proposed to go very deeply into variance analysis as such other than to explain the extent to which our treatment differs from the usual approach. A great number of excellent books have been written on conventional standard costing and variance analysis. The Institute of Cost and Works Accountants manual *Budgetary Control, Standard costing, Material control, and Production control*, for example, gives a detailed explanation of the layout of accounts for a standard costing system on traditional lines.

Here we are principally concerned to point out that many of the variances prepared in this way have a very limited meaning. Most of these variances—to restate our position—contain certain elements of cost due to external factors over which no control is possible. It follows that the first step must be to separate each variance into two parts. First, that part over which the person concerned has no control (and therefore cannot properly be judged), and second, that part over which he has control (and can therefore be properly judged). In practice, the division is not at all easy to make and each variance requires separate treatment. The split.up for each cost variance is discussed below.

Materials price variance: (A purchasing manager's performance appraisal variance.) The conventional expression of the materials price variance is:

$$\text{Actual price} - \text{Standard price}$$

If the actual price paid is in excess of the current marketing price then this would, prima facie, appear to be due to bad purchasing. So as a first step we split this variance into:

$$(\text{Actual price} - \text{Current marketing price}) + (\text{Current marketing price} - \text{Standard price})$$

The latter variance is uncontrollable from the point of view of the person concerned with prices, i.e., the purchasing manager. It is really a *planning* or *standard setters variance*. In the long run, all such variances must be taken out from the conventional variances and shown on a separate list; this way it will be possible to see how good the setting of standard costs has been. One additional advantage follows from this which has been noted before. The very fact that their own work will subsequently be the subject of the same type of analysis must make the standard setters more careful, responsible and accurate in their own work.

The former variance could be called a *purchasing managers' appraisal variance.* Left in this form, however, it is doubtful if it has much more significance than the original materials price variance. What we still have not taken account of, is that the difference is probably due to a deliberate policy of forward purchasing. This may well have been done, either with a view to getting bulk quantity discounts, or possibly in expectation of a general market increase; on the other hand it may be because of above average selective purchasing, i.e., an ability to jump in and clinch a bargain at the right time and place.

We cannot, therefore, appraise the true value of forward purchasing until the actual prices become available later. Moreover, we need to increase this actual price paid by the amount of those additional costs incurred by the forward purchasing. These costs will include all stockholding charges, such as additional insurance, warehousing and storing costs, interest on capital tied up, and any wastage or depreciation in value of the stock of materials held. There may be some additional savings made in bulk purchasing if the costs of making one large order are less than that of making several small orders. However, it is unlikely that these savings will be realized in the sense that they will actually result in any greater cash flow from profits. All that will probably happen is that the clerks in the purchasing department will have slightly less work to do; it is unlikely that they will be paid any less in wages.

When all relevant holding costs have been taken into account, the difference between the actual price and the current price will give a good indication of the effectiveness of the purchasing policy for comparison purposes. The absolute value of this variance is not as important as the ratio of the variance to the total amount of purchases which have been analysed. So that

$$\text{Variance} = \text{Actual price} + \text{Holding costs} - \text{Current market price}$$

$$\text{and the Variance index} = \frac{\text{Actual price} + \text{Holding costs} - \text{Current market price}}{\text{Purchases}}$$

It is evident that the variance index can usefully be calculated for each of the major types of materials purchased.

Materials usage variance: (A production manager's performance appraisal variance.)

The same approach can be used for the materials usage variance. The conventional variance is

$$\text{Actual usage} - \text{Standard usage}$$

and we can split this into

$$(\text{Actual usage} - \text{Optimum usage}) + (\text{Optimum usage} - \text{Standard usage})$$

To determine the optimum usage we must take into account only those machines, labour, and materials actually available to the production manager, and calculate from these figures the optimum usage which could have been obtained from using these resources to their maximum advantage. This calculation will have to be made at the end of the period under review, since the availability of these resources cannot be known in advance. Just to illustrate this briefly, consider the rather extreme example when either a power breakdown in the factory area or a National strike occurs. Or—more prosaically—consider the situation when poor materials are purchased. Even this will be beyond the control of the production manager. Any factors not within the manager's control must always be eliminated.

All these calculations will have to be made in the management information or management services centre—or whatever name may be used for the control department. As we shall see later, the work of this department will be central to the analysis of all management performance; in particular, it is absolutely vital when this appraisal work is being done through the use of controllable variances.

Once again the absolute value of this variance needs to be related to some measure of the quantities involved to have much meaning for control purposes.

Hence,

$$\text{Variance} = \text{Actual usage} - \text{Optimum usage}$$

$$\text{and Variance index} = \frac{\text{Actual usage} - \text{Optimum usage}}{\text{Usage}}$$

Mix variance: (Primarily a production manager's performance appraisal variance.)

At first sight it might seem that the accountants' mix variance, as it stands, would give a good guide as to whether the factory manager is using the optimum proportion of raw materials in production.

The calculation of a mix variance is based on a standard specification for each unit of output. To take an example, let us suppose this is

	£
2 lb of *X* at £3	6
1 lb of *Y* at £4	4
3 lb	£10

and let us further suppose that 100 units were produced and the actual quantities of raw materials used were 240 lb of *X* and 105 lb of *Y*. The conventional calculation of the mix variance is in two stages:

First, we apply the standard proportion (i.e., 2/3 and 1/3) to the total actual usage of (240 + 105 =) 345 lb to give 230 lb and 115 lb.

Second, we apply the standard price to these proportions and deduct the actual amounts used, also at standard price. This gives

		X		*Y*
		£		£
Actual	240 × 3 =	720	105 × 4 =	420
Standard	230 × 3 =	690	115 × 4 =	460
		30		(−40)

This traditional calculation has been worked through in some detail to see if, indeed, it is really as useful as it might seem to be.

First it must be noted that the mix variance ignores price variations. All prices are taken to be standard. What the mix variance does show is the difference between the cost as it is and the cost as it would be if the same total weight of materials had been used but in the standard ratio. But why make the comparison with the *standard ratio*? What we are really interested in is the optimum ratio (i.e., the ratio giving the lowest total cost, given the prevailing price of materials and availability of machines and labour). Once again the department that will have to work this out will be the management information or control centre. Inevitably this will be a tedious and costly job if the work has to be done by hand. Conversely, if access to a computer terminal is available then, once a suitable programme has been written, the information can rapidly be obtained. Any substantial company that is operating in competition with other large efficient organizations must, we are saying, have some central information collecting and planning department with access to a computer, if it is to survive in today's business world. The need for such an information and control department with access to a computer is thrown up more and more clearly as we realize how complex must be the analysis of the variances for them to have any real meaning for appraisal and control purposes. The standard setters' section will be separated from this information centre. This separation is important, since the management information centre must be in a position to be able to check on the effectiveness of the standard setting. The two functions are quite different and the departments must be kept apart.

Our conventional mix variance, that is

$$\text{Actual mix} - \text{Standard mix}$$

needs therefore to be split up into

$$(\text{Actual mix} - \text{Optimum mix}) + (\text{Optimum mix} - \text{Standard mix})$$

The former variance is a production manager's appraisal variance, and the latter is a standard setter's variance.

The factory manager's mix index is

$$\frac{\text{Actual mix} - \text{Optimum mix}}{\text{Mix}}$$

Determining the optimum mix for this variance must be based on those raw materials which are actually available to the factory manager. If optimum mix has been departed from because the purchasing department has not ensured that the requisite materials are available, then this will be a part of the purchasing manager's appraisal variance, and not part of the production manager's.

One final point remains to be made. Optimum mix could, perhaps, have been obtained, but at too high a price in terms of money paid out for skilled supervisory labour. A situation parallel to this occurs with the materials usage variance. There, good wastage figures may be obtained, but at the expense of excessive utilization of labour. It is clear that many variances are interdependent. To look at each only in isolation is to obtain a series of sub-optimal solutions.

Labour time (efficiency) variance: (A production manager's appraisal variance.)
The calculation of the conventional labour efficiency variance is

$$(\text{Actual hours} - \text{Standard hours}) \times \text{Standard rate}$$

which can be split into

$$(\text{Actual hours} - \text{Optimum hours}) \times \text{Standard rate} + (\text{Optimum hours} - \text{Standard hours}) \times \text{Standard rate}$$

The optimum hours can differ from the standard hours for a variety of reasons. The labour efficiency variance, indeed, provides a very clear example of the interdependence of variances. A good efficiency variance may easily be obtained, but at the expense of other factors. Specifically:

1. Quality may have suffered.
2. Spoilage/wastage may have increased.
3. Considerable overtime may have been worked because of increased production. During long overtime periods tiredness will inevitably reduce the efficiency of the labour force.
4. Hours worked are presumed in the calculation to vary directly with volume. If, for instance, the output is increased by 100 per cent, the standard hours will certainly be double, since they are based on a fixed standard for each unit of output. But will double the number of hours, in fact, have been worked in batch production? The initial 'set up' and 'ending' times will probably be much the

same whether 2 or 2000 units are to be produced. Moreover, if 2000 are put on the production line then it is likely that the later units will be put through much more rapidly as greater skill is acquired in dealing with the particular sequence of operations. This is the application of the 'learning' curve. Both these considerations are ignored in the conventional efficiency variance, yet they will both tend to make actual unit cost decrease with increased volume. These factors must be taken into account when arriving at a proper appraisal variance for the production manager.

The labour efficiency index, therefore, is

$$\frac{(\text{Actual hours} - \text{Optimum hours})}{\text{Hours}} \times \text{Standard rate}$$

Labour rate variance: (A personnel manager's appraisal variance.)
This variance is usually expressed as

$$(\text{Actual rate} - \text{Standard rate}) \times \text{Actual hours}$$

For appraisal purposes it is a little unfortunate that this rate is weighted by the actual hours worked. Standard hours would seem to be more suitable. However, it is normal to use actual hours since, if this is done, the labour efficiency variance and the labour rate variance, together, add up to the total labour variance.

The labour rate variance can be split up into

$$(\text{Actual rate} - \text{Market rate}) \times \text{Actual hours} + (\text{Market rate} - \text{Standard rate}) \times \text{Actual hours}$$

It might seem that our analysis of labour rate variance should follow a similar pattern to the materials price variance. After all the personnel manager, just like the purchasing manager, is trying to beat the market and should presumably be judged by how well he succeeds. The only difference is that one is operating in the labour market, and the other in the materials market.

It is doubtful, however, if labour rates and materials prices are at all analogous. A quantity of raw material to a given B.S. specification will be much the same whoever the supplier may be. Consequently, if the purchasing manager can buy at cheaper than market price, this difference is the precise measure of the benefit he has gained for his company. But people are not like materials. There will be no true gain to the company when the personnel manager engages men at under market price if they have to be given more training, their performance at work is less satisfying, and they leave after only a short time so that the whole cycle has to be started again. The costs that we need to take into account when appraising the performance of the personnel department must therefore include

(*a*) any additional expenses in the personnel department (caused by the necessity to continually take on replacement labour),
(*b*) additional costs of training, and
(*c*) any additional production costs due to the lower efficiency or skill of the labour.

Moreover, the effects of any alterations in the costs of welfare facilities (canteen, sports ground, rest rooms, etc.) must also be taken account of, as this money is spent with a view to getting and keeping staff. These considerations may not play much part in the decision of a prospective employee as to whether or not he will join the company, but they are likely to have some considerable significance as to whether he stays on as a satisfied member of the work force, or incurs further labour turnover expenses by seeking employment elsewhere.

From all this it follows that, in order to appraise properly the personnel manager's performance, we need to include certain changes in welfare costs, costs of his own department, and those changes in training costs caused by differing levels in capacity and skill of the newly engaged labour.

Overhead variances

So far the pattern of our analysis has been to break down the relatively simple conventional variances into much more complex variances for control purposes. The position is different with overhead variances since those overheads which are *allocated* to production, sales, personnel, purchasing, and other departments will be, by definition, not under the control of the various departments. They, therefore, play no part in the appraisal of the departmental manager's work. A few overheads may, indeed, be controllable by some sections of the head office administration, e.g., rents payable are the responsibility of the legal department. However, most sections of the head office, e.g., the accounts department, have their own separate functions. Their output, though not exogenous, can best be measured and costed by techniques such as regression analysis. These are dealt with earlier in this chapter.

The conventional treatment of overheads in variance analysis involves the computation of overhead recovery and its division between efficiency and volume or capacity variances. There seems to be what amounts to almost a major conceptual error in this approach. Many overheads are fixed for any level of production within a reasonable range (though this may be fairly narrow in practice). To divide these overheads by the budgeted production and then to explain the difference between this figure and the corresponding figure obtained by dividing these actual overheads by the actual production as being an *overhead* variance, must be wrong. What this sort of variance does show is that there has been a change in the number of units produced. But change has already been directly explained in the materials and labour variances. It is obviously wrong to complicate differences in fixed overheads by involving them with differences in volume of output. The first is a result of irrevocable major decisions made in the past as to the size of the factory, number of machines available and so on; the second is governed by how well things are going at the moment. The former is a sunk cost and is irrelevant for decision purposes. The latter is exactly what we are concerned to analyse. Conventional overhead variance analysis often inextricably combines the two. Many of the calculations made to arrive at these variances are highly involved and give, perhaps, a certain intellectual satisfaction. The chief executive would be well advised to accept that this is all it really amounts to. If he likes pretty intellectual patterns for their own sake, his time would be better spent on an Ximenes crossword puzzle. At least the clues there never pretend to do anything else than enable one to fill up the squares correctly!

Sales volume variance: (A sales manager's performance appraisal variance.)

The conventional calculation of the sales volume variance is

$$(\text{Actual volume} - \text{Standard volume}) \times \text{Standard price}$$

This can be split up into

$$(\text{Actual volume} - \text{Optimum volume}) \times \text{Standard price} + (\text{Optimum volume} - \text{Standard volume}) \times \text{Standard price}$$

The latter variance is, of course, a standard setter's performance appraisal variance. It is the former variance which is of especial interest to us. At the very beginning of this chapter the problem of arriving at estimates for both sales and profit was considered at some length. The two are often treated together since it is a fact that in many companies the over-riding factor is the level of sales that can be achieved. Other restraints, e.g., materials, labour, availability of factory space and machines, are usually regarded as subsidiary. If the sales can be made, then the materials, etc., can usually be found. The really difficult problem, therefore, is to find what sales could possibly have been made in the prevailing circumstances. Market share is probably the most important single indicator of what this figure should be. If 10 per cent more, for instance, is available to the industry as a whole, then our company should get its share of this 10 per cent. The underlying assumption here is that the company and its competitors, who form the rest of the market, are operating under similar conditions. Sometimes, however, this just is not true. It may be that more money has been injected into our company, e.g., by way of new factories or heavy T.V. advertising. It may be that strikes, lack of materials, or lack of factory space have after all held up production. If the industry is an obvious growth sector, more firms may have decided to enter the field, and some of these may represent diversifications of powerful industrial leaders and will, therefore, have strong financial support. Even if the pie is a little larger, when there are many more people to eat it, each individual's share will be less rather than more. But perhaps our company—after massive expenditure on research and development over the past few years—is now in a position to exploit this lead over its competitors. Clearly, under such circumstances, we should expect a good deal more than a market share just based on our comparative size in this particular growth sector. From all this it follows that, though market share is probably the best single guide to optimum sales volume, it needs to be qualified by a number of factors.

In the light of all this it may well be argued that to arrive at any meaningful figure for the optimum sales volume is a well-nigh impossible task. However, we have to bear in mind that we are only concerned to assess the possible sales' figures that could be achieved by the sales manager if he exploited the possibilities available to him to the full. This is why market share does provide such a good basis for assessment. If our sales manager does as well as the average sales manager in the industry, then almost by definition he must get his market share. The problem of finding the precise figure by which he should be judged is a difficult one, but market share adjusted for any special factor beyond the control of the sales manager, does seem to give the best guide.

In order to be able to provide these details, the management information centre must include both a trained economist and a trained statistician. For a small or medium sized firm these services will have to be obtained through a consultancy firm; for a large firm these specialists should be available on the spot.

The sales manager's appraisal variance is, therefore,

$$(\text{Actual volume} - \text{Optimum volume}) \times \text{Standard price}$$

and his sales volume index is

$$\frac{(\text{Actual volume} - \text{Optimum volume}) \times \text{Standard price}}{\text{Sales}}$$

Sales price variance: The conventional sales price variance has little or no significance as a performance appraisal variance and, indeed, little real meaning of any sort. Unlike labour time, mix, and other variances, if prices have been altered it has almost certainly been as the result of a conscious decision, generally made by the sales director, probably after discussion at board level. All that the sales price variance is doing in this case, is to remind the sales director of these decisions.

In many industries prices are dictated by the market and—apart from allowing discounts—the sales staff have little discretion in altering prices. If there is a sales price variance, then this probably reflects a market change, most likely initiated by the market leaders. Clearly this sales price variance is effectively uncontrollable from the point of view of the sales director, or indeed of anyone in the company. In these circumstances, sales price variance as such can be ignored, and the sales volume variance, calculated on the lines shown above, is the appropriate variance to use for the appraisal of the sales manager's performance.

When prices can be altered, the position is more complex. In some industries pricing policy is a major weapon in the sales' armoury. Lowering the price is done with a view to producing greater sales volume and conversely increasing prices usually brings a lower sales volume. It might seem, therefore, that the aim of pricing policy should be to maximize total sales' revenue in money terms. In this case, we could rely on the total sales revenue to record this change, and certainly not bother to confuse the issue by analysing it into a volume variance and a price variance.

However, the benefit from sales is not truly measured by the income in money terms. If demand is elastic, a slight reduction in prices may bring a substantial increase in volume. To take the increase in total revenue as the criterion of the gain to the company, is to ignore the additional costs incurred in producing the extra volume. It follows that any analysis should be based on the total *contribution* from sales.

By way of illustration, suppose that at a standard price of £10 per unit our rate of selling is just 100 units per month. Variable expenses are, we suppose, £4 per unit, so that the contribution is $(10-4) = £6$ per unit. When the price is dropped to £9 per unit, a 50 per cent increase in sales' volume is actually achieved. Figure 8.2, which shows the position, can also be regarded as a particular example of the situation shown earlier in Fig. 3.1.

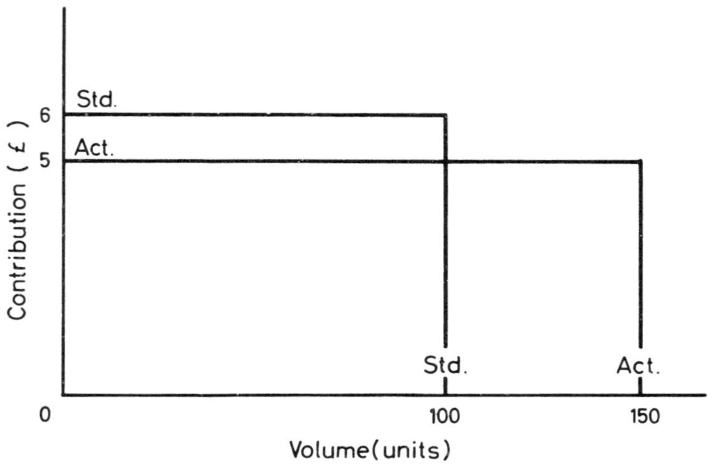

Figure 8.2.

The calculation of the real gain to the company is

				£
	Actual	$150 \times (9-4=)\ 5$	=	750
Less	*Standard*	$100 \times (10-4=)\ 6$	=	600
	Gain			150

This can be analysed into:

Volume variance

(Actual volume − Standard volume) × Actual contribution

$$= (150-100) \times 5 = 250$$

Contribution variance

(Actual contribution per unit − Standard contribution) × Standard volume

$$= (5-6) \times 100 = (-100)$$

If we were to follow the general line of argument that we have been taking so far, it is evident that we would wish to compare the actual performance with some measure of the optimum reasonably possible under the prevailing market conditions, rather than with the laid down standard performance. However, with this variance such an approach, though theoretically correct, is almost impossibly difficult to achieve in practice. To start off with, how can anyone, even with the benefit of hindsight, tell what the sales would have been at any price level other than the actual price? Without such knowledge, there are no facts available on which to base the choice of the optimum price, i.e., the price which gives the highest gain from contribution. Realistically speaking, the only possible yardstick that is practical to use for comparison purposes is the present price level, (i.e., the standard). If the sales director, by making a price change, can show any real gain from this position, then this difference must be the best available measure of his performance in the period under consideration.

The conclusions arrived at in these two sections on sales' variances can be stated as follows:

1. If the firm is operating in an industry in which the market determines the price, then sales price variance can be ignored. The calculation will follow along the lines shown in the section headed 'Sales volume variance' and the measure of the sales manager's performance will be

$$\frac{(\text{Actual volume} - \text{Optimum volume}) \times \text{Standard price}}{\text{Sales}}$$

2. If price discretion is available, then conventional sales volume and price variances can be ignored. The calculation will follow along the lines shown in the section headed 'Sales price variance' and the measure of the sales manager's performance will be

   Actual Contribution (i.e., at actual price and volume) −
   Standard Contribution (i.e., at standard price and volume)

   No further split up of this variance (e.g., into a volume, and contribution per unit variance) is of any help at all.

Summary of controllable variances

Table 8.1., shows the variances for each of the managers whose performance we wish to assess. Since all the entries in this table are in money terms, our measure of managerial efficiency will be in money terms too.

Table 8.1

Purchasing manager

Actual price + Holding costs − Current market price

Production manager

1. Actual usage with Actual mix − Optimum usage with Optimum mix

   Specifically:

   Actual usage − Optimum usage
   Actual mix − Optimum mix

2. (Actual hours − Optimum hours) × Standard rate

   where Optimum Hours takes account of such factors as reduction in labour output rate, if substantial overtime is worked, and the application of the learning curve to the production process.

3. Increase in spoilage/wastage/returned goods.

Personnel manager

(Actual rate − Market rate) × Actual hours + Changes in training costs, etc., due to quality of labour employed.

Sales manager

If no price discretion available:

(Actual volume − Optimum volume) × Standard price

If price discretion available:

Actual contribution − Standard contribution

where the term 'contribution' means total contribution and not unit contribution in this context.

Appendix: A new view of the profit and loss account and balance sheet

Introductory

In this appendix we are concerned to show that, using a new style of preparation and presentation of accounts, it is possible to record most assets, even to some extent human assets.

Although it is in the balance sheet that these values will ultimately be noted, the method of assessing these values relies heavily on an accurate, impartial, recording of profit. Attention is therefore concentrated in the first place on the conventional profit and loss account, with a view to its revision.

Profit and loss account

To understand how the present format of accounts arose it is necessary to go back some while in time. In the U.K., shortly after the initial period of the Industrial Revolution, it became evident that it was beyond the capacities of the owners of the new factories to pay for the comparatively expensive land, plant, and machinery involved. Clearly, the funds had to come from persons not directly concerned with running the business. To induce these people to part with their money they had to be given more participation and more expectations, than that offered by fixed interest lending. Hence, the growth of the joint stock company. Because the funds were supplied by shareholders who really had little or no control over the company, it was felt that their interest should be looked after by 'independent' experts. It is the job of auditors to perform this function.

Industries grew up haphazardly in locations which were generally geographically quite separate, and although all book-keeping was based on the double-entry principle, it was inevitable that many different styles and methods of book-keeping were evolved. Many of these differences in accounting methods have persisted, and in practice it is possible to arrive at many different ideas as to the correct profit of a company today. For a variety of reasons auditors find it difficult to argue against some of the more extreme versions of the profit figure, suggested, for example, by the directors. Although protected to some extent by law, auditors are paid by directors and they may well *feel* that their continued existence as the companies' auditors depends partially on how they stand with the directors. Auditors, though they are required by law to state whether the accounts represent a 'true and fair' view of the company's situation know that present accountancy practice is so flexible that any reasonable figure can be justified on some basis. Examples of this abound and have given rise to a good deal of criticism of the accountancy profession. Recently in the U.K., one public company reported duly audited earnings of over £2 m, later assessed at around £1 m, and later still reduced to a mere £140 000. When highly reputable auditors can disagree (even with the benefit of hindsight) to this extent, it seems that almost any figure for profit can be regarded as acceptable on the basis of current accounting practice.

One final point remains to be made. Profits are book figures. Whatever reasonable profit figure is agreed to by auditors, will not directly affect the cash supplied by the shareholders. It can be argued that auditors may well feel that they have looked after the principal interests of shareholders if they can be reasonably sure that no misuse of funds has occurred.

Basic profit

Most, though not all, of the problems in arriving at a good figure for the profit of a company arise because a profit and loss account covers an artificial period of time and it is therefore necessary to allocate costs, which really relate to a much longer period of time, to the period of the profit and loss account. Typical problems relate to the allocation of items such as:

(*a*) Fixed assets.
(*b*) Massive advertising expenditure.
(*c*) Research and development expenditure.
(*d*) Initial, financial, or promotional expenditure.

Let us concentrate on the first of these. How do we allocate expenditure on, for example, heavy machinery, which will probably last over many years, to one particular year? There is, of course, no absolutely right way. For a start, no one knows how long the machinery will last, whether technological advances will suddenly render it obsolescent in a few years time or not. However, even granted the impossible, and supposing that such information were available, we would still have grave conceptual problems. What method of allocation over these years should we use? Straight line—on the basis that the firm will use it for so many years and each year should be treated equally? This is the conventional book-keeping method in the U.K. But there are many others, e.g.:

(*a*) Straight line, but adjusted for differences in its usage each year.
(*b*) Reducing balance (which does tie up with the commonsense approach that a machine loses more of its value in the early years of its life than in the later years).
(*c*) Market value—say, net realizable value.
(*d*) Tax written down value (a reducing balance method, but based on the externally generated rules laid down by the Inland Revenue—that is *standard* rules).

Much the same can be said about the other period costs. Here, too, there are wide differences in accounting practice. Sometimes R. and D. expenditure is written off as it occurs. Sometimes it is capitalized as a period cost and written off over a number of years. The effect of these differences on the profit and loss account can be very substantial, indeed in a few cases almost catastrophic. What should we do? As we have seen, there can be no absolutely right answer. But surely this should not be an excuse for allowing almost any figure for profit to be shown in published accounts.

The only profit figure that can have much meaning, either for reference or comparison purposes, must be one that is prepared on a standard basis. Such a figure could be called BPBT—basic profit before tax. In order to arrive at BPBT we need, first, a uniform method of allocating long-term expenditure to a profit and loss period. Depreciation is the example that we have been using all along, and fortunately there is an agreed independent yardstick available to all firms. This is the depreciation figure as laid down by the tax authorities, i.e., the statutory capital allowances. (In any country where inflation is material, the cumulative capital allowance figures should be adjusted each year by the national price level rise. This allows for a rise in replacement cost.) This method is used effectively in the U.S.A. and now that we, too, have a Corporation Tax structure, there is no real obstacle to its adoption here. The only possible disadvantage is that occasionally alterations are made in the Finance Acts (e.g., changes or the abolition of investment grants). However, the general basis of writing down allowances appears to be firmly established. Even if changes* are made to accord with fiscal policy, the incidence of these alterations on comparable companies will be the same.

The allocation of other long-term expenditure will also need to be in accordance with accepted yardsticks. In many cases these could be the guidelines laid down by an independent authority such as the Inland Revenue, or failing that, could be the practice accepted and used by the best firms in any particular industry. This latter method would be particularly suitable for dealing with the valuation of work in progress, the one substantial factor affecting profit not so far mentioned.

All in all, techniques such as these would seem to be adequate to achieve the aim of producing a single meaningful profit figure, useful not only to shareholders, managers, and creditors, but also to employees, take-over candidates, and financial analysts. Although the BPBT figure will be arrived at by methods which will be much more precisely determined than those leading to the conventional net profit figure, it does not mean that there will be no areas left in which the accountant will have to apply his judgement. This is certainly not the case. His work will, however, be restricted to the task of deciding whether expenditure has been properly dealt with in accordance with the laid down guidelines. Research and Development expenditure has been much in the news recently, particularly after the problems of companies such as Rolls-Royce. Here the guidelines should indicate precisely what qualifies as research, and what as development expenditure. Each of these main divisions will be further subdivided, e.g., into pure and applied research and various types of development expenditure. For each subdivision the rules will state over how many years the expenditure should be written off, or how it should be dealt with. Deciding under which section each item of expense should come is the job of the accountant and it is here that his judgement will be most needed. He will have to decide, for example, how to deal with an apportionment of overhead, charged as part of support for a new product.

In conclusion it must be added that basic profit may not be, in every circumstance, the best measure of a company's performance—because it is so inflexible. If, in the event, directors felt that their own accounts, prepared on traditional lines, gave a better picture of the profit position, then their version could be included as well. However, basic profit is likely to be a fairer measure for comparison purposes, whether this be with last year's figures or with similar companies in the same line of business. Indeed, for all such purposes it is the only measure which has much real meaning.

The balance sheet

The present layout of the balance sheet is equally unsatisfactory. Set out as it generally is, with one side headed 'assets', the other side headed 'liabilities', and both sides balancing, it has a spurious sense of accuracy and completeness. The fact that it balances is tautological. Any set of balances taken at any time from a set of books kept on double-entry principles will always balance. This does not prove that the figures are necessarily correct or complete. Many of the figures, indeed, in a balance sheet do not mean what they appear to mean. 'Fixed assets', for instance, will be at book value and not true value. Many assets which should appear in any complete list of assets are omitted. Trade prestige, know-how, the value of employees, etc., are examples of these.

* Unfortunately the recent changes in tax allowances in the U.K. were fairly substantial.

In view of this, it seems best to break with the conventional layout entirely and present such figures as are available in a more helpful and less misleading form under the title 'funds and assets statement'. Employees and shareholders are likely to be interested primarily in profit, and basic profit will supply this need. Banks, intending shareholders, and institutional investors, will be more interested in the financial structure and the availability of funds. To assess these matters, ratio analysis is the accepted tool. Accordingly, the first two sections of the revised 'balance sheet' presentation show the sources of long- and short-term funds respectively, set out in ratio analysis form. The third section shows the visible assets. In this section the book value figure, that is, cost less accumulated depreciation, will be shown, just as in normal accounting practice. Additionally, it should be mandatory for all land and property, and as well, plant and machinery above a certain laid down figure, to be valued by professional valuers at least once every four years, and for this information to be included as well.

The fourth section shows the invisible assets, and it is here that problems really occur. Conventionally, goodwill is only introduced into accounts on merger or take-over. The figure for goodwill is just the excess of the cost of acquisition over the book value of the assets acquired. Commonly, this figure is written off over a short number of years by charging the profit and loss accounts. Such book entries are highly artificial and possibly would be better not made.

Most of the excess of the real value of a company over and above its net asset value arises on account of its trade relationships and the skill of its managers. For a small family commercial concern trade relationships may well be the more significant of these two. For any medium-sized or large public company the managerial skill is likely to be much the more important. All the available evidence to date points to a good management team as being the outstanding invisible asset that a company can possess, and this far exceeds in importance, either any particular management skill, even that of selling, or the possession of new product ideas, or the managerial efficiency of one man, with the possible exception of the chief executive.

Fortunately, the establishment of the basic profit figures as a fair and impartial measure of a business's performance in the past, gives us the means, at least, to indicate the value that the management team has shown in the past. The relevant figures will be the basic profit, expressed as a return on investment, for those recent years for which management has been together as a team, compared with the return obtained by comparable companies in the same or similar industries. Students of accountancy theory will recognize that this concept is similar to that of valuing goodwill on the basis of so many years superprofits. This approach is different, however, for two reasons. First is uses a measure of profit which is impartial, since the same rules have been applied in assessing the profit figure for all the companies entering into the comparison. Second, the normal superprofits formula ignores the fact that some of the managerial team may have left. Basing goodwill at the current balance sheet date on the skill of people who are no longer with the company hardly seems valid. This highlights one of the major problems in valuing 'human' assets. In a conventional balance sheet, a fixed asset is 'fixed' in the sense that its disposal or otherwise is in the hands of the directors of the company. A management team, though equally an asset in the revenue-earning sense, is different in that the decision as to whether to retain this asset may not be entirely in the hands of the directors. Managers—unless on a long-term arrangement and the practical value of even a cast-iron legal contract is doubtful—can walk out, singly or *en bloc*. However highly automated machinery may be, it cannot, as yet, do this on its own!

Because it is so difficult to determine what constitutes a 'management team', e.g., whether the departure of one key man is significant or not, it is doubtful if any attempt should be made to give money figures for this admittedly crucial aspect of a company's value. Instead, it would seem best to provide all the available details, i.e., the return on investment figures, the salaries, and contract terms of service for all the managers in recent years. This, unfortunately, is as near as we can get at the moment to recording human values in accounting terms.

Funds and assets statement.

	This year's figures	*Previous year's figures*
1. *Long term funds*		
(*a*) Return on invested capital $= \frac{\text{Basic profit before tax}}{\text{Invested capital}} \times 100 =$	—	—
(*b*) Gearing $= \frac{\text{Long term debt}}{\text{Invested capital}} \times 100 =$	—	—
Note: Invested capital is made up of:		
Ordinary shares —		—
Revenue reserves —		—
Capital reserves —		—
Debentures —		—
2. *Short term funds*		
(*a*) Liquidity ratio $= \frac{\text{Debtors}+\text{Cash}}{\text{Current liabilities}} =$	—	—
(*b*) Current ratio $= \frac{\text{Stock}+\text{Debtors}+\text{Cash}+\text{Quoted investments}}{\text{Current liabilities}} =$	—	—
Note: Current liabilities is made up of:		
Trade creditors —		—
Dividends payable —		—
Interest payable —		—
Taxation —		—
Other items —		—

	Method of valuation		
3. *Visible assets*			
Property		—	—
Plant and machinery		—	—
Motor vehicles		—	—
Furniture, fixtures, and fittings		—	—
4. *Invisible assets*			
Copyrights		—	—
Patents		—	—
Goodwill		—	—
Research and development		—	—
Trade investments		—	—

Employees, including working directors, by categories:

	Number	*Salary (average)*	*Age (average)*	*Years service (average)*	*Contract years unexpired (A. and B. only)*	
A	—	—	—	—	—	↑
B	—	—	—	—	—	*Ditto*
C	—	—	—	—	—	
D	—	—	—	—	—	↓

(*Explanatory Note:* Category *A* is the chief executive only. Category *B* is for the top 1 per cent, by salary, of all the employees. Remaining categories are for managers and workers, split either by salary groups or by trades within trade unions. For these categories salaries or wages should be split up into basic and overtime earnings.)

Return on investment:

	This company	*Industry average*
This year (Y)	—	—
Last year Y-1	—	—
Y-2	—	—
Y-3	—	—
Y-4	—	—

9. Technological forecasting

9.1. Introduction

In the opening remarks, at the beginning of chapter 1 of this book, it was argued that accountants and controllers nowadays do look at the *future* prospects of their company. Estimated profit and loss accounts are prepared with a view to giving an assessment of the company's future position for the next year or so. Of more importance still—since after all a business can survive without showing a book profit, but cannot survive without cash to pay its bills—cash budgets are produced. These are usually prepared in detail, month by month, for the next financial year, and also, in outline only, for the following few years. In these long-range budgets, only the major items are considered, and the short-term ebb and flow of cash from creditors and trade debtors is 'smoothed out', or regarded as virtually self-cancelling.

These budgets or forecasts are the corner stones of business decision making. All major decisions are made within the framework that they allow. Their accuracy is crucial to the success or failure of the company. In making these forecasts accountants themselves rely on other forecasts, principally market forecasts, but also many others. Financial managers, indeed, are not unique in accepting the significance and validity of forecasts. Every April the Government issues a white paper giving their forecasts of expenditure and income in detail for the coming year. Even in our private lives we acknowledge the validity of forecasts when we take our umbrella on 'full many a glorious morn', because the weather man says that 'anon the basest clouds' will appear. And more and more we come to rely on his prognostications as the techniques of scientific weather forecasting improve. Not long ago, even forecasts for the following day were often wrong. Now forecasts are given with considerable confidence for as much as a whole month in advance.

Every year some £500 million is spent by British industry on research and development. (Even this amount is probably not enough. It has been estimated that a growth rate of around 10 per cent a year in R and D expenditure is necessary to maintain a growth rate of 3 per cent in an individual company's sales.) Without some fairly accurate estimate of technological trends much of this money could be wasted. Fortunately, technological forecasting is capable of a formulation which is probably more precise than any of the foregoing forecasts. Even so, there is still some reluctance to accept it as a technique of equal reliability for decision-making purposes. Almost certainly this is due to a basic misconception as to the *aim* of technological forecasting. The object is not to identify a particular invention or an exact form of technological innovation. This aim, in any case, must be self-defeating. For if the invention can be precisely foreseen, then it no longer remains to be invented. However, the likely *forms* that it will take and the economic and commercial consequences that will follow, can be forecast with some accuracy.

Allied with this misconception is the idea that inventions are spontaneous, one-off flashes of genius, and that technological improvements are made in sudden discontinuous and magical jumps. Occasionally this is the case; indeed, it is just these brilliant exceptions which catch the eye. Generally, however, the steps are very small and progress in any technology takes the form of a nearly smooth curve. It is this factor which makes forecasting a viable proposition.

In a business forecast, such as a market forecast, the precise value of the sales figure in the future cannot of course be accurately predicted. In practice, what will be estimated is the most likely figure and also the range within which the final figure is almost certain to be. Much the same remarks apply to technological forecasting. The precise time when some commercial breakthrough occurs and its precise details cannot be estimated exactly, but this prediction can nevertheless be made within fairly narrow limits. The business and commercial consequences can then be determined and exploited.

Since forecasting is of such importance, how do we go about it? Clearly, to understand it, we must first determine the *reason why* any invention or innovation is made. The question can be stated like this:

Is the invention caused by knowledge itself breaking through the barriers at some point or is the change caused by the need? Is it supply or demand which is the critical factor in this situation?

9.2. Demand assessment

Several recent studies have suggested that it is clearly perceived demand—not excess technological capacity—that tends to be the primary force stimulating technological change. Therefore, in order to analyse future technological innovations, we should look first at likely future demands. Such demands or needs will arise from one of two sources:

1. *Natural* human needs, e.g., food, clothing, warmth, protection, communication, desire for self-advancement.
2. *Imposed* demands, e.g., those which arise from Government or local authority restrictions or rules.

To illustrate the first group, let us consider briefly two fairly recent examples. Leather is needed both to shoe and help clothe the population of this country. There is certainly no decline in the popularity of leather as a fashion material—rather the reverse. It follows that, with the increase in population over the next decade or so, there must be a big increase in demand for leather. But the supply of leather is decreasing since the animal population is dwindling. Hence, we have a need for a synthetic leather, such as Corfam.

Again, let us consider the explosive growth of education in recent years. Of course more people are being educated but, much more significantly, the level to which they are being educated is increasing rapidly. To teach higher education requires better books, better teachers and better means of communication from teacher to student. Let us concentrate on the last of these three. How do teachers communicate? At one time, just by means of 'chalk and talk'. Some still say this is the best! Others, however, do not agree and use a huge variety of visual aids such as overhead projectors, closed-circuit television, cine and slides, plastigraphs, whyteboards, feltboards, neck microphones, and tape recorders. The technological rate of advance of some of these, *made in response to the demand*, has been staggering. Only two or three years ago, overhead projectors were reasonably effective but unpleasant affairs, reflecting blinding light back into the eyes of the lecturer and pushing a stream of hot air (required for cooling the bulb) backwards into anyone unfortunate enough to be within range. The I.B.M. overhead projector now has none of these disadvantages and is, as well, much lighter. The need was there, the technological innovation to satisfy the need, was quickly found.

Today, however, we live in a period of increasing Government spending and Government control. It is not surprising that many of the needs for technological innovation arise not from free market demand, but from Government legislation. In many cases, the direction in which Government control is moving has long been clear. It follows that it is easy to forecast the demands and the innovations that will be required.

Car safety legislation provides a good example to explore in some depth. For many years and for obvious reasons, it has been evident that more and more restrictions and requirements are going to be placed on the motorist. The latest moves in this direction in the U.K. are:

1. The undertaking by the car manufacturers to fit anti-theft locks to steering columns on all new models brought out after 1st January, 1970.

2. The compulsory fitting of seat belts on all new cars produced since 1965.
3. The legislation making it an offence to use a tyre with less than one millimetre of tread (recent surveys indicated that half the cars on the road have at least one defective tyre).
4. Legislation standardizing dipping mechanisms and windscreen wipers, providing for spot checks on defective silencers, provisions relating to new lights for elderly vehicles, and so on.

It is easy to see that many firms should benefit from this existing legislation. For example:

1. *Anti-theft*	Wilmot Breeden Trico Excelsior
2. *Seat belts*	Kangol Wingard Britax (Excelsior)
3. *Tyres*	Dunlop Firestone Goodyear Michelin Pirelli Avon
4. *Sundry*	Lucas Tudor Trico Quinton Hazell Harmo and many small manufacturers of silencers.

However, it is not only the present legislation which will force technological change but future legislation as well. Again, not only the direction that this will take, but even its form, can be assessed pretty accurately.

The starting point in this calculation must be the fact that some European countries and the U.S.A. (in some respects) already have regulations in force in advance of ones in the U.K. Quite likely our own forthcoming legislation would, in any case, follow along the same general lines. It is almost *certain* to do so, however, for two reasons. First, a substantial car export business is essential to our economy. For practical purposes it is obviously far easier for the car manufacturers if they have only one set of regulations to comply with. Second, when we do eventually join the Common Market (or if we have a Channel Tunnel), a common set of legislative requirements will be a logical necessity.

To sum up, we have seen in this example:

1. A clear general trend (more car safety legislation).
2. The form it will take (European and U.S.A. measures and, no doubt, other extensions of our own existing regulations, such as seat belts at the back, special provisions for children's safety, better braking, e.g., discs on all new cars, collapsible or compressible steering wheels, and so on).

9.2.1. Conditional demand assessment

Sometimes there is some doubt as to whether a particular field of technology will need to be developed or not. Whether this is so or not will depend on whether the costs of an existing technology remain competitive and on whether an existing source of supply has the capacity to continue to satisfy the demand. To illustrate:

Shale oil recovery techniques will be required under any of several circumstances:*

1. If shale-oil mining, retorting, and transportation costs can be reduced so that shale crude at the refinery costs less than other crude sources.
2. If foreign crude supplies are severely curtailed.
3. If shale oil permits the refinery to produce an output mix of sufficiently greater value than other hydrocarbon sources.
4. If international hydrocarbon finding, lifting, and transportation costs exceed certain levels.
5. If pegged international crude prices become too high.

Each oil company can calculate the points at which each of these events would affect its operations. The conditional probability, timing, and impact of each event can be predicted by Bayesian and/or trend analysis techniques. Although no one contingency may justify research, development, or other actions, the combined probabilities and impacts of several contingencies might.

Potentialities of various shale mining and liquifaction processes can be assessed by analysing trends in technical progress and by forecasting the probability that each will overcome specific remaining barrier problems. Then the final forecast can predict:

1. Whether there is a strong enough need to justify seeking some form of technical solution.
2. The performance requirements any solution must meet if it is to be successful under various conditions.

* This example is taken from, 'Technological forecasting', by James Brian Quinn, *Harvard Business Review*, 1967. (as are Figs. 9.1 and 9.2).

3. How rapidly present technical advances—and the vulnerability of anticipated road-blocks—indicate that shale can substitute for other resources under specific circumstances.
4. The probability of each circumstance occurring by some future date.
5. The pay-off if the event occurs and if the state of the art is as anticipated.

9.3. Theoretical limits analysis

Although we have emphasized that the demand side of the 'technology supplying a need' situation is surprisingly often the dominant factor, we must not ignore the other side. Research staff at work in a given technology, equipped with considerable specialized knowledge, and emotionally involved in the projects they are bringing to completion, will naturally show a strong tendency to operate in accordance with Newton's Third Law of Motion and continue in a state of 'uniform motion along a straight line'. Unless, therefore, there is established a new need, technological invention will continue to develop along existing lines.

What are these existing lines? A very short, but general list includes:

Lasers.

Atomic propulsion and controlled thermonuclear power.

Sophisticated computery, such as:
automated language translators, and direct reading devices.

Transplanted organs and implanted artificial organs.

Economically useful water desalination and oceanology.

Commercially produced synthetic protein food.

(Every individual will be able to provide additional detailed examples taken from his own particular industrial field and these are the ones that will be of importance for him.)

The technique of theoretical limits analysis is simply to take any appropriate existing technology, push it to the ultimate limits of its possible attainment, and then consider what the implications of this will be. Let us consider two fairly prosaic examples.

Steadily throughout the years chemical electrical cells have become more and more efficient, both in the technical sense of converting a higher proportion of their chemical energy into electrical energy, and in the commercial sense of being cheaper, lighter, and more robust for a given output of power. A graph showing efficiency against time would provide a good example of the 'smooth' curve that is, as we have said, the usual characteristic of technological growth. All this is good news for manufacturers of torches, toys and those household appliances that use a battery or cell. However, there is an application of the electric cell, now well within the bounds of possibility, which has revolutionary consequences.

Not long ago a research project at the Massachusetts Institute of Technology into the future patterns of transport in the 'North East' corridor of the U.S.A. (the area covering Washington and New York) came to some startling conclusions. The starting-off point was the fact that, in order to accommodate the modern motor-car, a city has to be nearly ten times as spread out as it would otherwise be. Now motor-cars certainly do not travel in crowded city streets more than ten times as fast as people walk. Consequently, even if everyone has a motor-car, there is little gain in time. People are just travelling ten times as fast over ten times the distance. But there is yet another and probably more powerful argument against the large fast modern car, and this is the rising social cost it has in terms of driving strain, noise, accident rate, air pollution, etc. A small electric car—just for city travel (it is not being argued here that there should be any replacement for the conventional petrol driven status symbol for travel outside the cities' boundaries) would, if economic, provide all the answers. Very shortly it seems, the electric cell will in fact be able to provide adequate economic power for a small compact car.

The accountant, whether in commerce, or in the profession, is not directly concerned with the development of any technology as such, but the technology of quite overriding significance to him is computery. The growth in the use of computers by businesses is fantastic. In the U.S.A. the first electronic computer actually to process business transactions was the UNIVAC (1954). By mid-1962, the number of computers in use had reached nearly 6000; by the end of 1964 it was around 12 000. In 1968 it was nearer 60 000. Conventional computers are likely to pose many problems to the accountant and auditor, with the advent of on-line real time systems and the virtual elimination of not only past balances but the need for most original documents as well.

However, some of the most important practical advances being made in this technology at the moment are in the small visible on-line record computers. These have a direct keyboard input simple enough to be operated by a typist after only a few hours training. The output is on typewritten, readable, records. These records usually incorporate a magnetic strip which enables them to be used for input into a conventional computer system. Visible record computers produce simple routine statistics as a by-product of their normal accounting operations.

If we extrapolate this situation only a little into the future, it seems likely that all conventional accounting machines, from ledger posting machines to punched card installations, will be replaced by these desk-top computer installations. Debtors and creditors control accounts, routine statistics, financial statements including profit and loss accounts, cost accounts, stock control figures, and cash budgets will all be readily available and capable of continuous updating.

The consequences of this revolution in small accounting machinery are considerable. To push it to its theoretical limits we have to imagine that every firm, however small, has its own visible record computer or terminal. Makers of traditional office machinery will no longer be in business. All managers, even the most junior, will need to know much more about statistics, accounting, and operational research techniques. Since costing figures, for instance, can be obtained immediately, it follows that prices can be quoted, even for complex one-off jobs, right away. The availability of the materials can be checked from up-to-date stock records. Production can be planned by P.E.R.T. or L.O.B. For branches and divisions of large firms, no reference to head office will be operationally necessary. The local manager can be given greater responsibility and freedom from control. Inevitably, therefore, he will need to have a far greater knowledge of sophisticated quantitative techniques than he has at the moment.

9.4. Trend analysis

Repeatedly in this chapter we have referred to the need to extrapolate or continue an existing trend some distance into the future, and it is worth while looking briefly at the appropriate techniques.

Where the existing curve is fairly clearly defined, the standard approach in mathematical trend analysis is first to construct a moving average curve. This is intended to iron out the short term ebbs and flows and present a reasonably smooth curve.

Sometimes it is easy to continue this curve by eye. This is certainly the case if the 'curve' is a straight line. Generally, however, it is not obvious which way the curve will turn.

Long-term forecasting using mathematical trend analysis has its most effective use in market research for an *industry*. Demand is plotted against time, and the suitable period for extrapolation is for some three to ten years in advance. Such forecasting can only be successful where past sales figures have been truly representative of demand (that is they have not been kept down by artificial restrictions—imposed by the Government or the trade—below their free market level). Forecasting national electrical consumption by different consumer groups is a good example of the proper use of mathematical trend forecasting.

The technique of mathematical trend analysis consists of:

1. a preliminary survey to see that adequate figures are available in a suitable form for fitting a trend curve;
2. the selection of the right type of curve to fit these figures; and
3. the calculation of the best fitting curve of this type.

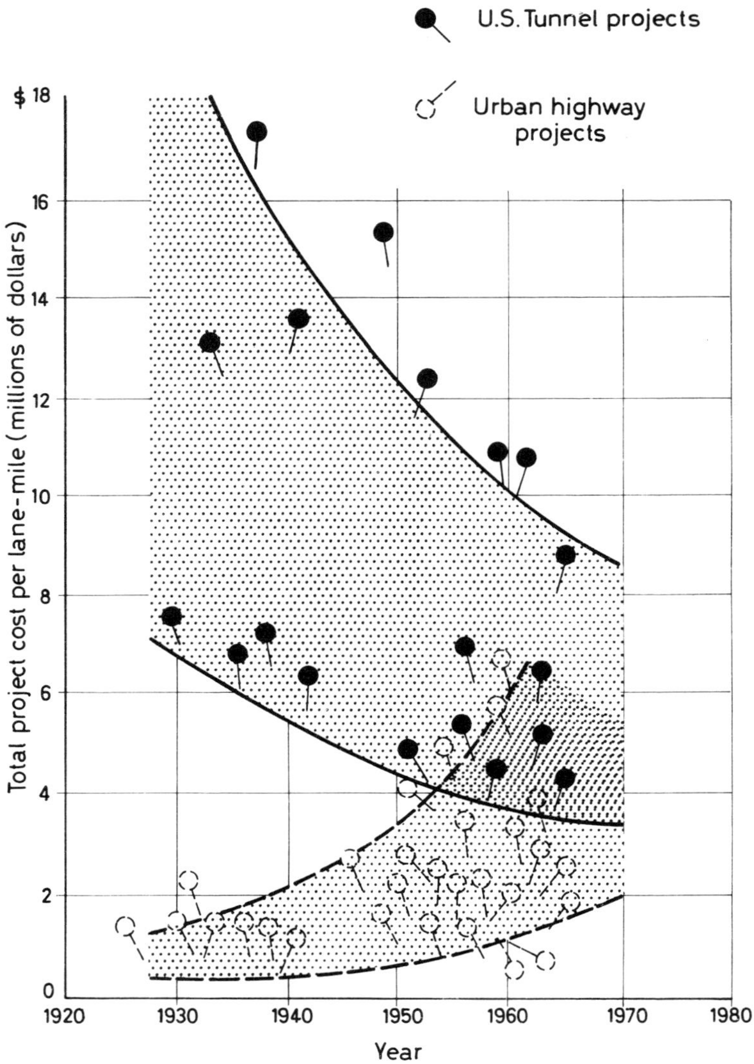

Figure 9.1. (Source: *G. A. Hoffman,* Urban Underground Highways and Parking Facilities, *Santa Monica, California, RAND Corporation, 1963)*

It is not proposed to go very deeply into the complex mathematical details of trend curve fitting.* Briefly, the method is to work out and plot, first the slope of the demand curve against time, then the ratio of the slope of the demand curve divided by the demand itself, against the time, and so

* See also the appendix to this chapter.

on. Eventually, some result of this plotting should be a straight line. When that occurs, the type of the curve will be known. The final step in the analysis is to calculate the likely amounts by which the estimated future figures will differ from the actual. Clearly, the further we go into the future the larger will be this gap. Usually, calculations are based on 90 per cent confidence limits; that is to say, there is a 90 per cent chance that the actual figures will turn out to be within these calculated limits. Series of tables are available to simplify the work. It is, however, quicker and easier to program the whole of this work, i.e., the calculation of the trend curve and the calculation of the figures for the future using this curve, and the 90 per cent confidence limits.

9.4.1. Technological trend forecasting

Plotting a series of points on graph paper to represent past commercial applications of a specific *technology* usually gives a somewhat widely distributed pattern with no clear indication of a central line or curve on which all the points lie. Generally, however, the direction of the trend is clear, and very often this can be shown diagrammatically by shading in or colouring a band which covers all the points. A Rand Corporation survey of the comparative costs in recent years of above ground motorways and underground tunnels (see Fig. 9.1) shows this quite clearly. Tunnel costs are obviously decreasing, and above ground highway costs are increasing rapidly. The crossover point has apparently just been reached. 'Predicting the technological changeover point'—as this position is called—is obviously of great importance in planning the commercial consequences for the takeover technology.

9.4.2. Substitution growth curves

Analyses of the growth of one technology, as it takes over from its predecessor, show that the pattern is remarkably constant. The standard shape of the curve is a somewhat stretched S, and this gives rise to the term 'S' curve.

Initially, growth along this curve is slow, at least until the technology gains some sort of acceptance. Then follows a period of rapidly increasing growth. This part of the curve is certainly exponential in form, that is, the rate of growth varies directly with the performance characteristic to date. The greater, for instance, the number of people who have colour television (see Fig. 9.2) the greater will be the demand from those who haven't in order to catch up with those who have. After a while the rate of growth will begin to slow down, as saturation is reached. (Partly this is because there are only a certain number of people in the world; even if they all went in for colour television, the demand must have a limit.) In practice,

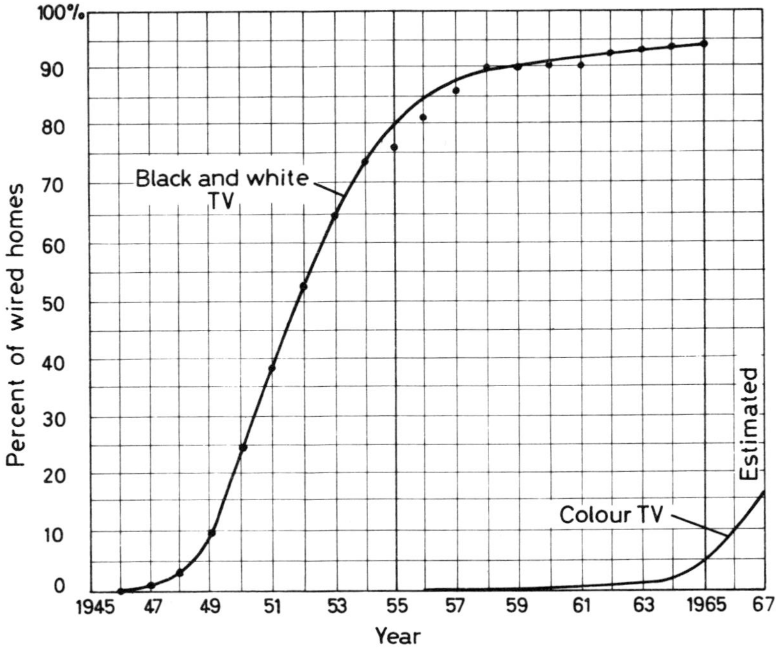

Figure 9.2. *(*Sources*:* The Economic Almanac 1964, *New York, National Industrial Conference Board, 1962, p. 414;* Electronic Industries Yearbook 1966, *Washington, Electronic Industries Association, 1966, p. 6;* Financial World, *August 24, 1966, p. 6. Figures derived by R. C. Goldstein)*

to use a substitution growth curve for realistically forecasting the future trends of a technology, substitution must already have reached the stage when the initial upturn is clearly visible. The exponential and 'S' curves are discussed further in the appendix to this chapter.

Since all technological growth curves seem to follow this pattern, it is interesting to speculate whether technology as a whole—civilization or human progress might be better, although more dramatic, terms—is following the same trend. The rate of increase of both knowledge and techniques seem to get faster all the time. Are we well into the initial upturn? How long before progress begins to slow down? Some constraints, which will come into force as saturation is neared, seem obvious enough—just our own physical and intellectual limitations.

9.5. Sources of technological knowledge

One result of this explosive growth in technology is a corresponding growth in the volume of published material relating to these technologies. The availability of such material is itself a spur to increased technological invention. This is indeed another example of the 'exponential' growth syndrome. Many of these particular constraints are already being felt by librarians, research readers, and so on, when they complain of the overpowering array of technical publications and literature available today.

The available sources of supply are:

1. Newspapers (e.g., the 'Technical Page' of the *Financial Times*).
2. Scientific and technical surveys.
3. Social and demographic analyses (outlining the nature of future needs such as food, clothing, communications, drugs, medicines, entertainments, and problems such as air pollution, racial discrimination, detergent disposal, etc.).
4. Economic analyses.
5. Statistics.
6. Government white papers and so on.

For an individual company, the most important job of all is to monitor competitor's activities. From publications, patents, and information passing along the commercial grapevine, an excellent map of competitor's strengths and weaknesses can be drawn up. This can save many a costly investment in plant, which, in a year or two, may well prove to be obsolescent.

9.6. Problems and limitations of technological forecasting

There is a temptation in technological forecasting to become excited about some of the wilder long-term possibilities which come under consideration. Such 'science fiction' stuff must be rejected out of hand in any commercial assessment. Anything which is unlikely to mature within ten years or so at the outside, should be set aside for the present.

Although a tight grip has to be kept on the time limits of technological forecasting, within this constraint a high degree of freedom must be given to the staff actively engaged in forward research. Boffins—to use the wartime phrase, or 'wild men' or 'wild birds' in current American technology—are people who need to be left alone to work out the implications of their own ideas. By nature they do not easily fit in to the formalized management structure of a company. However, the conclusions they arrive at, and the state of their work on any project, must be considered and evaluated at regular intervals by long-range planning or technical information committees. Groups of scientists, technologists, and marketing managers will get together in some brainstorming session—in which the wildest possibilities are actively encouraged, and then coolly assessed. These provide the necessary stimulation for research into new and original channels.

Appendix to chapter 9

The exponential and Sigmoid curves
The exponential is the curve of normal uninhibited growth. A good economic example of this is the overall rate of growth of a developing country. At the start, the few factories in existence will mean a slow rate. When more factories are available, more equipment for new factories can be produced from these. The rate of growth will, therefore, rise directly in proportion to the number of factories already in existence.

The population of a developing country (or the 'germ' population in a culture) also tends to grow according to an exponential curve. For the more persons there are, the greater will be the number of births. Where, as is usual, there are limiting factors, e.g., the inability of the country to support the people, this curve will not apply once these limiting factors begin to operate.

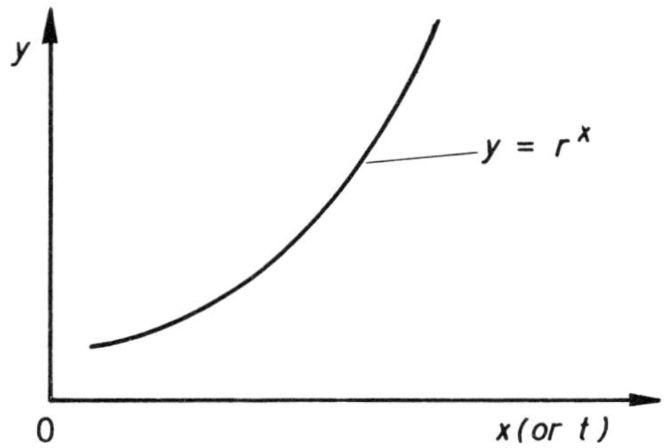

Figure 9.3.

The equation to an exponential curve (see Fig. 9.3) in its simplest form, is

$$y = r^x$$

where r is a constant

If $$y = r^x$$

then $$\frac{dy}{dx} = \log_e r \cdot y$$

Since dy/dx is the slope or gradient of the tangent at a point, it follows that the rate of growth of this curve (measured by the slope) varies directly with the value of y at that point.

For our purposes we make x the time base t, so that steady movement along the horizontal axis represents the passing of time, and y is the measure (using any suitable performance characteristic) of the technology we are dealing with.

At a certain point in the development of any technology, various limiting factors come into play. These factors arise for two separate reasons. First, the demand for the products of the new technology begins to slow down, in other words, market saturation is being approached. Second, the rate of growth cannot continue to be maintained because of the physical limitations of the materials from which the products are being made. Even a technology which transmits or passes information from one part to another at the speed of light has to accept that this speed cannot be exceeded. Trying to reduce the effect of this constraint is one of the problems of computery today.

The general category of curves which seem to fit best this combination of the two factors representing growth and constraint or decay are the 'general modified exponentials'. Their equation is

$$y = (a \pm br^t)^\phi$$

where a, b, ϕ are constants and r is a constant which must be between 0 and 1.

Three commonly-used curves of this family are

1. The simple modified exponential

$$y = a - br^t$$

This is obtained by putting $\phi = 1$ in the general modified exponential. The simple modified exponential can only be applied to that part of the S curve which lies to the right of the point of inflexion (see Fig. 9.4).

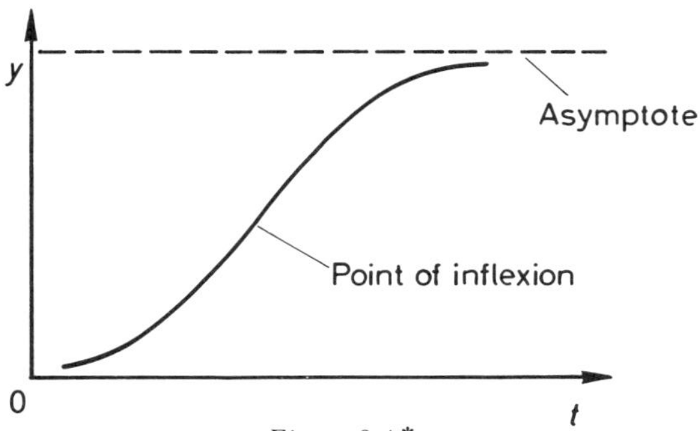

Figure 9.4.*

2. The logistic curve

$$y = \frac{1}{a - br^t}$$

3. The Gompertz curve

$$\log y = a - br^t$$

* The terms 'Sigmoid' or 'S' curve are often used for curves of this shape.

The general modified exponential is asymptotic to a^{ϕ} and the simple modified exponential, the logistic and the Gompertz curve are asymptotic to a, $1/a$, and e^{a} respectively.

For our application, therefore, these values represent the market saturation figure.

Finding the precise curve which best fits the figures either of technological development, or of demand for the products of a technology to date, is not easy. Trend-curve fitting requires specialist mathematical knowledge. The method has been briefly indicated in §9.4, the section on trend analysis.

10. Expenditure on marketing

by *Melvyn Hirst**

10.1. Introduction

British companies spend millions of pounds every year to market the products and services they produce, and many more millions to develop new products. The money is spent in advertising, personal selling, and distribution, as well as in collecting marketing information to help marketing management make better decisions. Despite the high level of expenditure on marketing research, however, it is well known that many of the decisions are made in an information void. Furthermore, there is at the moment, very little normative theory to guide the marketing manager in his decision making.

10.1.1. The need for a theory of marketing decision making

Marketing management is in need of a comprehensive theory of decision making to provide assistance in the following decision areas:

(*a*) What is the best product mix?
(*b*) What is the best level of total marketing effort?
(*c*) What is the best allocation of marketing effort over products, territories, and customers?
(*d*) What is the best mix of different types of marketing effort?
(*e*) What is the best timing of marketing effort?

These questions have to be answered because most business firms are multiproduct organizations, and each one of these products of the firm shares a different market with competing products of other firms. Also, every product requires more than one kind of marketing effort; a marketing mix of several kinds of effort is normally expended on each product. Finally, companies usually sell to several different types and size groups

* Lecturer in Marketing, School of Industrial and Business Studies, University of Warwick.

of customers, and they generally market in a number of different sales territories.

Given the need for a comprehensive theory of marketing decision making, why has such a theory not emerged during a period in which the methodologies of operational research and management science have found a number of successful applications in production and finance? A number of factors have contributed to this slow rate of development. The major reason is that marketing problems are very complex and many of the important variables involved are not quantifiable. For example, the shape of the market response function to additional expenditure on marketing is usually unknown. In general, it tends to be nonlinear, to exhibit threshold effects, to have carry-over effects, and to decay with time. Also the consumer-oriented nature of marketing makes response relationships almost impossible to measure. Recourse is often made to indirect measures of response, such as changes in attitudes. If this is not enough, there are also problems caused by interaction between the various elements of the marketing mix, the unpredictable reactions of competitors, and the traditional incompatibility between operational research workers and marketing personnel!

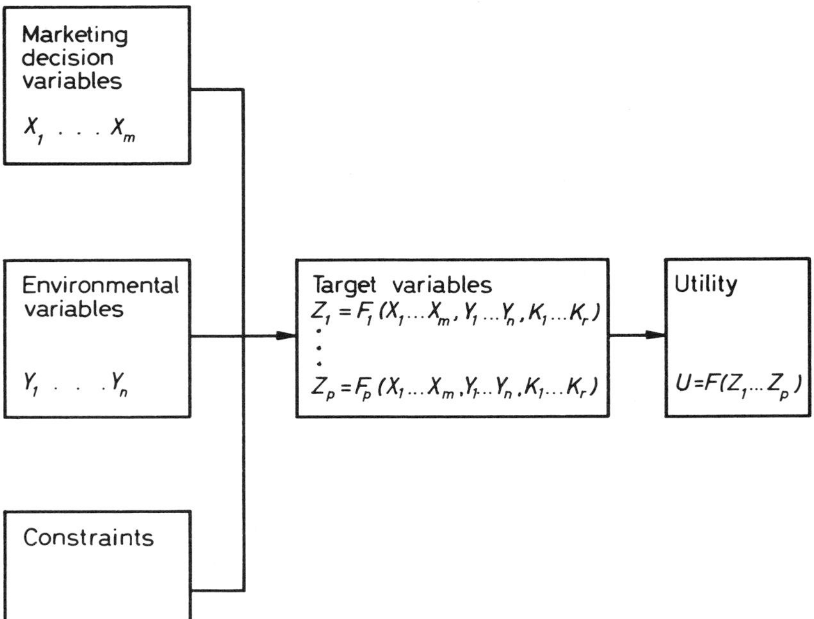

 Figure 10.1 *Framework for a theory of marketing decision making*

10.1.2. Formulation of a theory of marketing decision making

A framework for a theory of marketing decision making has been developed by Philip Kotler.* His statement of the problem is given below and illustrated in Fig. 10.1:

> Marketing management seeks to determine the best setting of various marketing decision variables *X* under their control (price, promotion, distribution, and product quality) over time, space, and product lines, in the face of environmental variables *Y* not under their control (the economy, competitive activity, and so on) that will maximize the firm's utility *U* over a set of target variables *Z*, all this subject to a set of constraints *K*. Marketing management must decide on these settings in the face of imperfectly known effects of marketing decision variables and imperfect projections of the future levels of environmental variables.

Under this concept the company is regarded as an entity that continually adjusts the variables under its control—the marketing decision variables—in the interest of maximal achievement of its objectives. These objectives are shown in Fig. 10.1 as the firm's target variables and include profit, and non-profit things such as sales and market share. Typically, the firm cannot simultaneously maximize all of its objectives. Some of them, for example sales and profit, inevitably conflict with one another if attempts are made to maximize them at the same time. To overcome this problem of conflicting objectives, the company has to place a value (utility) function over its objectives and seek to maximize this function. It might, for example, give a weight to each objective and then attempt to find a combination of marketing decision variables that would maximize the weighted combination of its objectives.

The results obtained by the company not only depend on its own marketing decisions, but also on environmental variables that are beyond its control, such as market potential and the activities of competitors. Hence, the firm must decide on the best levels of its own decision variables in the light of forecasts of the levels of the environmental variables. Also, this decision making must be carried out within a set of constraints. For example, there may be legal restrictions on the amount a firm can charge for a new product, or the amount by which it can change the price of an existing product.

An ideal theory of marketing decision making should allow the marketing manager to achieve an optimum solution to the problem of how to maximize the firm's objectives, subject to the constraints under which it operates. That is, it should provide a simultaneous solution to the best product assortment and level, allocation, mix, and timing of marketing effort in the light of its objectives and constraints. Although this ideal

* Kotler, P., 'Some Needed Extensions in the Theory of Marketing Programming', *1968 Fall Conference Proceedings of the American Marketing Association*, pp. 57–62.

has not been achieved, for the reasons given earlier, some progress has been made in developing decision-making models* in each of the decision areas. These models usually ignore interactions with the other elements of the marketing mix, and this is their greatest drawback. Nevertheless, viable models have been developed and are being used in such marketing decision-making areas as:

(*a*) new products,
(*b*) distribution,
(*c*) pricing,
(*d*) advertising, and
(*e*) personal selling.

In subsequent parts of this chapter we shall examine some specific applications from each of these areas.

10.2. New product decisions

The decision to introduce a new product is part of the continuous process of product planning, which attempts to ensure that the product mix of a company exactly matches the requirements of the market. Product planning ensures a successful matching of products with markets by answering the following questions:

(*a*) what products should be modified,
(*b*) what products should be dropped from the company's product mix, and
(*c*) what products should be added to the company's product mix.

All companies run the risk of adding new products that are not profitable, of retaining products that are no longer profitable, and of ending up with a product mix that cannot be regarded as optimum. Product planning seeks to minimize these risks through a careful appraisal of actual and potential markets, together with an evaluation of the company's resources.

Changes in the product mix have to be introduced because current company products cannot hold their market positions indefinitely. The lifetime sales of many products and industries reveal a typical pattern of development known as the product life-cycle. The shape of this life-cycle has been generally understood for many years. Brockoff,† for example, has developed a model which expresses sales at time t as

$$S_t = at^b \, e^{-ct} + dR_t$$

* Mathematical models, as we shall see, have been found of great use in solving marketing problems.

† Brockoff, K., 'A Test for the Product Life-Cycle'. *Econometrica*, Vol. *35*, July–October, 1967, pp. 472–484.

where a, b, c, and d are parameters, and the variable R is the sum of sales of related products manufactured by the same company. The length of the cycle depends on such factors as the rate of technological change, the rate of market acceptance, and the ease of competitive entry. What is not often realized, however, is that profits reach a maximum well before sales volume reaches a peak because of pressures from costs and profitless price competition. Consequently, product strategy is often better planned around the profit curve rather than the sales curve.

Most of the formal decision-making models that have been developed to assist product planners have concentrated on the problems of new products. There are several good reasons for this concentration of effort. According to a survey made by the Brookings Institution of the one hundred largest U.S.A. corporations from 1909 to 1948, few companies that had retained their traditional products and methods grew in stature.* The report concluded:

> There is no reason to believe that those now at the top will stay there except as they keep abreast in the race of innovation and competition.

The survey showed that it was those companies which grew, mainly as a result of new product development, that survived. New products are essential, therefore, to growth and hence survival of the firm. At the same time, however, it is extremely expensive and risky to innovate. The major reasons are:

(*a*) most product ideas which go into product development never reach the market,
(*b*) many of the products that do reach the market are not successful, and
(*c*) successful products tend to have a shorter life-cycle than new products once had.

For new products that are developed within the company, as against new products that are acquired by merger or take-over, the following six stages have been distinguished in the process of new product evolution:†

(*a*) Exploration—the search for product ideas to meet company objectives.
(*b*) Screening—a quick analysis to determine which ideas are pertinent and merit more detailed study.
(*c*) Business analysis—the expansion of the idea, through creative analysis, into a concrete business recommendation including product features and a programme for the product.
(*d*) Development—turning the idea-on-paper into a product-in-hand, demonstrable and producible.

* Kaplan, A. D. H., *Big Enterprise in a Competitive System*, The Brookings Institution, 1954.
† *Management of New Products*, 4th ed., Booz, Allen & Hamilton, Inc, 1965.

(*e*) Testing—the commercial experiments necessary to verify earlier business judgements.
(*f*) Commercialization—launching the product in full scale production and sale, committing the company's reputation and resources.

The next two sections will demonstrate the use of decision-making models at the screening and business analysis stages of new product evolution, respectively.

10.2.1. Screening of new product ideas

When the exploration stage of the new product evolution process has generated a set of potential product ideas, either from within the firm itself or from external sources, the next step is to screen out those products that are obviously not compatible with company objectives and resources. In general, four factors have to be taken into account for screening purposes:

(*a*) market size,
(*b*) market growth,
(*c*) competition, and
(*d*) compatibility.

In other words, is the potential market for the new product idea really big enough to make entry worthwhile? Is the market likely to grow? What other firms, if any, are already competing in it? And, finally, is the new product idea really compatible with the existing business resources, such as physical plant, current channels of distribution, financial strength, and personnel.

Various techniques have been developed for screening new product ideas, but the most commonly used method is that of product profile analysis. This procedure was first suggested in the mid-'fifties,* and it has been modified and made more sophisticated several times since then. It consists of listing the important factors to be considered, assigning weights to reflect their relative importance, and scoring each factor for every product idea under consideration. The magnitude of the score for each factor depends on how well the product idea meets the ideal for that factor. By multiplying the factor scores by the factor weights, and summing these products, a single weighted score is obtained which measures the desirability of the product. Thus, in mathematical terms, the firm may form a weighted score for product idea i as

* Kline, C. H., 'The Strategy of Product Policy', *Harvard Business Review*, July–August, 1955, pp. 91–100.

$$S_i = \sum_{j=1}^{f} W_j F_{ji}$$

where

S_i = product i's total weighted score,

W_j = weight associated with factor j where $0 = W_j = 1$, and $\sum_{j=1}^{f} W_j = 1$ and

F_{ji} = product i's score on factor j

The establishment of a lower cut-off value for the index will help to eliminate the apparently unsuitable products, and make sure that only relatively viable propositions are sent to the business analysis stage for a detailed profitability analysis.

A useful illustration of the procedure has been given by O'Meara,* in which four major factors are used as criteria for evaluating a new product idea. The four factors and their relative weights are shown in columns 1 and 2, respectively, of Table 10.1. The first factor, marketability, is concerned with the relation of the new product to the firm's present product line and its channels of distribution. In addition, it also relates to the compatibility of the product with the company's merchandising strengths, its quality-price relationship to competing products, and the production implications of the number of sizes and grades that will be required. The second factor, durability, is designed to assess the extent to which:

(*a*) there is a broad and lasting demand for the product,
(*b*) the product's design can be protected, and
(*c*) the product is affected by cyclical and seasonal variations.

Productive ability, the third factor, takes into account the availability of production knowledge, personnel, and equipment to produce the product, plus the availability of the appropriate raw materials. Finally, growth potential is concerned with the expected growth in the number of users, the growth of competition, and the product's place in the market.

To obtain a weighted score for the product idea, the weights in column 2 of Table 10.1, which represent the evaluator's judgement of their importance in relation to each other, are multiplied by the scores or assigned factor values given in column 3 for each factor. Multiplying the weights by the scores for each factor yields the quantities in column 4. Summing this final column provides the measure of product desirability which we are looking for—in this example it has a value of 72·2. But how are the scores or assigned factor values given in column 3 obtained? The procedure is as follows. (For the sake of brevity, only the marketability

* O'Meara, J. T., 'Selecting Profitable Products', *Harvard Business Review*, January–February, 1961, pp. 83–89.

Table 10.1. Example of product profile analysis

(1) *Factor*	(2) *Factor weight*	(3) *Assigned factor value*	(4) *Final factor evaluation*
I. *Marketability*	0·4	71·4	28·6
A. Relation to present distribution channels			
B. Relation to present product lines			
C. Quality-price relationship			
D. Number of sizes and grades			
E. Merchandisability			
F. Effects on sales of present products			
II. *Durability*	0·3	68·6	20·6
A. Stability			
B. Breadth of market			
C. Resistance to cyclical fluctuations			
D. Resistance to seasonal fluctuations			
E. Exclusiveness of design			
III. *Productive ability*	0·1	91·6	9·2
A. Equipment necessary			
B. Production knowledge and personnel necessary			
C. Raw materials availability			
IV. *Growth potential*	0·2	69·2	13·8
A. Place in market			
B. Expected competitive situation—value added			
C. Expected availability of end users			
		Final index	72·2

factor is used to illustrate the method.) Each of the subfactors that make up marketability are shown in column 1 of Table 10.2, and weights are assigned to them in column 2. Along the top of the table are verbal and numerical measures of how closely the ideal for each subfactor might be achieved. These measures relate to columns 3 to 7, inclusive. In the body of the table are estimated probabilities (EP) that the product in question will equal the description of 'very good', 'good', 'average', 'poor', or 'very poor'. For example, the evaluator believes there is a 0·5 chance that the merchandising characteristics of the product will meet the definition of 'very good'; probabilities of 0·4 and 0·1 are entered for 'good' and 'average', with no allowance for 'poor' and 'very poor'. Note that the probabilities in each row always sum to unity. Multiplying each probability figure by the numerical value attached to each rating (for example, the numerical value of 10 corresponds to 'very good') gives the values of expected value (EV) in columns 3 to 7. The total EV for each subfactor is shown in column 8. Multiplying the quantities in column 8 by the weights in column 2 yields the figures in column 9, which when added give the total factor value of 71·4 for marketability. A similar approach is used for the remaining three factors—durability, productive ability, and growth potential.

There are some important deficiencies in the method just described. Paul Green,* for example, has offered the following criticisms:

(*a*) The factor weights may not be independent of a product's scores on the various factors.
(*b*) The factors themselves may not be independent, as has been implicitly assumed above.
(*c*) The procedure assumes more knowledge on the rater's part about product characteristics than might be apparent at first glance.

The second of these criticisms appears to be of particular importance. Factor weights are usually assigned on the basis of either singular or combined subjective evaluations by managers and staff involved in the problem. They may be assisted in this task by a method such as that suggested by Dean,† which is based on ranking procedures. Whatever the method used, the weights given to the individual factors are treated as the probabilities of a set of mutually exclusive events. This is clearly not an accurate representation of the situation. Freimer and Simon‡ have suggested an approach that takes into account the interactions between the factors using the technique of multiple discriminant analysis.

* Alderson, W., and Green, P., *Planning and Problem Solving in Marketing*, Irwin, 1964, pp. 205–206.
† Dean, B. V., and Miskey, M. J., 'Scoring and Profitability Models for Evaluating and Selecting Engineering Projects', *Operations Research*, July–August, 1965, pp. 550–569.
‡ Freimer, M., and Simon, L., 'The Evaluation of Potential New Product Alternatives', *Management Science*, February, 1967, pp. B-279–B-292. Also, see Freimer, M., and Simon, L., *Analytical Marketing*, Harcourt, Brace & World, Inc, 1970, pp. 63–79.

Table 10.2. Evaluating the assigned factor value for marketability

(1) *Subfactor*	(2) *Subfactor weight*	(3) *Very good* (10) EP	EV	(4) *Good* (8) EP	EV	(5) *Average* (6) EP	EV	(6) *Poor* (4) EP	EV	(7) *Very poor* (2) EP	EV	(8) *Total* EV	(9) *Subfactor evaluation*
Relation to present distribution channels	1·0	0·1	1·0	0·2	1·6	0·5	3·0	0·2	0·8	—	—	6·4	6·4
Relation to present product lines	1·0	0·1	1·0	0·2	1·6	0·4	2·4	0·2	0·8	0·1	0·2	6·0	6·0
Quality/price relationship	3·0	0·3	3·0	0·4	3·2	0·2	1·2	0·1	0·4	—	—	7·8	23·4
Number of sizes and grades	1·0	0·1	1·0	0·2	1·6	0·5	3·0	0·2	0·8	—	—	6·4	6·4
Merchandisability	2·0	0·5	5·0	0·4	3·2	0·1	0·6	—	—	—	—	8·8	17·6
Effects on sales of present products	2·0	—	—	0·2	1·6	0·5	3·0	0·3	1·2	—	—	5·8	11·6
	10·0									Assigned factor value			71·4

Note: EP = estimated probability as judged by management; EV = expected value computed by multiplying the rating's numerical value by the estimated probability.

10.2.2. Evaluation of new product proposals

The new product ideas which pass through the screening process are subjected to detailed evaluation at the business analysis stage. In practice, this evaluation is often performed in the following way. First, the person or persons responsible for new product planning develop what they believe to be an optimum marketing mix for each product, using intuition and past experience as a guide to setting prices, determining advertising appropriations, and so on. Next, two estimates of sales volume are made. One is an estimate of the sales required to break-even, and the other is the likely sales volume which will be generated by the marketing mix chosen. If the margin between these two estimates is considered to be sufficiently large to meet the company's profit objectives, then the product is sent forward to the development stage. Alternatively, if several product proposals are being considered, the best one or two of these may proceed to development.

In recent years, more sophisticated procedures have been devised. They introduce additional factors into the analysis, such as marketing mix variations, product life-cycle considerations, discounted cash flow, and the consideration of uncertainty. With regard to marketing mix variations, Philip Kotler* has outlined an approach which provides a simultaneous evaluation of the profit potential of several marketing mixes in a break-even analysis framework. He derives three equations which are used to find the optimum marketing mix:

$$Z = (P-10)(Q-Q_B) \qquad (a) \text{ profit equation}$$

$$Q = 100\,000P^{-2}A^{1/8}S^{1/4} \qquad (b) \text{ demand equation}$$

$$Q_B = \frac{38\,000+A+S}{P-10} \qquad (c) \text{ break-even volume equation}$$

where

Z = annual profit
P = unit selling price
10 = variable cost per unit
Q = expected sales volume per year
Q_B = break-even volume
100 000 = a scale factor
-2 = the price elasticity
A = advertising budget
1/8 = the advertising elasticity
S = personal selling budget
1/4 = the personal selling elasticity
38 000 = nonmarketing fixed costs per year

* Kotler, P., 'Marketing Mix Decisions for New Products', *Journal of Marketing Research*, February, 1964, pp. 43–49.

His analysis proceeds by finding the unique set of values of P, A, and S which maximize Z. This is a problem in differential calculus, from which the following values emerge:

$$\begin{aligned} P &= 20 \\ A &= 12\,947 \\ S &= 25\,894 \\ Z &= 26\,735 \end{aligned}$$

Kotler himself points out the drawbacks in this method of analysis. Many of these drawbacks relate to the fact that the analysis is deterministic and static. Also, there are major problems involved in constructing the three equations that are required for obtaining a solution. Some of these shortcomings are alleviated by the approach to new product analysis known as DEMON* (DEcision Mapping via Optimum go-no Networks). The DEMON model consists of two distinct parts:

(*a*) A procedure for the development and analysis of the effect of marketing mix decisions on estimated demand and profits.

(*b*) A decision system for deciding whether to continue evaluations of the product (On), drop the product (No), or proceed to full-scale commercialization of the product (Go).

Under the decisions system, the Go decision is specified when the expected value of profits from the new product is greater than a specified value and when the probability of a particular payback requirement (for example, that the anticipated profits pay back the initial outlays within three years) is greater than the Go criterion level specified by management. The No alternative is taken when the expected value of profit is less than a specified level or the probability of achieving a particular 'pay-back' requirement is less than the No criterion level. The remaining area is for the On decision. When the answer is On, the model indicates the marketing variables that should be improved and specifies the optimum marketing research required to verify that improvement. A new evaluation is then made of the Go-No-On alternatives. The entire decision system can be represented as a network, such as that shown in Fig. 10.2.

The other major part of the DEMON model is the marketing relationships uncovered by studying 200 packaged goods products in 16 product categories. Figure 10.3 also portrayed in the form of a network indicates how relationships between advertising expenditures, advertising copy, product performance, distribution, and so on, are used. Thus, advertising expenditures give rise to media audiences (gross impressions) and so on. Eventually, triers (of the product) are converted to users and next, via a

* Charnes, A., and others, 'DEMON: A Management Model for Marketing New Products', *California Management Review*, Fall, 1968, pp. 31–46.

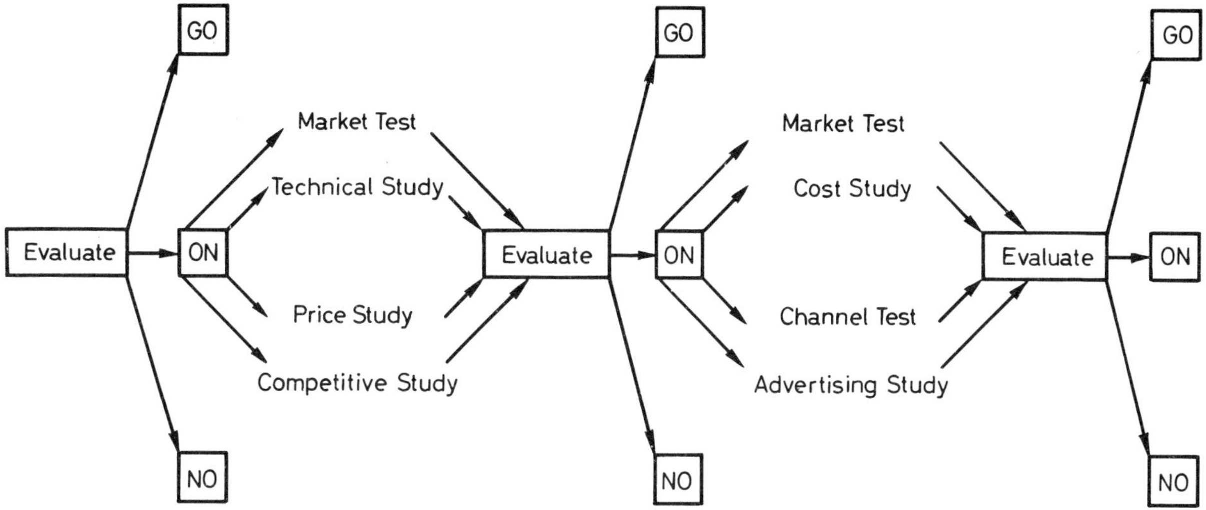

Figure 10.2. *DEMON decision network*

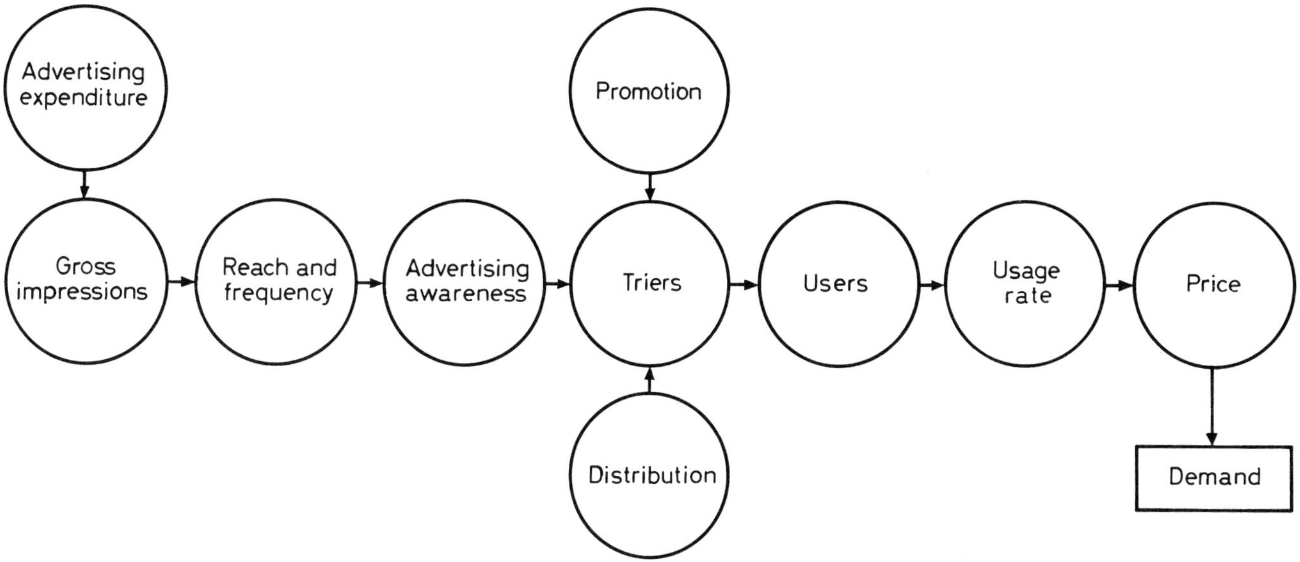

Figure 10.3. *DEMON relationships network*

unit price, the actual magnitude of consumer sales is obtained. Other routes to developing product trial are also possible, for example, 'promotion' and 'distribution'. Differing expenditures may be allocated to advertising and, in association with other factors, such as distribution, can affect usage rates. Using the estimated relationships between these elements, as estimated from the case studies, DEMON determines, at each evaluation, the combination of values for each of these variables which maximizes profits.

A recently developed model called SPRINTER* (Specification of PRofits with INteraction under Trial and Error Response) has all the characteristics of the DEMON model, plus a consideration of product interdependence. If a new product has demand and cost interdependencies with the other products in the company, the criterion for evaluation should be based on the differential profits of the whole product line, with and without the new product, not on the new product's absolute profits. The SPRINTER model incorporates managerial estimates of the demand and cost interrelationships between the new product and all other products in the line. In conclusion, it should be pointed out that the DEMON and SPRINTER models must be modified in some respects when the problem is not one of evaluating a new product proposal, but rather one of choosing from a set of new product proposals.

10.3. Distribution decisions

Distribution refers to the activities that take place between the time a a product is manufactured and the time it is bought by the customer. Problems of distribution are traditionally placed into one of two categories – problems of channels or problems of physical distribution. This distinction is a rather artificial one, however, and it is probably better to think in terms of the problems involved in constructing an integrated distribution system. To establish a distribution system, the marketing manager must undertake the following studies:

(*a*) Develop an understanding of retail and wholesale institutions, and the types of middlemen available in each group.
(*b*) Determine which channels to use, that is, the type or kind of middlemen (if any) to be used at each stage in the channel.
(*c*) Determine the intensity of distribution that is, the number of outlets desired in each stage.
(*d*) Select the individual middlemen.
(*e*) Determine the methods and procedures to be used in the physical distribution of the product.

* Urban, G. L., 'SPRINTER: A Tool for New Product Decision Makers', *Industrial Management Review*, Spring, 1967, pp. 43–55.

Steps (*a*) to (*d*) in the above sequence relate to the problems of channels. Distribution channels are the institutions through which title to goods is transferred from producer to ultimate consumer or industrial user. The channels always involve a flow of title and usually include a flow of goods. They form a total system and are best viewed as a series of independent firms that join together to develop a joint marketing opportunity.*

The institutions in a channel consist of middlemen—wholesalers and retailers. A wholesaler is a business enterprise which sells primarily to buyers other than ultimate consumers, and may be either a merchant or an agent. Retailers, on the other hand, sell primarily to ultimate consumers for non-business use, and they are almost invariably merchants. Merchant middlemen take ownership to the goods they are helping to market; agent middlemen do not take title, but they do actively assist in the transfer of title. The various channels of distribution which are available to a manufacturer or producer are shown in Fig. 10.4.

As mentioned above, the major channel decisions centre around which

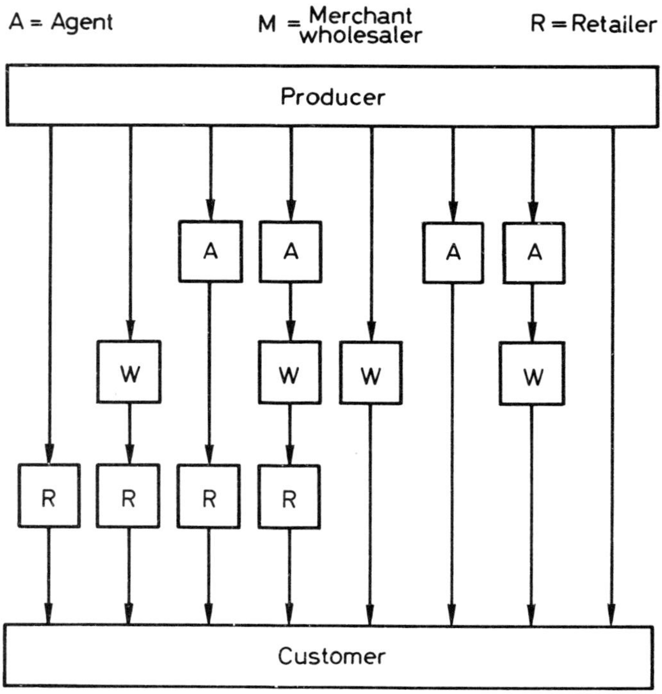

Figure 10.4. *Types of channels of distribution*

* Alderson, W., 'The Development of Marketing Channels', in Clewett, R. M. (ed.), *Marketing Channels for Manufactured Products*, Irwin, 1954, p. 30.

channel or channels to use, and what intensity of distribution to aim for at each stage of the channel. In practice, the decision on which channel to employ is usually based on a qualitative assessment of the following factors:

(*a*) the product and its characteristics, such as unit value, technical nature, perishability, and so on,
(*b*) the market and its characteristics, for example, the number of customers to be reached, order size, geographic concentration, and buying habits,
(*c*) the financial resources, reputation, and location of the company,
(*d*) the services provided and the availability of the desired middlemen, and
(*e*) the extent of competition in traditional channels.

Very few decision-making models have been developed in the area of channel selection for reasons which we shall discuss later. An example of one such model is briefly described in §10.3.1.

When making the decision on the level of intensity of distribution, a manufacturer has three main alternatives. He may elect for intensive distribution, and try to sell through as many wholesalers and retailers who will handle the product. This is usually the practice with heavily advertised, consumer–convenience goods. As an alternative to intensive distribution, the manufacturer may decide on selective distribution. The policy of selective distribution is one of carefully selecting only those distributors who meet certain requirements, in terms of their facilities for adequate distribution and servicing. Exclusive distribution, the third alternative, is similar to selective distribution, except that only one distributor is chosen in a particular market area. He is given exclusive distribution rights, often called a franchise, in an area.

After the manufacturer has decided on the number of middlemen he wishes to sell to directly, and also selected the specific middlemen he requires (assuming, of course, they are willing to handle his product), he is faced with the problem of getting the product to them in the right quantities at the right time. This brings us into the realm of physical distribution and step (*e*) of the establishment procedure. If there are a large number of middlemen to be supplied, and if they are scattered over the length and breadth of the country, it may be necessary for him to establish a chain of warehouses. This problem is particularly amenable to the techniques of operational research and management science, and in §10.3.2 we shall describe some of the methods that are available for deciding on the number and location of warehouses.

10.3.1. Selection of distribution channels

Very little progress has been made in constructing models which help the manufacturer to make decisions on which channels of distribution he should select for distributing his product or products. This is partly due to the fact that in many instances the manufacturer has very little choice in the matter; powerful groups of middlemen who hold the reins of a large distributive system make the choice for him! McVey has pointed this out in his classic paper on channels of distribution.* He says that the study of marketing textbooks may lead a reader to conclude that:

(*a*) middlemen of many types are available to any manufacturer in any market to which he wishes to sell, and within each type there is an ample selection of individual firms,
(*b*) the manufacturer habitually controls the selection and operation of individual firms in his channel, and
(*c*) middlemen respond willingly as selling agents for the manufacturer rather than as purchasing agents for a coveted group of customers to whom the middlemen sell.

Yet none of these conclusions is entirely valid, particularly the second one. He goes on to argue that a manufacturer may not even consider himself at the head of a channel, but only as occupying a link in a channel that begins with his suppliers.

Because a channel of distribution is a group of firms which constitute a loose coalition engaged in exploiting joint opportunity in the market, some kind of joint decision-making by all the firms in the channel on how to structure themselves is perhaps the only logical approach to channel selection. Some decision-making models have considered this possibility.† The simple problem described by Artle and Berglund compared the relative merits of a group of manufacturers distributing direct to retailers or selling through wholesalers, using costs and profits as criteria.‡ To illustrate their method, the two authors used a hypothetical market in which there were four manufacturers supplying ten retailers with goods. Each manufacturer produced and sold one kind of product. Three alternative channels of distribution were considered:

(*a*) selling directly,
(*b*) selling through one wholesaler, and
(*c*) selling through two wholesalers.

* McVey, P., 'Are Channels of Distribution What the Textbooks Say?', *Journal of Marketing*, January, 1960, pp. 61–65.

† Artle, R., and Berglund, S., 'A Note on Manufacturers' Choice of Distribution Channel', *Management Science*, July, 1959, pp. 460–471, and Stasch, S., 'A Method of Dynamically Analysing the Stability of the Economic Structure of Channels of Distribution', described in Kotler, P., *Marketing Management: Analysis, Planning and Control*, Prentice-Hall, 1967, pp. 414–415.

‡ See Buzzell, R. D., *Mathematical Models and Marketing Management*, Harvard University, 1964, pp. 136–156; for a related example on the allocation of personal selling effort between wholesaler and final customers.

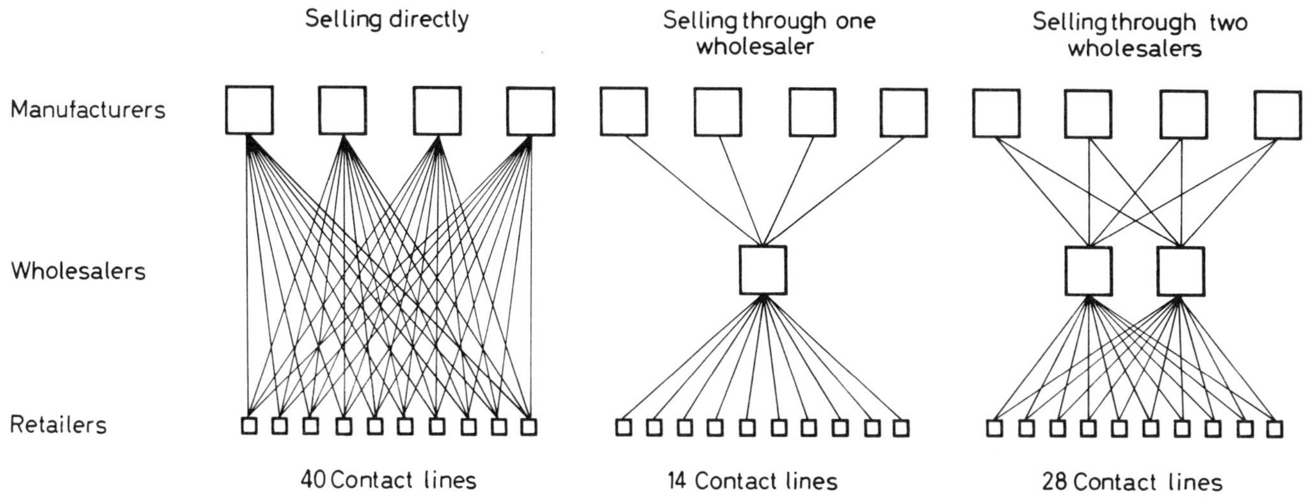

Figure 10.5. *Three possible channels of distribution with four manufacturers and ten retailers*

These alternatives led to 40, 14, and 28 contact lines, respectively (see Fig. 10.5). For the sake of simplicity, the only costs considered were those of selling.

When the direct sales force of the manufacturers and the calling force of the wholesalers were assumed to be equally effective in selling to retailers, the channel which used one wholesaler gave minimum total costs. However, when the direct sales force was considered more effective, which would probably be the case in practice, the sales volume varied between channels and profit was used as the criterion for choosing among them. Artle and Berglund extended their example to take this into account.

10.3.2. Number and location of distribution facilities

Having decided on the channels of distribution that are to be used for a product, marketing management must decide on the required number, size, and location of distribution facilities. The classic models that have been developed for solving this kind of problem employ their own particular vôcabulary. The sources of the goods which are being distributed are referred to as plants, and it is usually assumed that the number of plants, their locations, and the quantity of goods which each plant can supply is known. The ultimate destinations of the goods are called consuming centres, and it is further assumed that their requirements and locations are also known. Warehouses are the storage facilities between the plants and the consuming centres, and the problem is to determine the number, size, and location of the warehouses in order to minimize the costs of transportation from plant to warehouse and from warehouse to consuming centre, plus the costs of operating the warehouses.* The examples we shall describe will concentrate on the problem of distributing a single product and will assume that potential warehouse locations are restricted to a finite number of fixed sites. However, models are available which consider multiple products,† and which do not assume the number of sites to be fixed. The latter type of model is based on the well known centre of gravity analogy.‡

The problem of minimizing the cost of the distribution system can be integrated within the framework of mathematical (linear) programming. We must minimize the total cost:§

* An alternative formulation of the problem is to attempt to maximize profits, rather than minimize costs. This alternative approach assumes that total demand is not fixed, as assumed in the classic models, but is itself affected by the distribution system and the functions it performs. Little work has been done in this direction.

† Hurt, V. G., and Tramel, T. E., 'Alternative Formulations of the Transhipment Problem', *Journal of Farm Economics*, August, 1965, pp. 763–773.

‡ Cooper, L., 'Location-Allocation Problems', *Operations Research*, May–June, 1963, pp. 331–343.

§ Simon and Freimer, op. cit., p. 149.

$$\sum_i a_i y_i + \sum_i \sum_j b_{ij} x_{ij} + \sum_i \sum_k d_{ki} z_{ki}$$

where a_i = fixed cost of operating a warehouse at location i
y_i = 1 if a warehouse is placed at location i, 0 otherwise
$b_{ij} = c_i + t_{ij}$ = unit cost of operating a warehouse at location i plus unit cost of shipping from location i to consuming centre j
d_{ki} = unit cost of shipping from plant k to warehouse at location i
z_{ki} = quantity shipped from plant k to warehouse at location i
x_{ij} = quantity shipped from warehouse i to consuming centre j

Also, the following restrictions apply:

$\sum_k z_{ki} = \sum_j x_{ij}$ for all locations i; further restricted to 0 if $y_i = 0$

$\sum_i z_{ki} = S_k$ = supply at plant k

$\sum_i x_{ij} = R_j$ = requirement at consuming centre j

This is a mixed integer programming problem, because of the 0–1 variables y_i, and the problem we have formulated cannot be solved by ordinary programming methods, even if the cost functions are assumed to be linear. Early attempts to solve the problem did not consider fixed costs, that is, $a_i = 0$ for all i, and the problem was treated as one of nonlinear programming.* This is a reasonable assumption to make if the manufacturer does not own the warehouses. Developments in the theory of mathematical programming, however, have enabled the problem to be tackled using more complex methods.

A relatively simple approach to the problem, even though it involves a large amount of computational effort, is based on the idea that if the y_i are specified in advance the resulting problem can be treated as a transportation problem. Using the transportation method, a solution is obtained for each possible combination of warehouse location in turn, and the optimum combination is found by inspection. Suppose we have the following data:†

$a_1 = 70$	$a_2 = 80$	$a_3 = 60$	
$c_1 = 3$	$c_2 = 4$	$c_3 = 2$	
$t_{11} = 3$	$t_{21} = 6$	$t_{31} = 4$	$R_1 = 10$
$t_{12} = 3$	$t_{22} = 6$	$t_{32} = 3$	$R_2 = 6$
$t_{13} = 4$	$t_{23} = 4$	$t_{33} = 1$	$R_3 = 8$
$t_{14} = 5$	$t_{24} = 2$	$t_{34} = 4$	$R_4 = 10$
$t_{15} = 7$	$t_{25} = 3$	$t_{35} = 5$	$R_5 = 6$
$d_{11} = 0$	$d_{12} = 5$	$d_{13} = 3$	$S_1 = 20$
$d_{21} = 5$	$d_{22} = 0$	$d_{23} = 4$	$S_2 = 20$

* Baumol, W. J., and Wolfe, P., 'A Warehouse Location Problem', *Operations Research*, March–April, 1958, pp. 252–263.
† Simon, L. S., and Freimer, M., op. cit., p. 150.

As can be seen, there are two plants, three warehouse locations, and five consuming centres. Except for the fixed costs, a_{ij}, all this information is used to derive Fig. 10.6a, which is the cost-requirement-supply tableau for the problem. In the body of the tableau are the appropriate costs; the use of ∞ is designed to preclude the warehouses from supplying each other and the plants from supplying direct to the consuming centres. The optimum solution to this transportation problem is shown in Fig. 10.6b. The upper left block shows the quantities to be shipped from plants to warehouses (z_{ki}), the lower right block shows the quantities to be shipped from warehouses to consuming centres (x_{ij}), and the lower left block shows

		Warehouse 1	Warehouse 2	Warehouse 3	Consuming centre 1	Consuming centre 2	Consuming centre 3	Consuming centre 4	Consuming centre 5	
Plant	1	0	5	3	∞	∞	∞	∞	∞	20 (Supply)
	2	5	0	4	∞	∞	∞	∞	∞	20 (Supply)
Warehouse	1	0	∞	∞	6	6	7	8	10	50 (Capacity)
	2	∞	0	∞	10	10	8	6	7	50 (Capacity)
	3	∞	∞	0	6	5	3	6	7	50 (Capacity)
		50	50	50	10	6	8	10	6	
		Capacity			Requirement					

(a)

		1	2	3	1	2	3	4	5	
	1	16		4						20
	2		16	4						20
	1	34			10	6				50
	2		34					10	6	50
	3			42			8			50
		50	50	50	10	6	8	10	6	

(b)

Figure 10.6. *Transportation formulation*

unused warehouse capacity (since the capacities were not given, they were set large enough for any warehouse to cope with total demand, if this were found to be necessary). In this solution, all three warehouses are used, so the total fixed cost is $70+80+60 = 210$. The variable cost is 250, obtained by multiplying the costs in Fig. 10.6a by the quantities in Fig. 10.6b and summing. The total cost is then, $210+250 = 460$.

Because it was computed ignoring fixed costs, the optimum solution shown in Fig. 10.6a need not be the best solution for the overall problem. The method proceeds, therefore, to study all other possible configurations of warehouse use. The results of this enumeration are shown below in Table 10.3. Two warehouses, at locations 1 and 2, produce the minimum total cost.

Table 10.3. Total cost of location configurations

Locations used	*Fixed cost*	*Variable cost*	*Total cost*
1, 2, 3	210	250	460
1, 2	150	258	408
1, 3	130	310	440
2, 3	140	292	432
1	70	392	462
2	80	426	506
3	60	356	416

The procedure just described involves the solution of approximately 2^N transportation problems, where N is the number of available warehouse sites. When N is very large, the amount of computation becomes prohibitive, and alternative methods are needed. One approach is to build up a warehouse network one warehouse at a time. In our example (see Table 10.3) this would start with a warehouse at location 3 (the lowest fixed cost). Because no improvement can be obtained by adding a warehouse at either location 1 or location 2, this would then be the solution. In a larger problem, with perhaps several hundred possible sites, more warehouses would undoubtedly be added. At the end of this forward selection procedure, this might result in some of the earlier sites selected at a previous stage being badly located or even superfluous. A second phase would then be necessary. Kuehn and Hamburger have developed such a procedure using the method of heuristic programming, a technique which is midway between mathematical (linear) programming and simulation.* In their model, certain arbitrary but plausible rules

* Kuehn, A. A., and Hamburger, M. J., 'A Heuristic Program for Locating Warehouses', *Management Science*, July, 1963, pp. 643–666.

(known as heuristics) are introduced which lead to quick and satisfactory, if not optimum, solutions. Their program is divided into two parts:

(*a*) the main program, which locates warehouses one at a time until no additional ones can be added without increasing total costs, and
(*b*) a 'bump and shift' routine which attempts to modify the distribution network arrived at in the main program by evaluating the profit implications of dropping warehouses or of shifting them from one location to another.

The program also includes the demand creation aspect of distribution as an opportunity cost. Other heuristic procedures have also been developed. For example, Feldman and his associates have developed a heuristic procedure that begins by including all possible warehouses and then dropping them one by one until no further cost reduction can be obtained.*

If the distribution system is to be modelled in all its complexity, then deriving an analytical solution through mathematical programming might not be possible. Similarly, the use of heuristic methods might not be appropriate. In this kind of situation, a satisfactory solution to the facilities location problem may be found through the use of simulation—the technique of experimentation applied to a model of the system. One of the most widely used simulation programs, developed by Shycon and Maffei, is capable of simulating a system of up to forty warehouses, 4000 customers or consuming centres, and ten plants.†

10.4. Pricing decisions

Deciding on the price to charge for a product is one of the most important decisions facing the marketing manager, in spite of the growing emphasis on non-price factors in the marketing mix.‡ As some type and level of profit is the normal goal of business, the price must be the right one or a firm will make less profit than it might have. This is as true if the price is too high as if the price is on the low side. Too low a price quite obviously gives away a lot of profit. The same is true of too high a price, although in this case it is brought about through a reduction of sales and is less obvious. Furthermore, the pricing decision has to be made in a variety of situations, and this tends to make the decision an extremely complicated one. Pricing is a problem when a new product is being introduced, when a

* Feldman, E., Leher, F., and Ray, T. L., 'Warehouse Location Under Continuous Economies of Scale', *Management Science*, May, 1966, pp. 670–684.

† Shycon, H. N., and Maffei, R. M., 'Simulation: Tool for Better Distribution', *Harvard Business Review*, November–December, 1960, pp. 65–75. See also, Gerson, M. L., and Maffei, R. B., 'Technical Characteristics of Distribution Simulators', *Management Science*, October, 1963, pp. 62–69.

‡ Udell, J. G., 'How Important is Pricing in Competitive Strategy?', *Journal of Marketing*, January, 1964, pp. 44–48.

price change is being considered in the face of uncertain customer and competitor reactions, and when a firm must react to a competitor who has just changed his price. It is also a problem in industries where companies submit sealed bids for jobs, as we shall see (in §10.4.2.). And it is a problem when the firm's product mix is subject to substantial demand and cost interdependencies. Because of this complexity and the importance of the pricing decision it might be expected that a useful theory of pricing exists to help the decision maker. Unfortunately, this is not yet the case, and a tremendous gulf exists between the traditional theories of the economist and the practices of the businessman.

One of the main objectives of competitive price theory is to explain by abstract analysis how prices are determined under various kinds of market structures, and economists have isolated several such structures in their attempts to explain how prices are determined in a free enterprise economy. Thus, sophisticated models have been developed which describe pricing under pure competition, pricing under pure monopoly, pricing under monopolistic competition, and pricing under oligopoly. As a result of this theorizing, an economist would probably define price, if asked, as the factor which equates supply with demand. He might also add that in a competitive market price will tend to settle at a level at which no excess profits are made by the manufacturers, whilst a monopoly will fix prices so that its profits are at a maximum. It is generally agreed that whether or not these statements are true, they are of no value whatsoever to the businessman. The businessman, on the other hand, would probably say that price is the cost of the product, plus his margin for profit. While this is undoubtedly true, it gives no guidance at all to the person or persons who have to set or administer a price. Clearly the definition depends on what is meant by cost and what is the actual size of the margin which is added to it.

Prices are generally arrived at in practice from a consideration of cost, demand, and competition. Each of these three factors has an important role to play in determining price, but the businessman usually places the greatest emphasis on cost or supply considerations. This is in contrast to the theory of the economist, which gives full and equal recognition to both supply and demand. The importance attached to cost-plus pricing by the businessman is probably a function of two things; first, an accurate demand schedule for the product is extremely difficult, if not impossible to obtain, and second, the accountant can supply cost data that has a comforting appearance of precision. However, cost concepts differ widely. A firm's accounting records describe what costs have been in the past, yet the determination of price should require a knowledge of what costs will be in the future. Also, there is the problem of what cost base to use and what size of margin to add. For example, two commonly accepted price formula which are based on costs are:

(*a*) prices equal to allocated total costs, plus a certain standard percentage mark-up, and
(*b*) prices equal to allocated direct or variable costs plus some amount added to cover allocated overhead and profit contribution.*

Whichever method is used, an estimate is required of sales volume to derive the price, and this is the major conceptual flaw of cost-based methods of pricing. Price itself is a factor that influences sales volume! If cost-plus pricing is being used, however, most authorities would recommend the use of direct costs as the base. This is particularly appropriate under conditions of excess plant capacity, when a product may be sold that covers less than full costs, provided no better use can be found for the facilities. The size of the margin might then be determined from a study of demand and competition.

Public explanations by companies of price changes usually give major emphasis to costs. Nevertheless, demand is of equal, and in some instances of greater, importance. For some products, sales can be increased by a relatively larger percentage than the decline in price (an elastic demand). The larger volume, in turn, tends to reduce unit costs by permitting the distribution of overhead costs over more units and sometimes by permitting the economies of large scale production. The pricing executive should attempt to establish the demand schedule for the product, which in the graphical approach, involves determining the level, slope, and shape of the demand curve. If this can be done, and the difficulty of this was mentioned earlier, then the boundaries of the pricing problem can be defined. At one extreme the price setter has a knowledge of costs, and at the other he knows something about the demand for the product, or what the traffic will bear. His task is to choose the right price in the gap between the cost 'floor' and the demand 'ceiling'. This depends upon such factors as the nature and type of competition, the overall marketing mix, and any legal constraints which may have to be observed. The reactions of competitors, in particular, is often the crucial consideration imposing practical limitations on pricing alternatives.

10.4.1. Decision theory in price modification

It is often said that in the face of declining demand, a firm should reduce its prices. Although a very high price elasticity of demand has to exist for this to be profitable, Buzzell† and Green‡ have provided an example of the application of decision theory to a price reduction problem where a

* Very often, the pricing objective behind these methods is to earn a 'target' level of profit or a target rate-of-return.

† Buzzell, op. cit., chapter 6.

‡ Green, P. E., 'Bayesian Decision Theory in Pricing Strategy', *Journal of Marketing*, January, 1963, pp. 5–14.

reduction was shown to be desirable. A large chemical manufacturer had been selling a plastic material known as Kromel to industrial users for several years, and had captured 40 per cent of the Kromel market; the three competing sellers were also large firms. Kromel was basically a modification of an older plastic material named Verlon, and because Kromel was superior in many respects its price was about 10 per cent per pound higher. The management of the company became concerned as to whether or not its present price of $1 per pound could be maintained much longer because of stagnant demand and an expected increase in the production capacity of the industry. It was felt that a solution to the problem lay in penetrating one of four market segments (segment A) which was closely held still by Verlon, the produce of six companies. The executives of the company were sure that if segment A could be penetrated then, for various reasons, demand in the other three segments (B, C, and D) would increase substantially. Therefore, it was decided to evaluate four alternatives; maintaining the price at $1 per pound, or reducing the price to $0·93, $0·85, and $0·80, respectively.

Clearly the decision on which price to adopt involved some risk. What the management needed was a prediction of what might happen if a given price change was introduced, as well as estimates of the likelihood of each possible series of events. A decision tree diagram of possible chains of events was drawn up, and a part of this diagram is shown in Fig. 10.7. Each

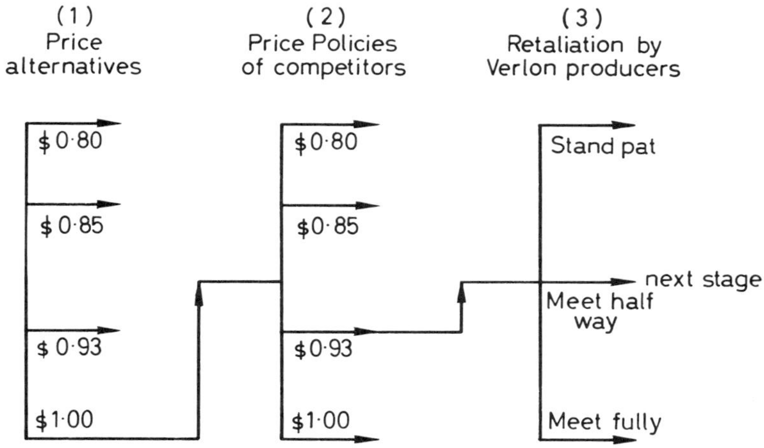

Figure 10.7. *Partial tree diagram of chains of events for alternative Kromel prices*

branch of the tree represents a specific series of possible events. For example, at stage 1 there are four alternative price strategies. If one of these were followed, then the three competing sellers might reduce their prices (stage 2) to any of the four alternative levels. (It was assumed that if any Kromel producer lowered his price, the others would follow.) For any of these four possible levels, the six Verlon producers might retaliate by meeting the reduction fully, by meeting it halfway, or by standing pat (stage 3). The tree was extended in this way to account for further uncertainties, such as what change in the Kromel industry capacity might take place, in what year penetration of segment A might be achieved, what the Kromel share of segment A might be, and finally, for any given market share in segment A, whether Kromel market shares in the other three segments might follow a basic (predicted) pattern of growth or might be speeded up a year.

For each possible series of events, the sales and profit consequences were traced out. Included in this analysis were three alternative forecasts (optimistic, pessimistic, and most probable) of combined Kromel-Verlon sales that had been made for the next five years—the analysis period which had been decided upon. Thus, by following each of these forecasts and any one of the complete chains of events, it was possible to arrive at a five-year forecast of the company's Kromel sales (making certain assumptions about the company's market share). As costs could be estimated from sales volume, the profits on Kromel sales could then be derived. The next step was to obtain estimates of the probabilities at each branch of the tree from the firm's sales personnel. Once these were obtained, the model was programmed on a digital computer for simulation of the various alternatives. The sequence of possible events was laid out for each price alternative, and the cumulative, compounded profit at the end of five years associated with each outcome was computed from

$$\sum_{i=1}^{5} (1+r)^{5-i} (D_{ij} - Z_{ij}) (K_{ij} M_{ij})$$

where r = rate of interest. In this particular study, rates of interest of 6 and 10 per cent were used to represent two possible opportunity costs on potential use of funds

D_{ij} = Kromel price per pound in year i, under the j'th outcome

Z_{ij} = total cost per pound of Kromel in year i, under the j'th outcome

K_{ij} = company's overall market share of Kromel sales in the i'th year under the j'th outcome

M_{ij} = total Kromel sales (in pounds) in year i under the j'th outcome

Probabilities for each outcome were computed by multiplying the probabilities of the events leading up to it. Then, for each price alternative ($1, $0·93, $0·85, or $0·80), the expected values of compounded net profits over the five-year period were computed from:

$$\sum_{j=1}^{n} P_j \text{(Profit of } j\text{'th outcome)}$$

in which P_j represents the probability of the j'th final outcome for the given price.

When the calculations were carried out using the 6 per cent interest rate, the most probable sales forecast for industry sales, and under the assumption that a price reduction would effectively discourage growth in industry capacity, the price of $0·80 yielded the higher expected profit. Furthermore, it was found from sensitivity analysis that the use of the alternative interest rate (10 per cent) and either of the other two industry sales forecasts (optimistic and pessimistic) did not affect the ranking of the four price strategies. A separate series of computations was then run on the assumption that price reductions would not discourage the growth of productive capacity. This led to $0·85 being the best price to charge and a drop in the expected profit of 21·5 per cent. Comparing these results, it became clear that the key factor underlying the differences in profits was the company's share of total Kromel sales. That is, if it were assumed that a price reduction would discourage additions to capacity, then the company would probably win a higher share of the expanding market by reducing prices.

10.4.2. Competitive bidding

A special type of new product pricing is where the company submits a sealed bid for a contract. In its purest form, the firm submitting the lowest bid is awarded the contract. The bidder has the problem of attempting to submit a bid that will help his company achieve its objectives, if the bid is accepted, while at the same time trying to beat competitive bids. To aid the price setter in such situations, competitive bidding models have been developed.*

As an example of competitive bidding, assume that a firm has as its objective the maximization of immediate profit. Profit (P) in this case is the difference between the Bid Price (B) and the Expense (E) of completing the project. Symbolically, we might express this as follows: $P = B - E$. If the company bids £10 000 on a project that will cost £9000 to complete and its probability of getting the contract is 50 per cent, then the expected value of profit, or expected profit, for short, is calculated as follows:

$$\begin{aligned} \text{Profit} &= £10\,000 - £9000 \\ &= £1000 \\ \text{Expected profit} &= 0{\cdot}5 \times £1000 + 0{\cdot}5 \times 0 \\ &= £500 \end{aligned}$$

* Friedman, L., 'A Competitive Bidding Strategy', *Operations Research*, February, 1956, pp. 104–112.

In formula form, the calculation of expected profit (EP) is:

$$EP = PR(B-E)+(1-PR)\times 0$$
$$= PR(B-E)$$

where PR = probability of receiving contract

To extend the theory further, assume that a firm has bid on 100 contracts in the past. It has kept a record of its estimated expenses to complete the project if it won the contract. It also has kept a record of all the winning bid prices. The probability of winning was calculated as shown in Table 10.4. There is no history of any winning bid being less than 80 per cent of the company's estimated expense, therefore if the company bids 79 per cent of its estimated expense it is assured of winning. The next row of the table shows that 1 per cent of the bids in the past have been between 80 per cent and 90 per cent of the company's expected expense of completion; therefore the probability of winning a bid if that bid price is 89 per cent of expense is 99 per cent. The same type of reasoning follows for the remaining rows in the table.

Table 10.4. Probability of winning a contract

Winning bid as a per cent of estimated expense (%)	*Frequency of occurrence*	*Probability of occurrence* (%)	*Bid as a per cent of estimated expense* (%)	*Probability of winning* (%)
80	1	1	79	100
90	5	5	89	99
100	10	10	99	94
110	14	14	109	84
120	30	30	119	70
130	22	22	129	40
140	18	18	139	18
150	0	0	149	0
	100 bids	100 per cent		

With this information an optimal bidding strategy can be developed. Taking all the possible bids the company could make, the profit or loss that bids would generate is expressed in terms of percentage above or below expense. For example, a bid of 79 per cent of expense would generate a loss of 21 per cent. The percentage profit or loss is then multiplied by the probability of its occurrence. The result is the expected profit in terms of a percentage over or below expense. In terms of our previous formula, and a bid of 109 per cent of estimated expense, we would have:

$$\text{Profit} = B - E$$
$$= 1{\cdot}09E - E$$
$$= 0{\cdot}09E$$
$$\text{Expected profit} = PR(B - E) = 0{\cdot}84 \times 0{\cdot}09E$$
$$= 0{\cdot}0756E$$

This figure is shown in percentage form in the first column of Table 10.5., together with the remaining calculations. From this exercise the company knows that in the long run it will maximize profit by bidding 119 per cent of its estimated expense in all competitive bidding situations.

Table 10.5. Expected profit

Bid as a per cent of estimated expense	*Per cent above or below expense*	*Probability of winning*	*Expected profit in terms of expense*
79	−21	100	−21
89	−11	99	−10·9
99	− 1	94	− ·94
109	+ 9	84	+ 7·56
119	+19	70	+13·3*
129	+29	40	+11·6
139	+39	18	+ 7·0
149	+49	0	0

*Optimal bid

10.5. Advertising decisions

The task of building an advertising campaign calls for considerable skill. For this reason, among others, advertising agencies are often appointed by manufacturers to handle their advertising problems for them, particularly the problems of creating advertising copy and selecting advertising media. However, in order to work efficiently with advertising specialists, the marketing manager should have an understanding of many of the functions which the advertising agency performs. With the growing emphasis on sophisticated decision-making techniques, the need for this understanding is doubly important. We shall consider in the following three sections the problems of deciding how much to spend on advertising (the advertising appropriation), which media to use, and how to measure the effectiveness of the advertising.

10.5.1. Determination of the advertising appropriation

The major recurrent advertising decision facing the marketing manager and his agency is how much to spend on advertising. This should, of course, be regarded as part of the larger questions of how much to spend on total promotion (advertising, personal selling, and sales promotion), and what share of the total promotional budget should advertising receive. In practice, however, the advertising appropriation tends to be arrived at independently.

Despite the various methods available for determining the advertising appropriation, this decision remains an extremely hazy one for most firms, and in view of the considerable amounts of money that are often involved it is not surprising that it was one of the first areas to be investigated by operational research workers. One of the earliest studies was that made by Vidale and Wolfe at Arthur D. Little, Inc.* After a lot of experimentation, they found that the relationship between sales, S, and advertising, A, could be represented by the differential equation:

$$\frac{\mathrm{d}S}{\mathrm{d}t} = [rA(t)\,(M - S(t))/M] - \lambda s(t)$$

where $S(t)$ = rate of sales at time t.
$A(t)$ = rate of advertising expenditure at time t.
M = the saturation level, i.e., the practical limit of sales that can be generated in response to a specific advertising effort. This is a function of the media used as well as of the character of the product.
r = the response constant, i.e., the sales generated per advertising dollar when sales equal zero. It is assumed that advertising affects only sales to noncustomers and not the retention of current customers. The difference between the saturation level of sales and the current level represents potential customers.
λ = the sales decay constant, or percentage decline in sales per period that would take place in the absence of advertising.

The task for the company is to estimate the three parameters M, r, and λ, for its product and campaign, from either historical information or from controlled experimentation. For example, λ can be measured by observing sales declines in areas where advertising has been set equal to zero for measurement purposes.

Given the parameters, the company can solve the equation for the level of advertising necessary to achieve a particular level of sales in the steady state, by setting $\mathrm{d}S/\mathrm{d}t$ to 0 and obtaining:

$$A = \frac{(\lambda/r)\,SM}{M - S}$$

* Vidale, M. L., and Wolfe, H. B., 'An Operations-Research Study of Sales Response to Advertising', *Operations Research*, June, 1957, pp. 370–381.

The equation shows that the company wishing to achieve a higher level of sales must spend more on advertising:

(*a*) the higher the ratio of the decay constant to the response constant,
(*b*) the greater the absolute level of sales, and
(*c*) the closer sales are to the saturation level.

Vidale and Wolfe also presented sales results for a constant advertising expenditure for a period of length T and for a pulse campaign. The model also enables some interesting comparisons to be made. For example, if a fixed sum is available for advertising (determined by some other method) the model can be used for comparing the effects of spending it in many different ways—a constant amount each month, the whole sum at the beginning of the year, half the sum now and half six months later, and so on. The limitations of the model, such as its failure to allow for competitor's actions and the notion that advertising only affects non-customers could be refined out of the model by introducing additional complexity.

More elaborate models of the advertising-sales relationships have in fact been developed since the pioneering efforts of Vidale and Wolfe. A model using the concepts of the linear learning model of consumer behaviour has been built by Kuehn,* in which sales are regarded as being made up of three components—sales due to habit, sales due to product characteristics, and sales due to advertising interacting with the product characteristics. In this model it is the third segment which is assumed to be affected by the advertising expenditure. The total sales function is dependent on:

(*a*) the percentage of brand-loyal customers and the rate of decay in this brand loyalty,
(*b*) the percentage of customers not committed to the company or its major competitors,
(*c*) the absolute size and growth rate of the market,
(*d*) the relative importance of price and distribution in the marketing process,
(*e*) the relative importance of the interaction of product characteristics and advertising in the marketing process, and
(*f*) the relative share and effectiveness of the advertising expenditure of the company.

Given the variables and the information required as input to the model, a competitive pay-off matrix can be constructed, and the standard expected

* Kuehn, A. A., 'A Model for Budgeting Advertising', in Bass, F. M., *et. al.*, '*Mathematical Models and Methods in Marketing*', Irwin, 1961, pp. 302–353. See also Kuehn, A. A., 'How Advertising Performance Depends on Other Marketing Factors', *Journal of Advertising Research*, March, 1962, pp. 2–10.

value concepts of game theory can be utilized to find the optimum advertising appropriation.

10.5.2. Media selection

Media selection, also known as media planning or media scheduling, is concerned with allocating the advertising appropriation among alternative media (television, newspapers, magazines, and so on) and also scheduling the insertion of the advertisements over time. From a conceptual standpoint, the total appropriation should be divided among the different media so that the marginal returns from each type of all media are equal.

Cost per thousand persons reached by a specific media vehicle is the traditional criterion used by media planners. In the case of newspapers, for example, it is possible to obtain figures of total readership, relate these figures to say the cost of a half-page advertisement, and so arrive at the cost of reaching 1000 persons. Under this approach the media planner would rank the various newspapers according to cost per thousand and place advertisements in those newspapers with the lowest rating. There are, however, several limitations to the simple cost per thousand approach:

(*a*) It uses the figure for the total readership of the newspaper instead of that part of the total readership representing target group members.*
(*b*) Only a fraction of the persons who are exposed to the advertisement will actually notice it, and an even smaller fraction will read it.
(*c*) It neglects qualitative differences which might exist in the impact of different newspapers.

These problems can be alleviated through the judicious use of what are known as target and media weights, which are invariably used in the decision-making models that we are about to describe.

Operational research workers and management scientists have been extremely active over the last decade in building decision-making models which assist the media planner in making his complex media decisions. It is probably safe to say that of all the marketing decision areas, the problem of media selection has received the greatest attention. All the various models that have been constructed fall into one of two groups. Some models take an optimizing approach, in which a mathematical algorithm† is used to determine the 'best' possible media schedule. The second class of models consist of heuristic and simulation models that evaluate the effectiveness of a given schedule, and compare it with other, alternative schedules. The latter group of models are less constrained than the optimizing models, but they do not yield a 'best' solution.

* A target group consists of those individuals at which the advertisements are directed. It may be made up of a number of smaller subsegments.

† An algorithm is a series of instructions, or procedural steps, for the solving of a specific problem.

The most publicized optimizing model is the linear programming model that was first launched by the American advertising agency Batten, Barton, Durstine, and Osborne (BBD & O).* In the model, the problem is stated as one of selecting the media mix which would maximize the total number of exposures† subject to constraints such as:

(*a*) the size of the total advertising budget, and
(*b*) the specified minimum and maximum usage rates of various media.

In practice, the model did not have the success BBD & O expected, because of its various limitations. Kotler‡ summarized the five most important of these:

(*a*) linear programming assumes repeat exposures have the same effect,
(*b*) it assumes constant media costs (no discounts),
(*c*) it cannot handle the problem of audience duplication,
(*d*) it says nothing about when advertisements should be scheduled, and
(*e*) it often requires poor or non-existent data.

The linear programming approach to media selection can be formulated mathematically as:

$$\text{maximize total exposure} = \sum_{i=1}^{I} R_i X_i$$

$$\text{subject to} \sum_{i=1}^{I} C_i X_i \leqslant A$$

$$X_i \leqslant U_i$$

$$X_i \geqslant 0 \quad \text{for } i = 1, 2, \ldots, I$$

where X_i = the number of insertions in medium i
C_i = the cost per insertion in medium i
A = the total advertising appropriation available
U_i = the physical upper limit of insertions in medium i
R_i = the rated exposure value of a single insertion in medium i.§

A further type of optimization model is the iteration or marginal analysis model.¶ Perhaps the best known models in this category are the 'High-

* Buzzel, op. cit., pp. 157–179.

† The various exposure measures such as total exposure, frequency, and reach, will be discussed in §10.5.3, together with a description of the related problem of audience duplication.

‡ Kotler, P., 'Toward an Explicit Model for Media Selection', *Journal of Advertising Research*, March, 1964, pp. 34–41.

§ The calculation of the number of rated exposure units (REU's) for a vehicle in the 'BBD & O' model, made use of target and media weights.

¶ Strictly speaking, an incremental model does not always yield an optimum solution. It may yield what is known as a 'local' optimum.

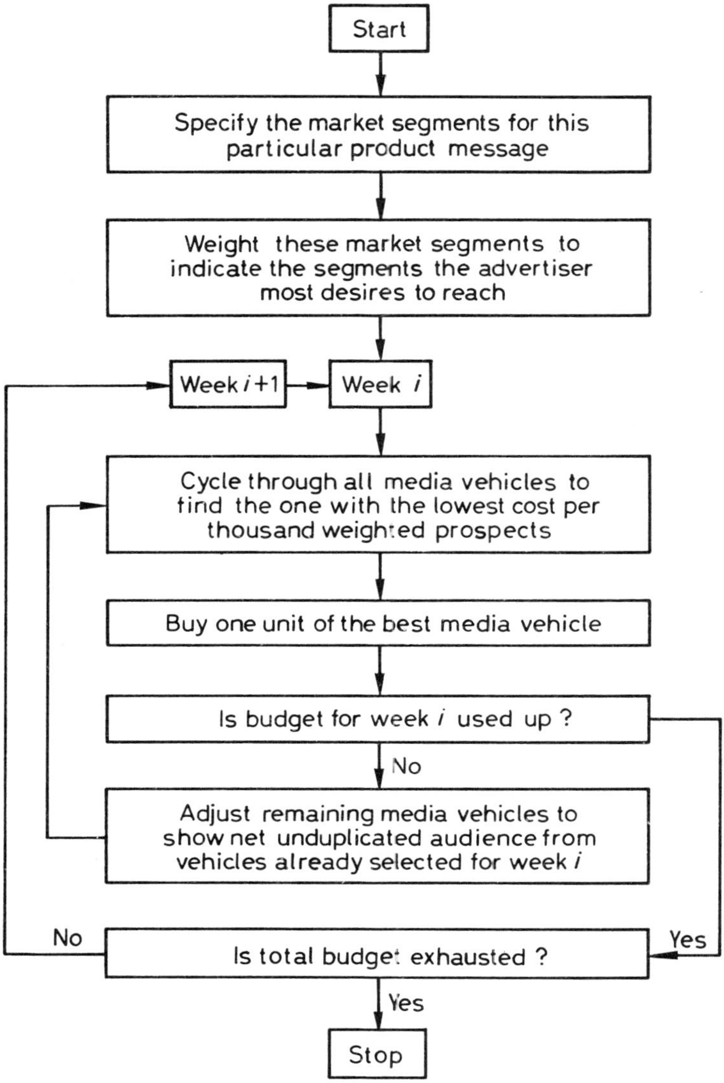

Figure 10.8. *Flow diagram for iteration model*

Assay' model of Young and Rubicam* (again, an American agency), and the model of Ogilvy and Mather† (British). The concept underlying the

* Moran, W. T., 'Practical Media Decisions and the Computer', *Journal of Marketing*, July, 1963, pp. 26–30.

† Philips, D., 'Schedule Building for Press and TV', in *Computers in Advertising*, Institute of Practitioners in Advertising, 1965.

iteration approach is to bring one vehicle into the solution at a time. The vehicle with the highest value is selected first. The list is then re-scanned, and the vehicle with the next highest value is selected. This process is continued until the appropriation is spent. A common feature of these models, which is an advantage over the linear programming formulation, is that the values of the remaining vehicles are recomputed after every stage to account for audience duplication. Figure 10.8 shows the basic structure of a media selection iteration model, in which the target group has been broken down into smaller subsegments or market segments, to which appropriate target weights are applied to reflect their relative importance.*

Many of the problems that appear to be inherent in the optimizing models can be circumvented through the use of heuristic and simulation models. The only reported heuristic model was developed by Lee and his colleagues at British European Airways.† There are, however, several simulation models in operation. The first of these to be publicized was the model of the Simulmatics Corporation, an American organization.‡ In common with all simulation models, it did not profess to find the 'best' media plan, but rather to estimate the exposure value of any selected media schedule. The most successful simulation model, however, appears to be the CAM (Computer Assessment of Media) model of the London Press Exchange,§ which attempts to simulate the process by which television and press advertisements reach individuals.

Work is progressing rapidly on media selection models. The original BBD & O linear programming model has been substantially refined,¶ and Little at the Massachusetts Institute of Technology has developed a dynamic programming model which specifies optimal solutions when the computational problems are not overwhelming.‖ One of the most interesting developments is the COMPASS (Computer Optimal Media Planning And Scheduling System) model which is supported by a group of agencies in the U.S.A. The project is in the hands of the Diebold Group,

* Gensch, D. H., 'Computer Models in Advertising Media Selection', *Journal of Marketing Research*, November, 1968, pp. 414–424.

† For a description of this model see Lee, A. M., 'Decision Rules for Media Scheduling: Static Campaigns', *Operational Research Quarterly*, September, 1962, 229–242; and Lee, A. M., 'Decision Rules for Media Scheduling: Dynamic Campaigns., *Operational Research Quarterly*, December, 1963, pp. 365–372.

‡ *Simulmatics Media-Mix: Technical Description*, The Simulmatics Corporation, October, 1962.

§ Broadbent, S. R., *Computer Assessment of Media*, London Press Exchange, 1965.

¶ Charnes, A., *et al.*, 'A General Programming Model for Media Planning', *Management Science*, April, 1968, B-423–B-430.

‖ Little, J. D. C., and Lodish, L. M., 'A Media Planning Calculus', *Operations Research*, January-February, 1969, pp. 1–35.

who have published a brief outline of the model.* In the U.K., the Operational Research Group of I.C.I. Ltd, have constructed a simulation model coupled with an optimizing search routine, which they call DYNAMO.†

10.5.3. Measuring the effectiveness of advertising

Measuring the effectiveness of advertising is a vitally important step in the entire advertising campaign, yet comparatively little attention is paid to it. There are several reasons for this. One such reason is that advertising research is invariably undertaken by an advertising agency, and it is very embarrassing for an agency to tell its client that their campaign has failed to achieve the desired results. Probably the major reason, however, is the sheer complexity of the problem!

In general, the creative department of an advertising agency requires answers to the following three questions:

(*a*) what should be said about the product,
(*b*) how should it be said, and
(*c*) after the campaign has run, how successful was it?

Pre-testing methods of measuring advertising effectiveness can help answer questions about the message content and the message presentation, whilst post-testing provides information on the success of the campaign.

One of the most common pre-testing methods, is the consumer-jury method, in which a small sample or 'jury' of prospects are exposed to alternative advertisements, and their opinions or reactions to the advertisement are recorded.‡ Various testing devices may be employed, for example, psycho-galvanometers and tachistoscopes. The former measures emotional responses to advertisements by means of changes in the electrical resistance of the informant's skin, while the latter exposes advertisements to the informant for a variable amount of time until the subject becomes able to identify the advertisements basic features.

Two other kinds of pre-testing are enquiry tests and local area tests, which involve post-measurement in a restricted area or restricted media to determine the advertisements to be employed in larger operations. In an enquiry test, the advertisement asks the customer to write or call for further information or to receive a gift or enter a contest. Enquiry tests with a split run allow the testing of two different advertisements in the

* Zinn, M., *The Use of Computers in the Media Selection Process*, The Diebold Group, 1965.
† *Dynamo-Media Scheduling Suite of Programs*, University of London Atlas Computing Service. See also Rawes, E. A., 'Media Models and Budget Decisions', in *Computers in Advertising*, Institute of Practitioners in Advertising, 1965.
‡ Cross, J. S., *et. al.*, 'The Consumer Jury Method of Measuring Advertising Effectiveness—A Case Study', *Journal of Marketing*, April, 1952, pp. 435–439.

same issue of a publication. Each advertisement appears in half the copies. Limited area sales tests use the experimental method of setting up an advertising programme in a test market and charting sales in relation to sales of a control market. Several interesting studies have been published in this field.*

The post-testing methods have one element in common—the advertising appropriation has been spent, and the value of post-testing lies largely in the provision of control information which will influence future decisions on advertisements and campaigns. The simplest techniques in measuring advertising effectiveness is counting sales that result from specific advertisements. However, mail order firms are the only type of organization that can accurately do this. For other organizations it is far more difficult to use sales results as the criterion of advertising effectiveness. The nearer the point is approached at which the customer makes a buying decision, the more difficult it becomes to assess the effectiveness of the individual advertisement which has played a part in that decision. Many other factors have played a part, including prices, distribution and the magnitude of competitive advertising. Consequently, such indirect measures as exposure, awareness, and attitudes are often used as criteria for setting advertising objectives and assessing effectiveness.

The three major exposure criteria are total exposures or gross impressions, frequency or impact, and reach (sometimes called cover or coverage). They are properly called 'potential' criteria, in that they generally reflect exposure to the medium that carries the advertisement, not simply the advertisement itself. Some kind of special study may be employed to estimate the amount of this audience contraction, and the information may then be used to adjust the measures of exposure. The total exposure or gross impressions is the sum total of the number of times any advertisement relating to the product is seen or heard by target group members in a given period. Let.

A_i = number of target group members exposed to an insertion in medium i ($i = 1, 2, \ldots, I$), and
N_i = number of advertisements in medium i during the time period of interest.

Total exposure is given by†

$$T = \sum_{i=1}^{I} A_i N_i$$

* See, for example, Becknell, J. C., and McIsaac, R. W., 'Test Marketing Cookware Coated With Teflon., *Journal of Advertising Research*, September, 1963, pp. 2–8.

† Montgomery, D. B., and Urban, G. L., *Management Science in Marketing*, Prentice-Hall, 1969, p. 97. The two authors also describe how to calculate a value of weighted total exposure, which takes into account the differing sales potential of target group subsegments.

The average number of advertisements for the product seen by each member of the target group during the given period is known as frequency or impact. If there are M individuals in the group, the frequency is given by

$$F = \frac{T}{M}$$

where F denotes frequency. An alternative definition of frequency is to call it the average number of exposures or impressions among the target group members who have been 'reached'. Reach or coverage is the total number of individuals exposed to at least one advertisement relating to the product in a given time period.

A problem which arises with the concept of reach is that of audience duplication. For example, some members of the target group could be exposed to several of the media which are carrying an advertisement, and the value of the combined audiences for two or more media is less than the sum of the individual values for the media because of this audience overlap. Thus, for the case of two media, say medium 1 and medium 2, the reach of a single insertion in each medium will be

$$R = A_1 + A_2 - A_{i2}$$

where R = the reach or number of persons exposed to one or more of the two insertions

A_{12} = the duplication, that is, the number of individuals exposed to an insertion in both medium 1 and medium 2

When the number of media is high, as is often the case in practice, the calculation of the unduplicated audience becomes extremely difficult, and the measurement problem is enormous. Agostini has done much to resolve this difficulty. He has examined the question in two different contexts: first, the case in which several different media are used* (net coverage), and second, the case in which there is use of multiple issues of a single medium† (cumulative audience). From a study of French magazines he obtained a formula for calculating the unduplicated audience, that included an empirically based constant which he called K.‡ The chief drawback in his method is that it is based on the assumption of similarity among the media vehicles; newspapers, magazines, and trade papers, for example, must all be treated separately, with no attempt to measure duplication among these major groups.

* Agostini, J. M., 'How to Estimate Unduplicated Audiences', *Journal of Advertising Research*, March, 1961, pp. 11–14.

† Agostini, J. M., 'Analysis of Magazine Accumulative Audience', *Journal of Advertising Research*, December, 1962, pp. 24–27.

‡ Claycamp, H. J., and McClelland, C. W., 'On Methods: Estimating Reach and the Magic of K', *Journal of Advertising Research*, June, 1968, pp. 44–51.

Determining whether or not an advertisement has actually been seen or heard involves a somewhat more difficult measurement process than measurement of the number of people who may have been exposed. However, since awareness of an advertisement is somewhat closer to the ultimate sales and profit objectives of advertising, it is obviously desirable that some attempt should be made to assess it. The most common way to determine if someone has been exposed to an advertisement is to question them about it, using what is commonly known as a memory test. These tests break down into two categories, those which stress recognition and those which stress recall. The recognition test consists of respondents looking through a selection of advertisements that have appeared recently, and reporting which ones he or she recognizes. The recall test, on the other hand, is less subject to inaccuracy and bias in that the respondents are not shown any advertisements. In the unaided form of test they are simply asked the open-ended question of which advertisements have they seen recently; in the aided form of test they are asked whether or not they recall seeing a particular advertisement. The drawback to many tests is that they succeed more in determining the creative effects of an advertisement than in assessing the actual noting.

Another measure of the communication-effect of advertising, which is further down the hierarchy of effects* towards actual purchase than awareness, is the consumers' attitude. The company may thus monitor attitudes to the product or the company, and design advertisements which are evaluated in terms of attitude changes that the firm believes will directly effect sales and profits. Yet despite the considerable progress that has been made in developing techniques of attitude measurement, there are many problems in applying them to the task of measuring advertising effectiveness. Not the least of these problems is the high cost and time-consuming nature of the techniques; also there is the problem of obtaining a representative sample from the population of target group members. Finally, the link between attitudes and buying behaviour is not a direct one, since it is known that attitude change may follow a purchase rather than precede it.†

Palda has reviewed the literature on the hierarchy of effects that purport to move the consumer from exposure to an advertisement to actual product purchase.‡ He concluded that it is, on balance, no more difficult or expensive to investigate the direct link between advertising and sales, than it is to concentrate on each step in the hierarchy and use the corres-

* One widely known formulation of this heirarchy is:

Attention → Interest → Desire → Action (AIDA)

† Raymond, C. K., 'Must Advertising Communicate to Sell?' *Harvard Business Review*, September-October, 1965, pp. 148–159.

‡ Palda, K. S., 'The Hypothesis of a Hierarchy of Effects: A Partial Evaluation', *Journal of Marketing Research*, February, 1966, pp. 13–24.

ponding measure of communication-effect to provide this link. Furthermore, the evidence he provides leaves considerable doubt about the existence of this hierarchy! This conclusion gives some comfort to the various researchers who have used sales as a criterion to evaluate advertising expenditures. Benjamin and Maitland, for example, made some empirical studies with four different models of sales response to advertising.* Two of the models used were:

(*a*) A logarithmic response curve, which is Weber's law of psychological response to stimuli:

$$S = b \log_e (A) + c$$

where S = sales response to A in units of product
A = advertising expenditure
b, c = parameters to be estimated

(*b*) An exponential response curve:

$$S = S'(1 - e^{-A})$$

where S' = the limiting value of S as A becomes infinitely large.

Of the four models the logarithmic response curve gave the best fit to the data, although the model predictions were significantly different from the data. Later work by Benjamin, Jolly, and Maitland described a time response function to an advertising pulse based upon an equation of the form:†

$$S = ae^{-bt}(1 + ct)^d$$

where S = weekly sales response following a single advertising pulse
t = time in weeks measured from the time of the advertising pulse
a, b, c, and d = parameters to be estimated.

This model was based on the theory of epidemics and rumours, and from an analysis of their data they concluded that the time–response function reached a peak very quickly and then gradually declined.

The carry-over effect of advertising is, of course, a well-known phenomena, and attempts have been made to explain why it occurs.‡ Using historical data, Palda has constructed a single-equation regression model

* Benjamin, B., and Maitland, J., 'Operational Research and Advertising: Some Experiments in the Use of Analogies', *Operational Research Quarterly*, September, 1958, pp. 207–217.

† Benjamin, B., Jolly, W. P., and Maitland, J., 'Operational Research and Advertising: Theories of Response', *Operational Research Quarterly*, December, 1960, pp. 205–218.

‡ Tull, D. S., 'The Carry-Over Effects of Advertising', *Journal of Marketing*, April, 1965, pp. 46–53.

which incorporates the carry-over effects of advertising via the distributed lag theory of Koyck.* The pitfalls of using a single-equation model for this type of application, however, where the direction of causality between sales and advertising is open to doubt, have been given by Quandt.† More recent work, such as that by Bass and his associates, has been based on a multiple-equation approach.‡

10.6. Personal selling decisions

Personal selling is oral presentation in a conversation with one or more prospective purchasers for the purpose of making sales. Unlike his role in advertising, in the matter of personal selling the marketing manager must ordinarily assemble his own pool of selling talent, develop its skills and direct its operations. It is, of course, possible for a manufacturer to shift the entire personal selling task to middlemen, but this is not so common a practice as it is to shift the advertising burden to an agency.

In the realm of personal selling, the marketing manager has to make decisions in the following areas:

(*a*) the type of sales force,
(*b*) the size of sales force,
(*c*) the selection and training of salesmen,
(*d*) the allocation of salesmen,
(*e*) the compensation of salesmen, and
(*f*) the appraisal of performance of salesmen.

We shall concentrate on the problems of sales force size and the allocation of salesmen.

10.6.1. Size of sales force

In deciding on the size of the sales budget and the optimum number of salesmen to employ, some knowledge of how sales respond to personal selling effort is required. As with price and advertising, the two most widely recommended methods of discovering this relationship are the analysis of historical data or some kind of experiment.

To illustrate the historical approach, we shall first consider the work of Semlow.§ He observed, in his analysis, that salesmen in territories having

* Palda, K. S., *The Measurement of Cumulative Advertising Effects*, Prentice-Hall, 1964.

† Quandt, R. E., 'Estimating Advertising Effectiveness: Some Pitfalls in Econometric Methods', *Journal of Marketing Research*, May, 1964, pp. 51–60.

‡ Bass, F. M., and Parsons, L. J., 'Simultaneous-Equation Regression Analysis of Sales and Advertising', *Applied Economics*, May, 1969, pp. 103–124. See also Bass, F. M., 'A Simultaneous Equation Regression Study of Advertising and Sales of Cigarettes', *Journal of Marketing Research*, August, 1969, pp. 291–300.

§ Semlow, W. J., 'How Many Salesmen Do You Need?' *Harvard Business Review*, May–June, 1959, 126–132.

greater potential generated more sales, but that the increase in sales was less than proportionate to the increase in potential. From the curve in Fig. 10.9, which is based on Semlow's analysis, it can be seen, for example,

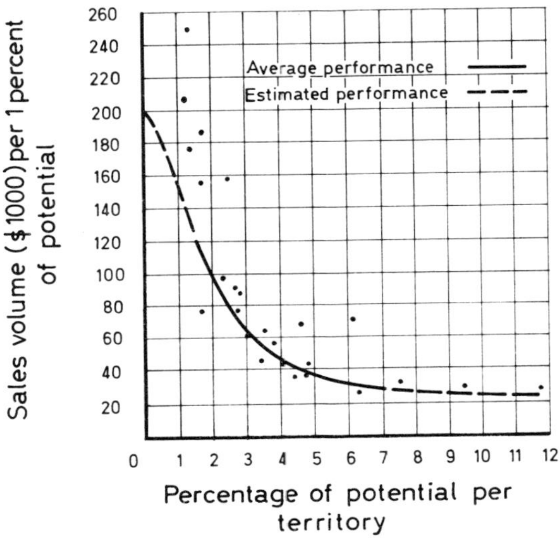

Figure 10.9. Sales potential per territory and sales volume per one per cent of potential

that sales in a territory with 1 per cent of total potential were \$160 000 (1 × \$160 000) and sales in a territory with 5 per cent of total potential were \$200 000 (5 × \$40 000). If the costs of personal selling were ignored, then it would be obviously desirable to employ a large number of salesmen, each operating in a small territory. However, when field maintenance costs are considered, this need not be the case. Semlow found in his example that the optimum number of salesmen to employ was sixty-five, and he suggested a simple marginal rule for adding salesmen:

$$S\bar{p} - C > 0$$

where S = sales volume generated by an additional salesman
$\bar{p}$ = profit margin per unit on this sales volume
C = cost of maintaining the salesman in the field

The approach adopted by Semlow incorporates several implicit assumptions. It assumes, for example, that good measures of potential are available, that the degree of competition is the same in all territories, that salesmen are homogeneous in their selling ability, and that territories are designed which have equal potential. As we shall see in the next section, however, the assumption on territories of equal potential is not realistic; territories are often designed which equalize the work-load of salesmen rather than the territorial potential. Designing territories of equal workload requires an explicit statement of the number of calls to make on customers of different sizes, and this call frequency is obviously related to the number of salesmen required. If optimum call frequency can be determined, this represents an alternative approach to determining the size of sales force.

Waid, Clark, and Ackoff made an interesting assessment of customer response to variations in the number of calls.* Their approach relied on a multiple regression analysis performed on the past sales data of the General Electric Lamp Division. Assuming an S-shaped response curve for cumulative sales volume against time spent with each customer, the authors concluded that the division was presently over allocating calls to customers. In other words, the division was operating in the saturation region of the response function. Consequently, General Electric were able to reduce the average number of calls per customer and maintain the same number of salesmen, despite an organizational change which would previously have meant an increase in the size of the sales force. Furthermore, the study recommended that some diversion of calls from existing accounts to new accounts was warranted, which could result in a substantial net increase in business.

To arrive at these conclusions, the researchers sorted customers into classes on the basis of similar characteristics. The customers or accounts in each group were sorted again into subgroups on the basis of call time spent with each customer (whether it had increased or decreased in the time period of the analysis). Then, the average value of sales was calculated for each subgroup. Finally, a curve was drawn to show the relationship between the average value of sales and sales-call time. The curve for each class of account lay in a basically positive direction, but the scatter was too great to permit the fitting of a statistically significant curve. Nevertheless, they concluded that uniform response curves do exist, but that the data in their particular study revealed only the upper plateau of the curves—the saturation region.

In an experimental approach to estimating the sales response curve to personal selling, a company investigated whether or not the productivity of personal selling could be improved by a different allocation of selling time to various sized groups of customers and prospects.† A preliminary survey discovered that over half the industry sales were concentrated in 4 per cent of all customers, and that 88 per cent of the customers concentrated their purchasing of the service with one supplier. The results of this survey provided a criterion for classifying customers as either current or

* Waid, C., Clark, D. F., and Ackoff, R. L., 'Allocation of Sales Effort in the Lamp Division of General Electric Company', *Operations Research*, December, 1956, pp. 629–647.

† Brown, A. A., Hulswit, F. T., and Kettelle, J. D., 'A Study of Sales Operations', *Operations Research*, June, 1956, pp. 296–308.

potential accounts. Each of eighteen of the company's thirty-five salesmen was assigned thirty-six customers for the experiment, so that about 550 customers were involved. Each customer was assigned either a low, medium, or high level of selling effort during the period of the experiment. Unfortunately, there were many violations of experimental design theory. In order to avoid lost sales opportunities, the greatest effort went to the largest customers, and the salesmen were allowed to select which accounts would receive the medium and low sales effort.

The reaction of the customer to the experiment was measured as follows. For each customer, the market survey established his potential, that is, the total amount currently spent by the customer on the service, either with the company or with its competitors. A customer was then considered to have 'responded' to the experiment if the company's share of his total potential increased by a 'significant' number of percentage points. Statistical analysis of the results provided an optimum rate of effort for personal selling.

10.6.2. Allocation of selling effort

The allocation of salesmen's effort is a class of problem which has been studied quite successfully by management scientists. The decision-making models which have been developed usually focus on one of three aspects of allocation:

(*a*) allocation to customers,
(*b*) allocation to areas or territories, or
(*c*) allocation over time.

Very few models have been constructed which consider two or more kinds of allocation simultaneously, although some progress is being made in this direction.* As we shall see, there is also considerable interaction between some of the allocation models and the size of sales force decision.

Allocating selling effort to customers is a problem that has attracted a great deal of attention. Buzzell reported a deterministic-static study in which a company attempted to decide on the extent to which it should go directly to customers versus the extent to which it should sell to wholesalers, who would then sell to final customers.† In other words, this application considered the question of allocation between direct and wholesale accounts. A stochastic-static model of sales effort allocation was developed by Magee in which he attacked the problem of the allocation of missionary sales effort to retailers by the manufacturer of a food product.‡

* Cloonan, J. B., 'An Analysis of Sales Tours', in Hertz, D. B., and Melese, J., eds., *Proceedings of the Fourth International Conference on Operational Research*, Wiley, 1966, pp. 284–292.
† Buzzell, op. cit., pp. 136–156.
‡ Magee, J. F., 'The Effect of Promotional Effort', *Journal of the Operations Research Society of America*, February, 1953, pp. 64–74.

The study by Brown, Hulswit, and Kettelle, mentioned in the previous section, included an attempt to estimate the deterministic-dynamic response functions of new and old customers and determine an optimal allocation between these two customer classes.*

An interesting type of stochastic-dynamic model which is directed at the acquisition of new customers is based on the theory of Markov chains. The first model to make use of this particular formulation was developed by Schuchman, in which new accounts were classified by the number of sales calls they had received.† A subsequent model, developed by Thompson and McNeal, described potential new accounts by the level of interest they displayed in the firm's product.‡ This second model is the one we shall describe here. Their Markov process involved two absorbing states and four transient or non-absorbing states. A description of these states is given in Table 10.6.

Table 10.6. Description of Markovian States

State	*Type*	*Description*
S_1	Absorbing	Sales completed during most recent call
S_2	,,	Sales lost during most recent call
S_3	Non-absorbing	New customer—no history
S_4	,,	Customer indicated low degree of interest during most recent call
S_5	,,	Customer indicated medium degree of interest during most recent call
S_6	,,	Customer indicated high degree of interest during most recent call

The absorbing chain transition matrix is shown in Fig. 10.10, and it is convenient to transform this into cononical form. This form is

$$P = \left[\begin{array}{c|c} I & O \\ \hline R & Q \end{array}\right]$$

where I is an identity matrix and 0 is a zero matrix.

Markov chain theory will yield, among other things, the probability

* Brown, Hulswit, and Kettelle, op. cit.

† Schuchman, A., 'The Planning and Control of Personal Selling Effort Directed at New Account Acquisition', in Preston, L., ed., *New Research in Marketing*, University of California, 1965, pp. 45–56.

‡ Thompson, W. W., and McNeal, J. U., 'Sales Planning and Control Using Absorbing Markov Chains', *Journal of Marketing Research*, February, 1967, pp. 62–66.

Prospect's state after new sales call

Prospect's state before new sales call		S_1	S_2	S_3	S_4	S_5	S_6
	S_1	1	0	0	0	0	0
	S_2	0	1	0	0	0	0
	S_3	P_{31}	P_{32}	0	P_{34}	P_{35}	P_{36}
	S_4	P_{41}	P_{42}	0	P_{44}	P_{45}	P_{46}
	S_5	P_{51}	P_{52}	0	P_{54}	P_{55}	P_{56}
	S_6	P_{61}	P_{62}	0	P_{64}	P_{65}	P_{66}

Figure 10.10. *An absorbing chain-call policy model*

that a prospect currently in state i ($i = 3, 4, 5, 6$) will ultimately be sold, that is, absorbed into state S_1. This is achieved by computing the matrix:*

$$B = (I-Q)^{-1}$$

Values in the B matrix give the probabilities of a prospect in one of the transient states eventually reaching one or other of the absorbing states. The rows of the B matrix sum to unity, indicating that eventually all prospects are either sold or deleted from the prospect list. Multiplying the B matrix by a column vector having revenue elements corresponding to the two absorbing states (0 in the case of lost sales), gives a vector R which has as its elements the expected revenue associated with customers in state i ($i = 3, 4, 5, 6$).

The expected number of calls required on a customer in state i ($i = 3, 4, 5, 6$) before a sale is made or lost is given by the column vector

$$T = (I-Q)^{-1} E$$

where E is a column vector with all unity elements. Multiplying the vector T by the cost of a salesman's call, assumed to be a constant, gives a column vector C whose elements are the costs required to absorb a customer in state i ($i = 3, 4, 5, 6$).

* For a detailed description of finite Markov chain theory see Kemeny, J. G., and Snell, J. L., *Finite Markov Chains*, Van Nostrand, 1960.

Thus, expected values of customers by states are given by

$$V = R - C$$

The relative values of prospects in each of these states then provides valuable information for allocating sales time. A salesman should first call upon the accounts that are in the state having the highest expected profit, as determined from the vector V. He should continue to allocate one call per customer in this state until either:

(*a*) he exhausts the time he has available during the call planning period, or

(*b*) he exhausts the set of customers available in this class or state.

If the company perceives its market in terms of areas and uses geographical control units, then it is likely that allocation of selling effort over territories will be made before allocation to customers. Two approaches to geographical allocation are possible. The first is the allocation of selling effort to specified territories; the second is the use of territorial design to allocate sales effort. Various decision-making models have been developed to solve the first kind of problem, and they may result in the assignment of a number of salesmen to a particular area.*

The second approach to geographic or area allocation is to treat territorial definitions as a variable and assume that only one salesman will be assigned to each territory. A simple solution can then be obtained by dividing the total market into N areas with equal potential, where N equals the number of salesmen available. This approach does not consider, however, such things as customer allocation or the routing and scheduling problems of sales allocation. Designing territories with equal work loads is a much more logical solution.† Given call frequencies for each customer, territories are assigned to salesmen in a heuristic manner so that the salesman's travel and sales call time provides him with a full work load.

Under this method, an estimate of the number of salesmen needed can be found. The number required is obtained from the formula:

$$N = \frac{\sum_{i=1}^{n} f_i C_i}{F}$$

* See, for example, Nordin, J. A., 'Spatial Allocation of Selling Expenses', *Journal of Marketing*, January, 1943, pp. 210–219; Howard, J. A., *Marketing Management: Analysis and Planning*, Irwin, 1963, pp. 475–479; Zentler, A. P., and Ryde, D., 'An Optimum Geographic Distribution of Publicity Expenditure in a Private Organization', *Management Science*, July, 1956, pp. 337–352.

† Talley, W. J., 'How To Design Sales Territories', *Journal of Marketing*, January, 1961, pp. 7–13. See also O'Shaughnessy, J., 'Work Study Applied to the Sales Force', *British Institute of Management*, 1965.

where N = number of salesmen
f_i = given call frequency on customer type i
C_i = number of customers of type i
F = average number of calls an average salesman can make during the planning period*

This provides an alternative approach to the methods given in the previous section, of deciding on the size of sales force. It also demonstrates the interdependence that exists between the decisions on sales force size and sales effort allocation.

The final aspect of sales allocation is the allocation of selling effort over time. This has been called the 'travelling salesman problem' by management scientists and operational research workers, and it is a special kind of scheduling problem. If a salesman has to visit n customers during a certain time period this means that there are n factorial possible routes. One of these routes would minimize the total travel cost; and another route (possibly the same) would minimize the total travel time or distance travel. The problem is to find the 'best' route in terms of the stated objective. A number of different models have been developed to tackle this problem.† The real challenge is to find a program which can solve the large n case without requiring excessive computer time. If, for example, there are 10 customers to visit, there are over 3 000 000 possible routes!

* The implicit assumption here is that salesmen have equal ability, which is obviously not the case. For a discussion of the problems in assigning specific salesmen to territories see King, W. P., 'A Stochastic Personnel-Assignment Model', *Operations Research*, January–February, 1965, pp. 67–81. This is basically an 'assignment' problem of linear programming.

† Little, J. D. C., Murty, K. G., Sweeney, D. W., and Karel, C., 'An Algorithm for the Traveling Salesman Problem', *Operations Research*, November–December, 1963, pp. 972–989, and Karg, R. L., and Thompson, G. L., 'A Heuristic Approach to Solving Traveling Salesmen Problems', *Management Science*, January, 1964, pp. 225–248.

11. Training

11.1. Introduction

In chapter 1, Table 1.2, we gave the basic layout for comparing three types of capital expenditure, and it is set out again here, for ease of reference (Table 11.1):

Table 11.1

Cash flow OUT	*Cash flow IN*	*Rate of return on investment (%)*
Additional production machine	Additional net revenue	8
Replacement automatic handling machine	Savings in labour costs	14
New factory	Increased profits	10

Of these three, the replacement machine shows the highest estimated rate of return. This will therefore be our choice provided we regard 14 per cent as a satisfactory rate, and provided also we have the investment money available. If, however, we are considering the alternative of expenditure on training, then, in order to justify this decision, we have to show that the return from training is likely to exceed the 14 per cent figure. For training in the U.K. there is one additional special factor to be taken into account, and that is that both the costs and benefits for an individual firm will be affected by the 1964 Training Act (if a training board has been set up for the industry in which our particular firm is operating). The grant will be an additional benefit: its size will depend on the amount of training undertaken, and whether the training qualifies under the regulations of the appropriate training board.

The main types of training are:

(*a*) Apprentice
(*b*) Operator
(*c*) Management

although, of course, there are others, and sub-divisions of these, such as—for example—supervisory training.

11.2. Apprentice training

A typical layout for comparing apprentice training with no formal training at all would be:

Cash flow OUT	*Cash flow IN*	*Rate of return*
1. Apprentices expenses: (*a*) Wages, gross (i.e., including tax, N.H.I., graduated pensions (*b*) Travel to and from work, if paid by the company (*c*) Accommodation (*d*) Other expenses (such as fees at technical colleges) subsidized by the company	1. Net increment in value of work done by a trained apprentice over that of an untrained man (taking scrap into account) 2. Grant	
2. Wages and salaries of training staff		
3. Costs of fixed assets used in training: (*a*) Buildings (*b*) Equipment (e.g., visual aids)		

It will be noted that no general, administrative, and selling overheads and, indeed, no training levy, have been added to the costs of training. This may seem surprising. After all, it could be argued that many administrative charges, for instance, are necessary for the good of all departments of the company and, therefore, all departments, including the training department, should bear their share of these costs. Why then do we omit these overheads? Why omit the levy? In this final chapter it is perhaps appropriate to summarize the position on decision-making that we have tried to make quite clear throughout. The approach is on these lines:

Granted that we have an ongoing business enterprise as the basis, what we have to consider is the effects of implementing our decision on this organization. What will be the additional costs? What will be the additional benefits? (At this point it cannot be too strongly emphasized that the incremental costs and benefits are determined from the one level that concerns us in practice—the present position of the firm. This is the only position that matters.) To continue: do the benefits outweigh the costs? Does the net benefit compare favourably with other possible expenditure? If so, and if the money is available, then, and only then, is a favourable decision indicated. Accountants will see that this approach is analagous to the use of marginal costing as a technique of costing. Marginal costing is, indeed, the appropriate technique to use in decision-making costing, because then the problem is whether to produce and sell *additional* units or not. It is true that the cost of any particular product which *has been produced* must bear its fair share of the fixed overheads. Similarly, to arrive at the cost of any training already in existence, we would have to include a proportion of overheads. Although all this is of no direct concern here, we should again note that it is not easy in practice to arrive at a fair proportion. The allocation of overheads, whether to a job, a process, or to a department—such as the training department, is always a difficult matter to determine. There is no absolute right or wrong. All that can be said is that some methods of allocation are obviously more sensible in a given set of circumstances than others.

11.3. Operator training

The term 'operator training' is not very clearly defined. In some industries its scope is restricted to semi-skilled workers; in other industries operator training is taken to include the work of quite highly skilled men and women. We are proposing to use the term in its broadest sense to include both semi-skilled and skilled training, provided there is no formal apprenticeship scheme in operation.

There are two basic ways in which the comparison can be made:

(*a*) Operator training compared with no formal training.
(*b*) Improved method of operator training compared with the present method.

11.3.1. Operator training compared with no formal training

This table will be similar to that for apprentice training:

Cash flow OUT	*Cash flow IN*	*Rate of return*
1. Wages and salaries of training staff	1. Net increment in value of work done (taking scrap into account)	
2. Cost of fixed assets purchased for training: (*a*) Buildings (*b*) Equipment	2. Grant	
3. Wages (gross) of operators for any period of training which is 'off the job'		

11.3.2. Improved method of operator training

This second type of comparison is of more practical importance. It requires further subdivision, since the precise ways of analysing the costs and benefits from improved methods of operator training will depend on whether the training is 'off' or 'on' the job, and also on whether the final rate which the trainee must reach is fixed for him or not.*

11.3.2.(1) Off the job training

In this event the operator is not put on production work until he is capable of maintaining a certain required output. The object is to teach the employee in such a way that he reaches a satisfactory performance level in the shortest possible time. Until such a position is reached then, by implication, the benefit from his work is small and can be ignored. In production line work this level of performance will be standard performance expressed in so many standard minutes. (In practice, it is useless to tell an employee that he is allowed—say 2·8511 minutes per job, but he will really understand if he is told that he is expected to produce 180 articles per day.)

The benefit in this case is given by the reduction in training time to reach the required level multiplied by the rate of pay of the trainee during training. If three weeks are saved, as in the diagram (Fig. 11.1), and the trainee is paid £11 per week, the benefit is £33.

* One further way of dealing with the costs of training which is not followed up here is by comparing these with the extra costs of hiring trained labour.

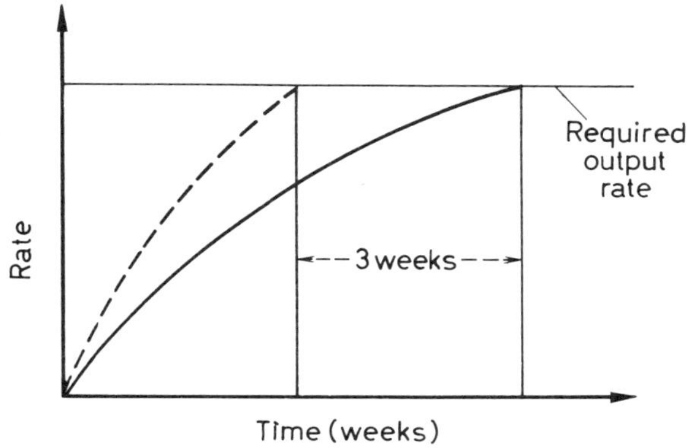

Figure 11.1.

11.3.2.(2) On the job training

Rate of production governed by some external factor, such as the fact that the unit produced is going to be used at a fixed rate in another part of the factory, or that the operation is part of a production line.

Since the aim of all operator training is to improve production we need to establish the cash benefit gained from producing that extra production unit. For each additional sale we get the benefit of the revenue, but the raw materials (and possibly some additional supplies, power, etc.) have to be paid out. Broadly, the net cash benefit is the sales revenue—less the raw material costs. This figure is almost certainly constant for each unit of production. Let us take an example:

The selling price of a torque limiter* is £13·72 and the cost of the metal used in its production is £1·22. The net cash benefit to the company from selling each additional unit is easy to calculate:

	£
Sales	13·72
Less Raw materials	1·22
Gain per unit	12·50

Figure 11.2 shows a typical operator learning curve. The learning curve under the present method of training is shown as a continuous line. From the graph it is evident that all the training given is 'on the job' training, since some units are produced right from the start.

The second dotted line shows the estimated learning curve under the improved method of training. It is obvious from the figure that this training

* Industrial type—the verbal type is difficult to price!

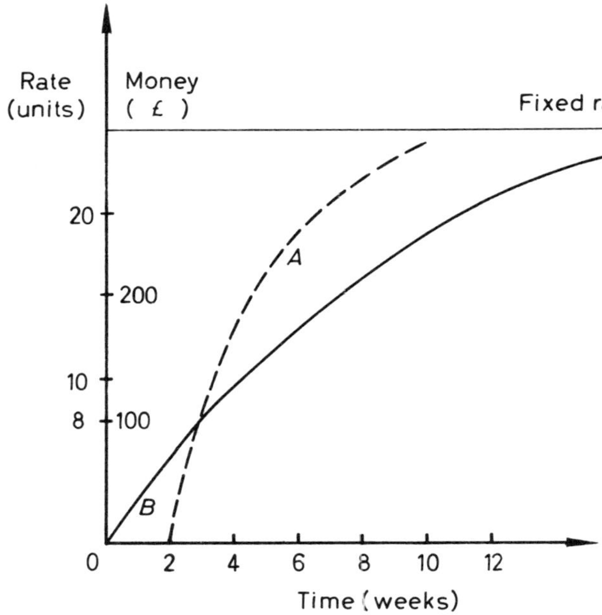

Figure 11.2.

starts off with a preliminary period of ten days or so spent at a training school before the trainee is allowed to get on with the job. Of course, the rate at which he then learns will be much faster than under the present system so that the learning curve corresponding to the proposed method of training is much steeper.

The horizontal axis in this figure represents time in weeks, and the vertical axis represents production expressed as so many units per week. It follows that the total production for either method of learning is shown by the area under that curve. The difference between the improved and present methods of learning will be the area *between* the two curves. The net benefit is therefore represented by $A-B$.

If, instead of taking the vertical scale to represent units of production per week, we replace it by a scale showing money units, then the difference in the areas will represent the benefit in money terms. In the torque limiter example we should use a money scale showing £100 ($= 8\times$£12·50) for every 8 units of production.

Where the operator is working at one machine which is part of a long production line, the net benefit is not always easy to isolate. We need to arrive at the contribution the operator makes from his work to the production line during this training period. To arrive at this benefit, the revenue, in the original calculation, must be replaced by a transfer price for his finished product. The calculation of this transfer price will generally be based on the standard cost of his work. If the operator received units which have already been through various processes the net benefit from his work is, therefore:

Transfer price of unit after its operation,
less transfer price of unit before operation
and raw material used in this operation.

At this stage it may be argued that to use a complex curve, such as the learning curve, shows a rather theoretical approach. However, drawing a learning curve is not too difficult. Let us call the production at any time (y) and the time, in weeks (t), and take it that the standard or fixed rate of production required is P units per week. The equation to the learning curve (in its simplest form) will be

$$y = P'(1-e^{-lt}) \tag{11.1}$$

Where l is a constant and is a *measure of the efficiency of training* and P' is the maximum rate of which the operator is theoretically capable. If the standard rate of production is high, P' may not be much greater than P and for a rough approximation can then be taken as equal to it. In that case we shall have only one constant to find and it will only be necessary to record the production rate at one or two points in time (for example after two and after four weeks of training). Substituting these values in eq. (11.1) will give us the constant l. We shall then have determined the exact equation to the curve.

There is, however, an even simpler approach. Equation (11.1), rewritten with $P' = P$, is

$$y = P(1-e^{-lt})$$

Differentiating with respect to t gives

$$\frac{dy}{dt} = Ple^{-lt}$$

Putting $t = 0$

$$\frac{dy}{dt} = Pl$$

or

$$l = \frac{1}{P}\frac{dy}{dt}$$

Hence *the learning rate* (dy/dt) *in the initial* (first week) *period gives the measure* (l) *of the efficiency of training.*

11.3.2.(3) On the job training

Rate not governed by production line or other external requirements. Since the operator's rate of production is not restricted by outside limitations then, ideally, it will continue to improve until it reaches the maximum of which he is physically capable. In practice, it is likely to reach the optimum figure fairly rapidly, and progress beyond this figure will not occur in stable conditions. Partly, it seems, this is because at a certain level the operator is personally satisfied with the rate he has achieved and does not wish to go above it. A number of other factors may also have some influence, e.g., the expectations of management, and the attitude of other operators to any substantial increase in the rate above their own.

For these reasons the optimum rate that an operator achieves may well be fairly constant whatever method of training is used. Of course, the time he takes to reach this rate—or something very near it—will depend on the efficiency of the training method. Figure 11.3 shows the position. It

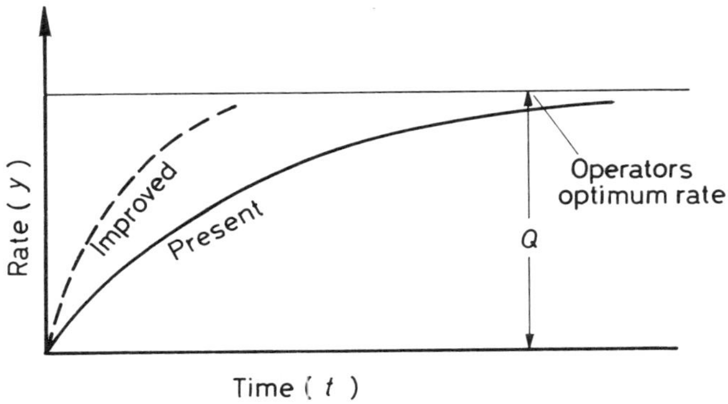

Figure 11.3.

differs from the previous diagram in two respects. First, it represents an *individual* operator's performance under the two types of training. Second, the optimum rate Q (say) is the individual's optimum rate, and hence will vary with each operator. The learning curves will be of the form:

$$y = Q(1 - e^{-lt})$$

Here we have two unknowns Q and l to find, and the solution is not quite so easy. However, trying to construct two learning curves for an individual operator is, in any case, conceptually unsatisfactory. No man can be trained *ab initio* by two different methods. One effects the other.

The only satisfactory approach is to work on a group basis and construct learning curves for the average worker under the present and improved systems. Statistical analysis will ensure that the control groups are as small as possible while still consistent with obtaining results accurate enough for decision purposes. The mathematical approach will be similar to that outlined in the previous section (at least two points will have to be taken in time). The average worker optimum rate (obtained from the control group) will replace the rate fixed by production line or other external requirements.

11.4. Management training

This term covers several different types of training. We can deal with them under the three headings:

(*a*) Induction of trainee managers.

(*b*) 'On the job' training.

(*c*) Outside training—e.g., at business schools, technical colleges, etc.

11.4.1. Induction training

The costs and benefits of induction training can be set out as:

Cash flow OUT	*Cash flow IN*	*Rate of return*
1. Trainees' salaries	1. Increase in efficiency of department due to the new managers having received the induction training, but—nominally measured by: increase in open market salary	
2. Any additional expenses incurred by the trainees		
3. Wages of the training staff		
4. Costs of any special equipment	2. Grant (although many Training Boards do not accept expenses on management training as an allowable cost for the grant, some do. The E.I.T.B. for instance, allow grants for internal or external seminars of any duration)	

The simplest measure of a manager's worth to a business is his market value, that is the 'at arms length' salary he can command. This is a very direct criterion for assessing his efficiency and hence the benefit he gets from training.

At first glance it may seem odd to regard an increase in open market salary as a benefit to a firm rather than as a cost. We are, of course, dealing with a nominal increase—that is, an increase he *could* command, on account of his better performance, in a free market.

This increase in open market valuation can sometimes be arrived at quite accurately; for example, many of the major computer companies, such as I.B.M., run a nine months' course to train newly joined accountants, engineers, and other qualified staff as systems analysts. After a successful conclusion of this course the market value of the trained systems analyst is considerably enhanced and is fairly precisely determined in the open market.

11.4.2. On the job training

This represents a high proportion of all management training (other than induction or introductory training). Figures as high as 90 per cent have often been quoted as good estimates of this proportion. The basic layout will be:

Cash flow OUT	*Cash flow IN*	*Rate of return*
1. Wages of training staff 2. Cost of equipment 3. Fees to outside lecturers	1. Increase in efficiency of department due to the manager having received the training, but—nominally measured by: increase in open market salary 2. Grant (if given)	

11.4.3. Outside training

The layout is similar:

Cash flow OUT	*Cash flow IN*	*Rate of return*
1. Cost of course, including all expenses paid by the firm 2. Costs of any additional services incurred by the absence of the manager on the course	1. Increase in efficiency of department due to the manager having received the training, but—nominally measured by: increase in open market salary 2. Grant (if given). (This grant may even include employee's salary. The C.I.T.B., for example, allowed: (*a*) 100 per cent of employee's salary (*b*) 75 per cent of course and accommodation fees (*c*) travelling expenses (*d*) additional supplementary grant of 20 per cent for attendance at their own approved courses)	

Although the manager will be away on the course, it is not strictly correct to charge his salary as a training cost because it is not an *additional* cost. If the department's efficiency is reduced because of his absence, then this—if it can be assessed—is a fair charge or addition to the costs.

We have seen that in some circumstances it is possible to find the incremental cash value of a manager on the open market as a result of his training. Generally, however, it is not easy to do so. In chapter 8 the following alternative methods of evaluating the benefit from management training were noted:

1. A direct test on the individual of the increase in his knowledge and aptitude following the period of training.
2. An assessment of the increase in the effective working capacity of the individual at his job.
3. An assessment of the benefit to the firm measured in terms of increased profitability, decreased costs, etc., as a result of the training.

It is evident that a wide range of measuring tools will be necessary. These include entirely non-quantitative techniques such as opinion surveys and attitude probes which will give a general feel as to the value of the training. At the other end of the spectrum there are objective tests which will measure increase in knowledge (e.g., by an examination). The results of such tests can certainly be quantified. The only problem is whether they are measuring that skill in management which the training is trying to impart.

Some of these techniques are applicable to a wide range of training methods. This makes comparison between the effectiveness of these methods of training possible. The De la Rue Index provides probably the most comprehensive application of this technique today.* This index employs a standard set of questions which are given to all managers who have been on any of the courses. The questions are simple tests of what the trainee thinks of the course. For instance, 'Were the objects of the course broadly achieved?', 'Do you think the lecturing was satisfactory?', and so on. The advantage of applying this rigid set of questions is that comparison between different external courses, e.g., ten-week management courses at business schools, universities, and technical colleges, is possible. There are two substantial disadvantages to this technique. First, although direct comparison is made between the benefits of varying courses, these results are not quantified, hence no direct comparison is possible between the costs and benefits. One course may clearly be judged the best, but we still do not know if expenditure on it is justified by the results. Second, this technique is only measuring the response of the individuals to the course. It may be that, although the group is certainly satisfied with a particular course, their work (that is the contribution that they make to the company) is improved much more by some other course which the members themselves do not rate so highly. Perhaps the unpleasant tasting pill really works better than the sugar coated placebo! It is important to keep in mind that what we are primarily trying to measure is the benefit that training brings to the firm and not to the individual, and *this has already been dealt with in chapter 8*. Here we have only been concerned to show that change in performance can be measured, and hence the benefits of training can be assessed.

To sum up both! Training a manager can be evaluated in a company which runs a comprehensive system of MBO based on target sales and standard costs (with suitable cost centres) in the production departments. In such a company, quantifying the benefits of management training, though difficult, is possible.

* The Confederation of British Industry now runs a similar scheme.

Table A. Present value of $1

Periods until Payment	1%	2%	4%	6%	8%	10%	12%	14%	15%	16%	18%	20%	22%	24%	25%	26%	28%	30%	35%	40%	45%	50%
1	0·990	0·980	0·962	0·943	0·926	0·909	0·893	0·877	0·870	0·862	0·847	0·833	0·820	0·806	0·800	0·794	0·781	0·769	0·741	0·714	0·690	0·667
2	0·980	0·961	0·925	0·890	0·857	0·826	0·797	0·769	0·756	0·743	0·718	0·694	0·672	0·650	0·640	0·630	0·610	0·592	0·549	0·510	0·476	0·444
3	0·971	0·942	0·889	0·840	0·794	0·751	0·712	0·675	0·658	0·641	0·609	0·579	0·551	0·524	0·512	0·500	0·477	0·455	0·406	0·364	0·328	0·296
4	0·961	0·924	0·855	0·792	0·735	0·683	0·636	0·592	0·572	0·552	0·516	0·482	0·451	0·423	0·410	0·397	0·373	0·350	0·301	0·260	0·226	0·193
5	0·951	0·906	0·822	0·747	0·681	0·621	0·567	0·519	0·497	0·476	0·437	0·402	0·370	0·341	0·328	0·315	0·291	0·269	0·223	0·186	0·156	0·132
6	0·942	0·888	0·790	0·705	0·630	0·564	0·507	0·456	0·432	0·410	0·370	0·335	0·303	0·275	0·262	0·250	0·227	0·207	0·165	0·133	0·108	0·088
7	0·933	0·871	0·760	0·665	0·583	0·513	0·452	0·400	0·376	0·354	0·314	0·279	0·249	0·222	0·210	0·198	0·178	0·159	0·122	0·095	0·074	0·059
8	0·923	0·853	0·731	0·627	0·540	0·467	0·404	0·351	0·327	0·305	0·266	0·233	0·204	0·179	0·168	0·157	0·139	0·123	0·091	0·068	0·051	0·039
9	0·914	0·837	0·703	0·592	0·500	0·424	0·361	0·308	0·284	0·263	0·225	0·194	0·167	0·144	0·134	0·125	0·108	0·094	0·067	0·048	0·035	0·026
10	0·905	0·820	0·676	0·558	0·463	0·386	0·322	0·270	0·247	0·227	0·191	0·162	0·137	0·116	0·107	0·099	0·085	0·073	0·050	0·035	0·024	0·017
11	0·896	0·804	0·650	0·527	0·429	0·350	0·287	0·237	0·215	0·195	0·162	0·135	0·112	0·094	0·086	0·079	0·066	0·056	0·037	0·025	0·017	0·012
12	0·887	0·788	0·625	0·497	0·397	0·319	0·257	0·208	0·187	0·168	0·137	0·112	0·092	0·076	0·069	0·062	0·052	0·043	0·027	0·018	0·012	0·008
13	0·879	0·773	0·601	0·469	0·368	0·290	0·229	0·182	0·163	0·145	0·116	0·093	0·075	0·061	0·055	0·050	0·040	0·033	0·020	0·013	0·008	0·005
14	0·870	0·758	0·577	0·442	0·340	0·263	0·205	0·160	0·141	0·125	0·099	0·078	0·062	0·049	0·044	0·039	0·032	0·025	0·015	0·009	0·006	0·003
15	0·861	0·743	0·555	0·417	0·315	0·239	0·183	0·140	0·123	0·108	0·084	0·065	0·051	0·040	0·035	0·031	0·025	0·020	0·011	0·006	0·004	0·002
16	0·853	0·728	0·534	0·394	0·292	0·218	0·163	0·123	0·107	0·093	0·071	0·054	0·042	0·032	0·028	0·025	0·019	0·015	0·008	0·005	0·003	0·002
17	0·844	0·714	0·513	0·371	0·270	0·198	0·146	0·108	0·093	0·080	0·060	0·045	0·034	0·026	0·023	0·020	0·015	0·012	0·006	0·003	0·002	0·001
18	0·836	0·700	0·494	0·350	0·250	0·180	0·130	0·095	0·081	0·069	0·051	0·038	0·028	0·021	0·018	0·016	0·012	0·009	0·005	0·002	0·001	0·001
19	0·828	0·686	0·475	0·331	0·232	0·164	0·116	0·083	0·070	0·060	0·043	0·031	0·023	0·017	0·014	0·012	0·009	0·007	0·003	0·002	0·001	
20	0·820	0·673	0·456	0·312	0·215	0·149	0·104	0·073	0·061	0·051	0·037	0·026	0·019	0·014	0·012	0·010	0·007	0·005	0·002	0·001	0·001	
21	0·811	0·660	0·439	0·294	0·199	0·135	0·093	0·064	0·053	0·044	0·031	0·022	0·015	0·011	0·009	0·008	0·006	0·004	0·002	0·001		
22	0·823	0·679	0·465	0·320	0·222	0·155	0·109	0·077	0·065	0·055	0·039	0·028	0·021	0·015	0·013	0·011	0·008	0·006	0·003	0·001	0·001	
23	0·795	0·634	0·406	0·262	0·170	0·112	0·074	0·049	0·040	0·033	0·022	0·015	0·010	0·007	0·006	0·005	0·003	0·002	0·001			
24	0·788	0·622	0·390	0·247	0·158	0·102	0·066	0·043	0·035	0·028	0·019	0·013	0·008	0·006	0·005	0·004	0·003	0·002	0·001			
25	0·780	0·610	0·375	0·233	0·146	0·092	0·059	0·038	0·030	0·024	0·016	0·010	0·007	0·005	0·004	0·003	0·002	0·001	0·001			
26	0·772	0·598	0·361	0·220	0·135	0·084	0·053	0·033	0·026	0·021	0·014	0·009	0·006	0·004	0·003	0·002	0·002	0·001				
27	0·764	0·586	0·347	0·207	0·125	0·076	0·047	0·029	0·023	0·018	0·011	0·007	0·005	0·003	0·002	0·002	0·001	0·001				
28	0·757	0·574	0·333	0·196	0·116	0·069	0·042	0·026	0·020	0·016	0·010	0·006	0·004	0·002	0·002	0·002	0·001	0·001				
29	0·749	0·563	0·321	0·185	0·107	0·063	0·037	0·022	0·017	0·014	0·008	0·005	0·003	0·002	0·002	0·001	0·001	0·001				
30	0·742	0·552	0·308	0·174	0·099	0·057	0·033	0·020	0·015	0·012	0·007	0·004	0·003	0·002	0·001	0·001	0·001					
40	0·672	0·453	0·208	0·097	0·046	0·022	0·011	0·005	0·004	0·003	0·001	0·001										
50	0·608	0·372	0·141	0·054	0·021	0·009	0·003	0·001	0·001	0·001												

Table Source: Anthony, Robert N., *Management Accounting: Text and Cases* (rev. ed.; Homewood, Ill.: Richard D. Irwin, Inc., 1960), p. 656.

Author's note: These values are obtained by compounding at the end of each period. Other tables use different schemes of compounding, without changing the magnitudes greatly.

Table B. Present value of $1 received annually

Periods to be Paid	1%	2%	4%	6%	8%	10%	12%	14%	15%	16%	18%	20%	22%	24%	25%	26%	28%	30%	35%	40%	45%	50%
1	0·990	0·980	0·962	0·943	0·926	0·909	0·893	0·877	0·870	0·862	0·847	0·833	0·820	0·806	0·800	0·794	0·781	0·769	0·741	0·714	0·690	0·667
2	1·970	1·942	1·886	1·833	1·783	1·736	1·690	1·647	1·626	1·605	1·566	1·528	1·492	1·457	1·440	1·424	1·392	1·361	1·289	1·224	1·165	1·111
3	2·941	2·884	2·775	2·673	2·577	2·487	2·402	2·322	2·283	2·246	2·174	2·106	2·042	1·981	1·952	1·923	1·868	1·816	1·696	1·589	1·493	1·407
4	3·902	3·808	3·630	3·465	3·312	3·170	3·037	2·914	2·855	2·798	2·690	2·589	2·494	2·404	2·362	2·320	2·241	2·166	1·997	1·849	1·720	1·605
5	4·853	4·713	4·452	4·212	3·993	3·791	3·605	3·433	3·352	3·274	3·127	2·991	2·864	2·745	2·689	2·635	2·532	2·436	2·220	2·035	1·876	1·737
6	5·795	5·601	5·242	4·917	4·623	4·355	4·111	3·889	3·784	3·685	3·498	3·326	3·167	3·020	2·951	2·885	2·759	2·643	2·385	2·168	1·983	1·824
7	6·728	6·472	6·002	5·582	5·206	4·868	4·564	4·288	4·160	4·039	3·812	3·605	3·416	3·242	3·161	3·083	2·937	2·802	2·508	2·263	2·057	1·883
8	7·652	7·325	6·733	6·210	5·747	5·335	4·968	4·639	4·487	4·344	4·078	3·837	3·619	3·421	3·329	3·241	3·076	2·925	2·598	2·331	2·108	1·922
9	8·566	8·162	7·435	6·802	6·247	5·759	5·328	4·946	4·772	4·607	4·303	4·031	3·786	3·566	3·463	3·366	3·184	3·019	2·665	2·379	2·144	1·948
10	9·471	8·983	8·111	7·360	6·710	6·145	5·650	5·216	5·019	4·833	4·494	4·192	3·923	3·682	3·571	3·465	3·269	3·092	2·715	2·414	2·168	1·965
11	10·368	9·787	8·760	7·887	7·139	6·495	5·937	5·453	5·234	5·029	4·656	4·327	4·035	3·776	3·656	3·544	3·335	3·147	2·752	2·438	2·185	1·977
12	11·255	10·575	9·385	8·384	7·536	6·814	6·194	5·660	5·421	5·197	4·793	4·439	4·127	3·851	3·725	3·606	3·387	3·190	2·779	2·456	2·196	1·985
13	12·134	11·343	9·986	8·853	7·904	7·103	6·424	5·842	5·583	5·342	4·910	4·533	4·203	3·912	3·780	3·656	3·427	3·223	2·799	2·468	2·204	1·990
14	13·004	12·106	10·563	9·295	8·244	7·367	6·628	6·002	5·724	5·468	5·008	4·611	4·265	3·962	3·824	3·695	3·459	3·249	2·814	2·477	2·210	1·993
15	13·865	12·849	11·118	9·712	8·559	7·606	6·811	6·142	5·847	5·575	5·092	4·675	4·315	4·001	3·859	3·726	3·483	3·268	2·825	2·484	2·214	1·995
16	14·718	13·578	11·652	10·106	8·851	7·824	6·974	6·265	5·954	5·669	5·162	4·730	4·357	4·033	3·887	3·751	3·503	3·283	2·834	2·489	2·216	1·997
17	15·562	14·292	12·166	10·477	9·122	8·022	7·120	6·373	6·047	5·749	5·222	4·775	4·391	4·059	3·910	3·771	3·518	3·295	2·840	2·492	2·218	1·998
18	16·398	14·992	12·659	10·828	9·372	8·201	7·250	6·467	6·128	5·818	5·273	4·812	4·419	4·080	3·928	3·786	3·529	3·304	2·844	2·494	2·219	1·999
19	17·226	15·678	13·134	11·158	9·604	8·365	7·366	6·550	6·198	5·877	5·316	4·844	4·442	4·097	3·942	3·799	3·539	3·311	2·848	2·496	2·220	1·999
20	18·046	16·351	13·590	11·470	9·818	8·514	7·469	6·623	6·259	5·929	5·353	4·870	4·460	4·110	3·954	3·808	3·546	3·316	2·850	2·497	2·221	1·999
21	18·857	17·011	14·029	11·764	10·017	8·649	7·562	6·687	6·312	5·973	5·384	4·891	4·476	4·121	3·963	3·816	3·551	3·320	2·852	2·498	2·221	2·000
22	19·660	17·658	14·451	12·042	10·201	8·772	7·645	6·743	6·359	6·011	5·410	4·909	4·488	4·130	3·970	3·822	3·556	3·323	2·853	2·498	2·222	2·000
23	20·456	18·292	14·857	12·303	10·371	8·883	7·718	6·792	6·399	6·044	5·432	4·925	4·499	4·137	3·976	3·827	3·559	3·325	2·854	2·499	2·222	2·000
24	21·243	18·914	15·247	12·550	10·529	8·985	7·784	6·835	6·434	6·073	5·451	4·937	4·507	4·143	3·981	3·831	3·562	3·327	2·855	2·499	2·222	2·000
25	22·023	19·523	15·622	12·783	10·675	9·077	7·843	6·873	6·464	6·097	5·467	4·948	4·514	4·147	3·985	3·834	3·564	3·329	2·856	2·499	2·222	2·000
26	22·795	20·121	15·983	13·003	10·810	9·161	7·896	6·906	6·491	6·118	5·480	4·956	4·520	4·151	3·988	3·837	3·566	3·330	2·856	2·500	2·222	2·000
27	23·560	20·707	16·330	13·211	10·935	9·237	7·943	6·935	6·514	6·136	5·492	4·964	4·524	4·154	3·990	3·839	3·567	3·331	2·856	2·500	2·222	2·000
28	24·316	21·281	16·663	13·406	11·051	9·307	7·984	6·961	6·534	6·152	5·502	4·970	4·528	4·157	3·992	3·840	3·568	3·331	2·857	2·500	2·222	2·000
29	25·066	21·844	16·984	13·591	11·158	9·370	8·022	6·983	6·551	6·166	5·510	4·975	4·531	4·159	3·994	3·841	3·569	3·332	2·857	2·500	2·222	2·000
30	25·808	22·396	17·292	13·765	11·258	9·427	8·055	7·003	6·566	6·177	5·517	4·979	4·534	4·160	3·995	3·842	3·569	3·332	2·857	2·500	2·222	2·000
40	32·835	27·355	19·793	15·046	11·925	9·779	8·244	7·105	6·642	6·234	5·548	4·997	4·544	4·166	3·999	3·846	3·571	3·333	2·857	2·500	2·222	2·000
50	39·196	31·424	21·482	15·762	12·234	9·915	8·304	7·133	6·661	6·246	5·554	4·999	4·545	4·167	4·000	3·846	3·571	3·333	2·857	2·500	2·222	2·000

Table Source: Anthony, Robert N., *Management Accounting: Text and Cases* (rev. ed.; Homewood, Ill.: Richard D. Irwin, Inc., 1960), p. 656.
Author's note: These values are obtained by compounding at the end of each period. Other tables use different schemes of compounding, without changing the magnitudes greatly.

Table C. Present value of $1/12 received monthly in year *N*

Year (*N*)	1%	2%	4%	6%	8%	10%	12%	14%	15%	16%	18%	20%	22%	24%	25%	26%	28%	30%	35%	40%	45%	50%
1	0·995	0·989	0·979	0·969	0·959	0·950	0·941	0·932	0·928	0·924	0·915	0·907	0·899	0·892	0·888	0·884	0·877	0·870	0·853	0·837	0·822	0·808
2	0·985	0·970	0·941	0·914	0·888	0·864	0·840	0·818	0·807	0·796	0·776	0·756	0·737	0·719	0·710	0·702	0·685	0·669	0·632	0·598	0·567	0·539
3	0·975	0·951	0·905	0·862	0·823	0·785	0·750	0·717	0·702	0·686	0·657	0·630	0·601	0·580	0·568	0·557	0·535	0·515	0·468	0·427	0·391	0·359
4	0·965	0·932	0·870	0·814	0·762	0·714	0·670	0·629	0·610	0·592	0·557	0·525	0·495	0·468	0·455	0·442	0·418	0·396	0·347	0·305	0·270	0·239
5	0·956	0·914	0·837	0·768	0·705	0·649	0·598	0·552	0·531	0·510	0·472	0·438	0·406	0·377	0·364	0·351	0·327	0·305	0·257	0·218	0·186	0·160
6	0·946	0·896	0·805	0·724	0·653	0·590	0·534	0·484	0·461	0·440	0·400	0·365	0·333	0·304	0·291	0·278	0·255	0·234	0·190	0·156	0·128	0·106
7	0·937	0·879	0·774	0·683	0·605	0·536	0·477	0·425	0·401	0·379	0·339	0·304	0·273	0·245	0·233	0·221	0·199	0·180	0·141	0·111	0·088	0·071
8	0·928	0·861	0·744	0·614	0·560	0·488	0·426	0·373	0·349	0·327	0·287	0·253	0·224	0·198	0·186	0·175	0·156	0·139	0·104	0·079	0·061	0·047
9	0·919	0·844	0·715	0·608	0·518	0·443	0·380	0·327	0·303	0·282	0·244	0·211	0·183	0·160	0·149	0·139	0·122	0·107	0·077	0·037	0·042	0·032
10	0·909	0·828	0·688	0·574	0·480	0·403	0·339	0·287	0·264	0·243	0·206	0·176	0·150	0·129	0·119	0·110	0·095	0·082	0·057	0·041	0·029	0·021
11	0·900	0·812	0·661	0·541	0·444	0·366	0·303	0·251	0·229	0·209	0·175	0·147	0·123	0·104	0·095	0·088	0·074	0·063	0·042	0·029	0·020	0·014
12	0·892	0·796	0·616	0·510	0·411	0·323	0·271	0·221	0·199	0·180	0·148	0·122	0·101	0·084	0·076	0·070	0·058	0·049	0·031	0·021	0·014	0·009
13	0·883	0·780	0·612	0·432	0·381	0·303	0·242	0·193	0·173	0·156	0·126	0·102	0·083	0·067	0·061	0·055	0·045	0·037	0·023	0·015	0·010	0·006
14	0·874	0·765	0·588	0·454	0·353	0·275	0·216	0·170	0·151	0·134	0·106	0·085	0·068	0·054	0·049	0·044	0·035	0·029	0·017	0·011	0·007	0·004
15	0·865	0·750	0·565	0·429	0·327	0·250	0·193	0·149	0·131	0·116	0·090	0·071	0·056	0·044	0·039	0·035	0·028	0·023	0·013	0·008	0·005	0·003
16	0·857	0·735	0·544	0·404	0·302	0·227	0·172	0·131	0·114	0·100	0·076	0·059	0·046	0·035	0·031	0·028	0·022	0·017	0·009	0·005	0·003	0·002
17	0·848	0·721	0·523	0·381	0·280	0·207	0·153	0·115	0·099	0·086	0·065	0·049	0·037	0·029	0·025	0·022	0·017	0·013	0·007	0·004	0·002	0·001
18	0·840	0·707	0·503	0·360	0·259	0·188	0·137	0·100	0·086	0·074	0·055	0·041	0·031	0·023	0·020	0·017	0·013	0·010	0·005	0·003	0·001	0·001
19	0·832	0·693	0·483	0·340	0·210	0·171	0·122	0·088	0·075	0·064	0·047	0·034	0·025	0·019	0·016	0·014	0·010	0·008	0·004	0·002	0·001	0·001
20	0·823	0·679	0·465	0·320	0·222	0·155	0·109	0·077	0·065	0·055	0·039	0·028	0·021	0·015	0·013	0·011	0·008	0·006	0·003	0·001	0·001	
21	0·815	0·666	0·447	0·302	0·206	0·141	0·098	0·068	0·057	0·047	0·033	0·024	0·017	0·012	0·010	0·009	0·006	0·005	0·002	0·001		
22	0·807	0·653	0·430	0·285	0·191	0·128	0·087	0·060	0·049	0·041	0·028	0·020	0·014	0·010	0·008	0·007	0·005	0·004	0·002	0·001		
23	0·799	0·640	0·413	0·269	0·176	0·117	0·078	0·052	0·043	0·035	0·024	0·016	0·011	0·008	0·007	0·005	0·004	0·003	0·001	0·001		
24	0·791	0·627	0·397	0·254	0·163	0·106	0·069	0·046	0·037	0·030	0·020	0·014	0·009	0·006	0·005	0·004	0·003	0·002	0·001			
25	0·783	0·615	0·382	0·239	0·151	0·096	0·062	0·040	0·032	0·026	0·017	0·011	0·008	0·005	0·004	0·003	0·002	0·002	0·001			
26	0·776	0·603	0·367	0·226	0·140	0·088	0·055	0·035	0·028	0·023	0·015	0·010	0·006	0·004	0·003	0·003	0·002	0·001				
27	0·768	0·591	0·353	0·213	0·130	0·080	0·049	0·031	0·025	0·019	0·012	0·008	0·005	0·003	0·003	0·002	0·001	0·001				
28	0·760	0·580	0·340	0·201	0·120	0·072	0·044	0·027	0·021	0·017	0·010	0·007	0·004	0·003	0·002	0·002	0·001	0·001				
29	0·753	0·568	0·326	0·190	0·111	0·066	0·039	0·024	0·019	0·014	0·009	0·006	0·003	0·002	0·002	0·001	0·001	0·001				
30	0·745	0·537	0·314	0·179	0·103	0·060	0·035	0·021	0·016	0·012	0·008	0·005	0·003	0·002	0·001	0·001	0·001					
40	0·675	0·457	0·212	0·100	0·048	0·023	0·011	0·006	0·004	0·003	0·001	0·001										
50	0·611	0·375	0·143	0·056	0·022	0·009	0·004	0·002	0·001	0·001												

Table D. Present value of $1/12 received monthly for *N* years

Years (N)	1%	2%	4%	6%	8%	10%	12%	14%	15%	16%	18%	20%	22%	24%	25%	26%	28%	30%	35%	40%	45%	50%
1	0·995	0·989	0·979	0·969	0·959	0·950	0·941	0·932	0·928	0·924	0·915	0·907	0·899	0·892	0·888	0·884	0·877	0·870	0·853	0·837	0·822	0·808
2	1·979	1·959	1·920	1·883	1·848	1·814	1·781	1·750	1·735	1·720	1·691	1·663	1·637	1·611	1·598	1·586	1·562	1·539	1·485	1·435	1·390	1·347
3	2·954	2·910	2·826	2·746	2·670	2·599	2·531	2·467	2·436	2·406	2·348	2·293	2·241	2·191	2·167	2·143	2·098	2·054	1·953	1·863	1·781	1·706
4	3·920	3·843	3·696	3·559	3·432	3·313	3·301	3·096	3·046	2·998	2·905	2·818	2·736	2·658	2·621	2·585	2·516	2·450	2·300	2·168	2·050	1·916
5	4·876	4·757	4·533	4·327	4·137	3·962	3·799	3·648	3·577	3·508	3·377	3·256	3·142	3·036	2·985	2·936	2·842	2·755	2·557	2·386	2·236	2·106
6	5·822	5·653	5·338	5·051	4·790	4·551	4·333	4·132	4·038	3·948	3·778	3·620	3·475	3·340	3·276	3·214	3·098	2·989	2·747	2·541	2·365	2·212
7	6·759	6·531	6·111	5·734	5·395	5·088	4·810	4·557	4·439	4·327	4·117	3·924	3·748	3·585	3·509	3·435	3·297	3·169	2·888	2·653	2·453	2·233
8	7·687	7·392	6·855	6·379	5·954	5·575	5·235	4·929	4·788	4·654	4·404	4·177	3·971	3·783	3·695	3·611	3·453	3·308	2·992	2·732	2·514	2·330
9	8·605	8·237	7·571	6·987	6·473	6·018	5·615	5·256	5·091	4·935	4·617	4·388	4·154	3·942	3·814	3·750	3·575	3·414	3·070	2·789	2·556	2·362
10	9·515	9·065	8·259	7·560	6·953	6·421	5·955	5·543	5·355	5·178	4·854	4·564	4·305	4·071	3·963	3·860	3·670	3·497	3·127	2·829	2·585	2·383
11	10·415	9·876	8·920	8·101	7·397	6·788	6·258	5·794	5·584	5·388	5·029	4·711	4·428	4·175	4·058	3·948	3·744	3·560	3·169	2·858	2·605	2·397
12	11·307	10·672	9·556	8·612	7·807	7·121	6·528	6·015	5·784	5·568	5·177	4·833	4·529	4·259	4·135	4·018	3·802	3·608	3·201	2·879	2·619	2·406
13	12·189	11·452	10·167	9·094	8·190	7·423	6·770	6·308	5·957	5·724	5·302	4·935	4·611	4·326	4·196	4·073	3·847	3·646	3·224	2·891	2·639	2·412
14	13·063	12·317	10·755	9·548	8·542	7·699	6·985	6·378	6·108	5·858	5·409	5·019	4·679	4·380	4·245	4·117	3·883	3·674	3·241	2·904	2·635	2·417
15	13·928	12·967	11·321	9·977	8·869	7·949	7·178	6·527	6·239	5·973	5·499	5·090	4·735	4·424	4·284	4·152	3·911	3·696	3·254	2·912	2·640	2·419
16	14·785	13·702	11·864	10·381	9·171	8·176	7·350	6·658	6·353	6·073	5·576	5·149	4·780	4·460	4·315	4·179	4·932	3·713	3·264	2·917	2·643	2·421
17	15·633	14·422	12·387	10·762	9·451	8·383	7·503	6·772	6·452	6·159	5·610	5·198	4·818	4·488	4·340	4·201	3·919	3·726	3·271	2·921	2·645	2·422
18	16·473	15·129	12·890	11·122	9·711	8·571	7·640	6·873	6·539	6·233	5·695	5·239	4·848	4·511	4·360	4·218	3·962	3·736	3·276	2·924	2·647	2·423
19	17·305	15·822	13·373	11·462	9·951	8·742	7·763	6·961	6·614	6·297	5·742	5·273	4·873	4·530	4·376	4·232	3·973	3·744	3·280	2·926	2·648	2·424
20	18·128	16·501	13·838	11·782	10·173	8·897	7·872	7·038	6·679	6·352	5·781	5·301	4·894	4·545	4·389	4·213	3·941	3·750	3·283	2·927	2·648	2·424
21	18·943	17·167	14·285	12·084	10·379	9·038	7·969	7·106	6·735	6·399	5·815	5·325	4·911	4·557	4·399	4·252	3·987	3·755	3·285	2·928	2·649	2·424
22	19·750	17·819	14·714	12·369	10·570	9·167	8·056	7·165	6·785	6·440	5·843	5·345	4·925	4·567	4·407	4·259	3·992	3·758	3·286	2·929	2·649	2·425
23	20·549	18·459	15·127	12·618	10·746	9·283	8·134	7·218	6·828	6·476	5·867	5·361	4·936	4·574	4·414	4·264	3·996	3·761	3·387	2·929	2·649	2·425
24	21·341	19·087	15·525	12·892	10·909	9·389	8·204	7·263	6·865	6·506	5·887	5·357	4·945	4·581	4·419	4·269	3·999	3·763	3·288	2·930	2·650	2·425
25	32·124	19·702	15·906	13·131	11·061	9·486	8·266	7·304	6·897	6·532	5·904	5·386	4·953	4·586	4·423	4·272	4·001	3·765	3·289	2·930	2·650	2·425
26	22·899	20·305	16·274	13·357	11·201	9·574	8·321	7·339	6·926	6·555	5·919	5·396	4·959	4·590	4·426	4·275	4·003	3·766	3·289	2·930	2·650	2·425
27	23·667	20·896	16·627	13·570	11·331	9·653	8·370	7·370	6·950	6·574	5·931	5·404	4·964	4·591	4·429	4·377	4·004	3·767	3·290	2·930	2·650	2·425
28	24·428	21·476	16·966	13·771	11·451	9·726	8·415	7·397	6·971	6·591	5·942	5·410	4·968	4·596	4·431	4·279	4·005	3·768	3·290	2·930	2·650	2·425
29	25·180	22·044	17·293	13·961	11·562	9·792	8·154	7·421	6·990	6·606	5·951	5·416	4·972	4·598	4·433	4·260	4·006	3·768	3·290	2·930	2·650	2·425
30	25·926	22·601	17·607	14·139	11·665	9·852	8·489	7·441	7·006	6·618	5·958	5·420	4·975	4·600	4·434	4·281	4·007	3·769	3·290	2·930	2·650	2·425
40	32·985	27·605	20·153	15·456	12·156	10·220	8·688	7·550	7·087	6·678	5·992	5·440	4·986	4·606	4·439	4·285	4·009	3·770	3·291	2·931	2·650	2·425
50	39·375	31·711	21·873	16·191	12·676	10·361	8·752	7·580	7·107	6·692	5·999	5·443	4·987	4·607	4·440	4·285	4·009	3·770	3·291	2·931	2·650	2·425

Formula: $\dfrac{1-(1+1)^{s}}{12[(1+1)^{1/12}-1]}$. Annual discounting is assumed.

Table E. Investment Incentives announced in October 1970

	First Year Allowance	Allowance for all later years
	%	%
New Machinery & Plant, and secondhand machinery and plant (arms length transactions)	60*	25

except that:

(1) new machinery and plant (other than mobile equipment) qualify for free depreciation; i.e. 100% allowance in the first year, IF in a development area.

(2) ships, and plant for scientific research, qualify for free depreciation; i.e. 100% allowance in the first year.

(3) motor cars (unless used in car hire or taxi business) qualify for 25% in the first year and all subsequent years.

(4) buildings qualify for rates which depend on whether they are at an ordinary location or in a development area and also on the date of acquisition. Grants are available for new industrial buildings in development areas, at a rate of 35% (45% in special cases) and in 'intermediate' areas at a rate of 25% (35% in special cases).

For full details see 'Investment Incentives' Cmnd. 4516, HMSO.

* 80% from 20 July 1971 to 31 July 1973.

Index

Filmset and Printed Offset Litho in Great Britain by
Cox & Wyman Ltd., London, Fakenham and Reading